# Development and Participation

## Operational Implications for Social Welfare

# Development and Participation

## OPERATIONAL IMPLICATIONS FOR SOCIAL WELFARE

PROCEEDINGS OF THE XVIITH INTERNATIONAL
CONFERENCE ON SOCIAL WELFARE
NAIROBI, KENYA
JULY 14–20, 1974

*Published 1975*
*for the* INTERNATIONAL COUNCIL ON SOCIAL WELFARE
*by* COLUMBIA UNIVERSITY PRESS
NEW YORK AND LONDON

Library of Congress Cataloging in Publication Data
International Conference on Social Welfare, 14th, Nairobi, 1974.
  Development and participation.
  1. Social service—Congresses.  I. International
Council on Social Welfare.  II. Title.
HV8.I56  1974      361      75-2099
ISBN 0-231-03972-7

# Foreword

BIENNIAL INTERNATIONAL conferences on social welfare—like human beings—develop their own personalities. The XVIIth Biennial, convened in Nairobi July 14 to 20, 1974, was no exception. The theme—Development and Participation: Operational Implications for Social Welfare—gave the Conference its special focus. Its distinctive characteristics were shaped by many additional factors.

Meeting for the first time in Africa contributed to a feeling more of impatient optimism than despair because, in spite of the obvious challenge for social and economic development, there was also undeniable evidence of progress. The physical environment undoubtedly made its impact. The benign Kenyan winter, the intriguing city of Nairobi, and the striking African architecture of the Kenyatta Conference Center combined to create a remarkable setting.

Kenyan hospitality, in the form of relaxed immigration procedures, social events sponsored by the Kenyan Government and the city of Nairobi, as well as countless individual courtesies, left an indelible mark on the Conference. The work of the Conference Organizing Committee members, their painstaking attention to detail, and the spirit of cooperation maintained throughout the Conference were of immeasurable value.

Finally, the close to two thousand participants from eighty-five countries and with a variety of backgrounds, professions, and disciplines were indispensable in creating the high quality of discussions.

While all these factors contributed to shape the personality of the Conference, the major determinant—its lifeblood—was the contribution made by the authors of the formal papers. It is for this reason that published proceedings—a collection of these documents—are such an essential follow-up to the Conference. Proceedings provide permanence and continuity;

they are the link between a certain event in history and future development in social thought, not only for the Conference participants but for thousands more of kindred mind who were unable to attend.

Development, as we were reminded again and again at the Conference, is an unfolding of the future—it is dynamic, not static. It is likely for this reason that no individual author, nor those who collectively formulated the Conference Working Paper or commission reports, claims to be the final authority in social thought. This is not to suggest that readers will find all points of view to lack conviction or simply be mutually reinforcing. Indeed, some contradict one another and some will offend. The wide range and divergence of viewpoints were also distinguishing characteristics of the Nairobi conference. Herein lies the major benefit of a world-wide forum, because it is this intellectual interaction which forces individuals to reconsider and perhaps redefine dearly held convictions in the relentless universal search for wisdom and truth.

REUBEN C. BAETZ
*President*

# Contents

# Development and Participation

## Operational Implications for Social Welfare

# Report of the Conference Working Party

## ZENA HARMAN

FORMER MEMBER, KNESSET, ISRAEL

THE WORKING PARTY, which on this occasion was organized to comprise a representative and a rapporteur from each region of ICSW, had, as a working document in addition to those national reports that reached its members, a synthesis prepared by each one of the rapporteurs. Although a Caribbean representative was present, the Latin American rapporteur was unable to attend and did not submit a synthesis, so that any special Latin American dimension is absent. The syntheses provided valuable material which brought together many of the achievements, problems, and viewpoints especially characteristic of the region, although each rapporteur admitted to injecting some of his or her own attitudes.[1]

In approaching its work, the Working Party took the position that by relating to the over-all theme without being confined to the chapter headings of the national reports or to the commission themes, it could make a more useful contribution to clarifying some of the implications for further discussion and investigation. Clearly, its work has been neither comprehensive nor exhaustive, and it is well aware of the limitations of the document, which should be regarded primarily as aimed at stimulating thought and, certainly, controversy.

It was generally agreed that the choice of theme was timely, indicating that ICSW is fully cognizant of the importance of involving itself more directly in over-all development strategies and the challenge they impose on a variety of disciplines, professions, and voluntary undertakings which contribute to social betterment and social welfare and social work. It was also felt that ICSW might take leadership in developing defi-

[1] These syntheses are available from ICSW.

nitions that would be in accord with today's new conceptions and needs in relation to the social aspects of development. Possibly a special committee might begin to consider this question during the Nairobi Conference.

The report, in fact, incorporates the gist of a number of reflections and concerns expressed by its members in five days of intensive discussion and exchange of views. The short time available for its work made it impossible to pursue ideas or consider their implications fully, or even to be meticulous as to fact and premise. No attempt was made to take definitive positions or do more than indicate the need for further investigation. There was no attempt to arrive at a consensus or even to determine common ground. Rather, there was an effort to highlight the complexity of the issues and tasks as they confront governments and peoples who are at different stages of development and have vastly differing resources, traditions, and cultures. It was felt that the most useful contribution that could be made toward the conference's deliberations would be to provide a background and, perhaps, a new stage setting to meet some of the fundamental changes and realities to which social welfare must relate.

DEVELOPMENT

The interpretation of "development" was considered crucial to the purpose of the whole conference. Although the definition given on the first page of the conference Bulletin, No. 34,[2] received wide acceptance, it was noted that the term has sometimes been used in a less comprehensive sense. For many people development means economic development, sometimes merely industrial development. The equation of devel-

---

[2] "Development is seen as a balanced and integrated process with targets derived from the aspirations of people for themselves and for their society. Economic growth alone is not a satisfactory objective, although for many people it is an indispensable part of development. Development also implies a greater command over goods and services by more people. This means in many societies a more equitable distribution of purchasing power amongst the population and an increasing capacity by more people to know how to use and benefit from the resources of the community. It means also equal access to basic social services, health, education, housing, adequate provision of and preparation for employment; increased ability to make choices and to assist in reaching decisions."

opment with growth of the gross national product (GNP) is considered misleading, as it tends to leave out the social and human dimension of development. Implicit in some concepts of development is that "big is better than small, and that wealth is better than poverty" irrespective of the effect on the human condition.

In North America and Europe there is beginning to be a shift from the emphasis on material development to an emphasis on increased human satisfaction. Many Third World countries believe that equating development to the higher standards of living attained in the industrial countries has set unrealistic and false targets. Development should mean a better standard of life. It should be understood as involving moral concepts and at the same time should be the basis for political action.

Development in practice has not been equated with equality of opportunity, removal of poverty, or improvement in the conditions of the poor. In Third World countries development has, in fact, been largely geared to serve the interests of the industrialized countries and has primarily benefited the elite. Sometimes the majority of the people are enjoined to wait their turn for development, or to make sacrifices today for the benefit of the next generation. In fact, the effect of development so far has been to accentuate the gap between the rich and poor with the Third World countries and between the Third World and industrialized countries, and even between rich and poor in developed countries.

Development should aim at increasing people's capacity to benefit from the resources of their community, to eliminate class distinctions and exploitation.

Many of the current trends in developement are self-defeating. What is required is a new "basket of goods and services" for the least advantaged. Development should be measured, then, in terms of the rate at which the poorest members of the community are able to develop. Indeed, a better word for development could be "liberation."

Development must be understood as a relative term, and no one definition will fit all circumstances. Essentially, it is a process that enhances the long-term capacity of a society to function for the well-being of all its members as understood and perceived by them, and that provides safeguards for the rights of the individual to an equitable share in the goods and services produced by the society.

Social development is a relatively new concept which, integrated with economic development, provides a more balanced process for improving the human condition by emphasizing community welfare, self-sufficiency, and self-fulfillment components.

PARTICIPATION

Participation, as a processs that provides for the participant a role in decision-making and in the implementation of programs, was seen as an essential element of development, as an end as well as a means, and as an important way of heightening consciousness and increasing knowledge of issues and available choices. The contribution to participation that could be made by social welfare in its widest connotation was seen as vital for development.

Participation can be considered purely in terms of the extent to which it promotes development. This approach, however, could justify restrictions placed on it if it is seen as a constraint on development. Some conceive of participation as a one-way process, in terms of people "cooperating" with the government and other authorities, and not as an exercise in shared responsibility for decisions and actions.

Participation as a means ensures involvement of people and approval for government policy and actions. As an end, participation becomes a condition for social development in the sense that "good government is no substitute for self-government," that people's right to express their consent for actions taken on their behalf is a continuing process, not a periodic exercise to determine who should rule or misrule them.

There is growing disenchantment with the representational democratic system. For many people, participation is restricted to periodic voting at elections. In some countries even this right has been suspended. Some political structures make participation difficult; hence the many protest movements against government decisions.

Scope for participation outside the electoral system is limited to voluntary organizations in many countries. The majority of the people are often bypassed and have little scope for participation. This could lead to alienation. Participation is a way of restoring common purpose and identity to a community.

What are the conditions for effective participation? Citizens must have access to a free flow of relevant information and knowledge to be able to participate meaningfully. They must also have the will and the willingness to give of their time and energy, and an attitude of mind that sees in voluntarism and personal service an essential element of self-help. Where structures and organizations are large and unwieldy, participation is difficult. It is usually only at the micro-level that most citizens are able to participate effectively. Therefore, decentralization of structures is desirable; it brings the decision-makers closer to the people.

The inadequacies of the representational system have led to some questioning, and a crisis in parliamentary democracy all over the world. Participation is more than mere representation. It ensures a continuing influence by people in decisions made on their behalf. At times participation may take the form of contesting policies and procedures of government and the authorities.

Participation is not only between people and government. It serves as a focus for decision-making in other sectors of human concern, within communities and organizations and in employer-employeee relations.

Participation between people and government is today sometimes preempted by the role of big organizations like corporations and trade unions. Some of these exert more weight with governments than the bulk of the poeple as a whole. Trade unions, for example, may sometimes act only in the interest of their members, oblivious of the interests of the larger community. Cooperative movements, another set of participatory organizations, are increasingly led by professionals who may effectively cut off their members' participation with government.

Some workers' councils that include representatives of government and the general public enable other than employers and union representatives to influence decisions. In general, however, consumers have no direct say in industry.

In private industry there are rarely opportunities for participation by the small shareholders other than at annual shareholders' meetings.

The right to have access to information from government and other authorities is essential for effective participation by the people. Participation by outside groups in government or industry is weak when the information flow is weak. There is need for consumers, for example, to have access to pertinent information.

It is important to develop new approaches to participation. It is not enough for the government to ask people to cooperate with it. Government must cooperate with the people. All participatory organizations need a two-way flow of information. Information should mean not merely facts but a correct interpretation of facts and opinions. To ensure this two-way flow, attention should be paid to the deliberate creation of machinery for this purpose.

Umbrella organizations, public councils, and government commissions are being used more frequently as a means of involving and consulting the general public. Their representative composition is often questionable, and they rarely permit participation in actual decision-making. Their function is usually limited to fact-finding. Although they are significant in assisting the two-way flow of information, they are often used as yet another medium for imposing views and policies.

Social welfare associations, usually voluntary organizations, provide services which can complement and even compete with public services. Some of them play an important vanguard role, compensating for state inaction. It is sometimes found that voluntary services are more personalized and better adapted to needs. If more services of the same kind were available, it would enable users to choose and express preferences.

The different organizations that require public participation in their decisions and sometimes in their activities are:

1. Central government (unitary, federal)
2. Local government (regional, district, or village)
3. Corporations, trade unions, and so forth
4. Voluntary organizations with open membership
5. Consultative and advisory councils.

It was noted that many voluntary organizations tend to be paternalistic and elitist with entrenched services that tend to perpetuate themselves. Opportunities for the majority of ordinary folk to participate in such organizations are not so open. Participation requires not only adequate information, and sometimes means, but also time. Many members of the working classes are usually too tired at the end of the eight-hour day to have the time or inclination to participate in many citizens' organizations.

One obstacle to participation, it was noted, is bureaucratization, usually a consequence of large-scale organization. This diffuses responsibility for decision-making and screens and excludes the public from influencing the decision-makers. It creates anonymity and absorbs the individual in the machine.

Despite the value and necessity for participation at all levels where decisions affect people, there are nevertheless certain risks of participation which must be borne in mind. For example, a multiplicity of private interest groups may lead to the domination of groups with the greatest bargaining power. Furthermore, they can cease to be spokesmen for the interests they purport to represent. Participation could become a privilege of those who have the time and the information to participate—usually the elite. As was noted earlier, the institutionalization of participation in very big organizations could alienate and separate the membership from the leadership and preempt the people from participation.

ASPIRATIONS

Development is considered meaningful only if it conforms to the expressed needs and aspirations of the people. But aspirations do not evolve in a vacuum. People's aspirations are often shaped by the elite and by their own perceptions of, and reactions to, the elite. Aspirations are also influenced by the social structure and people's perception of what is possible. Certain aspirations may be deliberately implanted by politicians, propagandists, and *animateurs.* Unrealistic aspirations can lead to much frustration and can be potentially dangerous, as happens, for example, when extreme wealth and poverty are juxtaposed.

The structure of people's aspirations has been greatly influenced by certain ideas implicit in current notions of development—that "what is good is urban and is industrialized." It is manifested in the rural-urban drift and the trend to industrialization. In such a structure of aspirations how, for example, does the rural-oriented citizen relate?

Contradictions can and do exist between the aspirations of the majority of the people and the aspirations of the government and the elite. Participation can help produce a consensus in aspirations that will make development decisions more acceptable and meaningful to all.

In societies where the majority of the people are illiterate and cut off from the developmental process, who is to help them know what development means and help shape their aspirations? It is contended that even where their stated aspirations are shaped by the elite, participation in development decisions and in the development process will lead to insights that will enable the people to redefine their aspirations more meaningfully.

What is done for people or on their behalf must conform to what they want. Participation is supposed to ensure this. But the determination of what people want is not easy. What people really want is supposed to be derived from their aspirations. Aspirations represent a way of life the people conceive for themselves. But this is a composite not only of how people see themselves, but of life styles, values, attitudes, and so forth, that they have internalized from school, from the mass media, from peer groups. Aspirations of people also change as their status alters, and as they perceive new opportunities. Programs for development would be meaningful to the extent that they are consistent with people's changing aspirations.

Decision-makers in determining what is good for all, and acceptable to all, have difficult choices to make. It is well-known that sometimes facilities and services demanded by people are not used when they are provided.

Development and welfare planners must acquire better insights into determining what people really want. The social worker with his special skills has a key role to play in articulating the needs of the people. What people say they want must be interpreted operationally in terms of their capacity or ability to use and to sustain their interest and derive benefit from what is provided. What may appear to government and other donors as services or opportunities offered to the people may only appear to them as "promised" opportunities and not actual opportunities which they can effectively utilize.

ECONOMIC GROWTH

Economic growth must be distinguished from economic development. The former is a purely physical phenomenon that may not confer benefits on its location. For example, there are factories established in many developing countries or depressed areas of developed countries which go through a full cycle of production but, like isolated enclaves, yield nothing to their locality beyond occupying space and sometimes distorting the price structures of land values and other material assets even though they provide some employment.

Economic growth, whether viewed as industrial expansion or as a great volume of production, does not automatically reduce the incidence of poverty or contribute to closing the gap between the haves and the have-nots.

Economic growth can result in waste of resources and the overproduction of goods which have little or no—and no direct—impact on social development objectives.

Under certain conditions economic growth may interfere with, impede, or even diminish other values which are essential to the growth and well-being of the people, as by maximizing profits at the expense of other objectives.

Economic growth in the developed countries is often accomplished at the expense of the developing countries and/or the underprivileged people of the developed countries themselves.

From the perspective of social development, expanded production may be necessary, at faster or slower rates, to provide the essential needs of all the people, but such growth should be viewed as a means and not as an end in itself. Where production is essential, care must be taken to insist that so far as possible it be in areas relevant to the basic and articulated needs of all the people.

Economic growth is meaningful only in so far as it contributes to social development. Planning for welfare must therefore not be considered an appendix to economic planning. Economic expansion must have as its immediate aim the elimination of poverty.

### ELIMINATION OF POVERTY

Development that does not aim at the elimination of poverty cannot claim to be aimed at the welfare of all. Poverty is, of course, a relative term. A starvation income in one country may be a comfortable income in another, and the resources required to keep a person in comfort in one area may differ from what can keep a person comfortable in another area.

In societies that claim to provide equal opportunities for all, poverty is sometimes seen as a sign of individual failure. That poverty is induced by the social structure, and those unfortunate enough to be caught in it are often in an inescapable vicious circle, is not readily understood by many.

In the same way, underdevelopment is not merely an absence of wealth, but the active result of certain economic and social forces. A government, for example, that makes a decision to maintain a certain level of unemployment in order to produce a certain economic effect condemns at once a number of people to a jobless and penniless state with no real options.

The major objective of all welfare effort should be the elimination of poverty. Poverty is not merely a shortfall in the material means to sustain an adequate living standard, it is also the undeveloped or restrained capacity to engage in the full social life of the society. However, the elimination of material poverty should be the first call on all development and welfare effort.

Mahatma Gandhi once said: "There is enough in this world for everybody's need; there is not enough for everybody's greed." Inequitable exchange and inequitable distribution of economic resources and goods have been the cause of persistent poverty. The function of poverty is to maintain affluence. If there is no poor there will be no rich. Social justice demands an equitable distribution of income and redistribution of resources.

In many countries taxation, especially progressive taxation, is a major instrument for reducing wide inequalities in income, and for closing the gap between rich and poor. However, studies conducted in some developed countries show that there has been only a narrow shift in income structures during the past three decades, and the gap between rich and poor has not narrowed appreciably.

Much has been said about the problem of poverty, and about the need to bridge the gap. Measures taken so far in many countries to achieve this aim, as noted, have not always been successful. Some would insist that it is not possible to correct the sharp imbalances in wealth and income without drastic changes in the social structure. Others believe that a set of progressive reforms could achieve a reasonable balance if efficiently implemented.

The Working Party is convinced that the time has come when social welfare workers must realize that their efforts at ensuring adequate welfare for everyone may well be ineffective in the long run and will merely provide palliatives unless the problem of poverty is attacked systematically and effectively. In this light, the Working Party puts forward certain postulates and principles for consideration as approaches toward certain postulates and principles for consideration as approaches toward solving the problem of poverty and reducing the sharp imbalances in income and other social requirements:

1. Development effort should be aimed primarily at the elimination of poverty.

2. Countries should determine basic minimum needs for all members of their population, and orient resources and production progressively to meeting these needs.

3. The provision for a person's basic needs and services should not depend necessarily on his occupation or earning capacity.

4. Wage structures should be progressively adjusted to narrow income gaps and raise low incomes.

5. Excessive use and acquisition of material resources and goods by individuals or groups must be considered inimical to the interests of mankind and must be controlled.

6. A ceiling should be placed on the share of the national wealth to which any one person is entitled.

7. Stringent measures must be enforced to reduce wastage of natural resources and resources in industry, agriculture, and so on, and the production of "false" goods.

8. Development should be measured by the rate of advance of the poorest in the population, and not only by the GNP or similar measurement.

9. Resource allocation must be directed first and foremost toward meeting the needs of all the people rather than meeting the needs of a minority.

10. Trade and economic relations between developed and developing countries must be adjusted and made more equitable.

These principles will be seen as prerequisites to successful attainment of today's development needs, and without their acceptance social welfare action cannot but be the remedial treatment of preventable conditions and the patching of a development system that requires fundamental restructuring, even though in every society the inept and the handicapped will require special consideration and services.

It was considered that in principle, policies aimed at reducing poverty and narrowing the gap between rich and poor are widely acceptable, and, in fact, form part of many political manifestoes. But when it comes to the practicalities of implementation any severe curtailment of income of groups that have a surplus leads to serious resistance. In other words, is there the political will to effect fundamental changes in the structure of incomes and property? A conference devoted to the consideration of development and the welfare of mankind cannot shy away from the responsibility of suggesting that, if necessary, people should be prepared to give up some material comforts and make adjustments in their way of life in order to correct past injustices or to give unfortunate brethren a chance for a better life.

EDUCATION

Education is considered crucial to both development and welfare. Conceived of as a major catalyst to social change and development, educational expansion has not fulfilled its promise. The opportunities created by education have reached their peak too soon. Is this failure due to faults in the educational system, curricula, and so forth, or is it due to faults in the social structure within which the educational system operates?

Attempts to attain the goal of functional literacy, a minimum aim of education, appears to have failed even in highly developed countries that have had compulsory education for decades. The failure of education to fulfill the high promise held out for it calls for careful review of both its form and content. This exercise has been going on for some time now, and new insights are being gained. One of the problems facing educators is that they are expected to provide training to fit people into a future society and to prepare them better to fulfill their aspirations in life. The future society envisaged is a dynamic concept, and the perception of people's aspirations is difficult for the same reason.

Current issues in education relate to: (*a*) its relevance; (*b*) its orientation; and (*c*) its duration and cost. The problem of relevance has sharpened the debate as to whether people are educated for jobs or are educated for general enlightenment. Elementary and secondary schools and universities do not see themselves primarily as job trainers. In this sense, some of the criticism of modern education is misplaced. Job training should be done in vocational schools or through well-organized apprenticeships.

Most formal education has geared to serve the system that sponsors it, the establishment. So long as the system trained a small number of people *from* the establishment *for* the establishment there was no crisis. Now, however, large numbers of people question the relevance of what they are taught to their aspirations, and to their prospects in life.

The orientation of education reflects to some extent class prejudices, with values tending to be upper-middle- and middle-class-directed to white-collar jobs. It creates distortions in aspirations, builds up frustrations because of its diminished relevance, and fails to take account of the needs of the society. It contributes to the rural-urban drift, the demoralization of the rural areas, and the urban crises. The schools are thus confronted with issues of relevance and caught in a crisis of values which are partly responsible for the present moral malaise.

Finally, the long duration of schooling and its high cost are questioned together with the relevance and function of much information that young people absorb in their years of schooling. For developing countries in particular, universal and conventional schooling sets unattainable targets. It should be possible to give people a reasonable education in shorter time and at less cost.

*Education as a Condition for the Promotion of Participation.* Everybody underlined the important role which education could play at all levels in evolving attitudes favorable to development of participation. In the past, education achieved the opposite, rather, by emphasizing notions of selection, competition, and hierarchy. The methods did little to prepare the young for work in groups or for behavior based on a sense of community. Consequently, we must insist upon the importance of a basic training which emphasizes autonomy, responsibility, and sense of community.

A major part of the child's first social experiences is obtained through school. The type of organization and functioning of the school system will therefore heavily color his or her vision of the social system as a whole. The teaching is now to be based on the desire to let the child's own originality develop. The child should not be seen as a subject for training, but as an actor in his own educational process.

In many countries, an increasingly important place is being accorded to participation in school organization. Parents' and pupils' councils have been set up to take part in discussions concerning school affairs. They often have limitations in that the more vocal middle classes play the dominant role. Conversely, deprived families tend to be excluded from participation. The establishment of teacher-pupil councils at the secondary education level is also helping to encourage the participation of those primarily concerned in the scholastic institution.

Meanwhile, some new insights have emerged to show that the crucial period for learning to relate socially is that between birth and three or five years of age. In view of this, it is suggested that more attention should be paid to expectant mothers and mothers nursing young babies. Preschool education should receive more funding. It is possible that in developing countries the institutional atmosphere of nursery school may not be a good substitute for the extended family home.

Preschool education can help to correct inequalities arising out of family background right from the start. Surveys conducted in underprivileged groups have shown that parents' attitudes toward the education of their children play a vital role. Thus, within the framework of educational priorities, and considering the importance of the needs of socially and culturally deprived children, emphasis is placed on sensitizing parents to the schooling of their children. In fact, the family, as an instrument for the transmission of handicaps or privileges, is far more powerful than the corrective force of schooling.

The social function of education as a catalyst in social mobility has not been too manifest. Social class constraints have proved more resilient. The much vaunted "meritocracy" in education has succumbed to "heritocracy." Clearly, there is need to do more for people from disadvantaged families than provide them with free education. Their aspirations and motivations need to be shored up.

That education has a central function to perform in the achievement of social development goals is not being questioned. What the foregoing discussion proposes is that the institution of education must itself undergo some major changes in order to fulfill its essential function more effectively. The educational system of a community must be careful not to contribute to the dysfunctional aspects of its society. For example, the fact that in some countries schooling keeps young people out of gainful and productive participation far too long results in difficulties for some of them when they do enter the adult world. Education, once considered for the young, must now serve man throughout his life cycle. Education must be flexible to meet the needs of its constituency and to grow or change as these needs change.

MASS MEDIA: COMMUNICATION AND INFORMATION

Development requires the transmission of new ideas, skills, attitudes, and a great deal of information to people. Modern techniques of mass communication can with great advantage be utilized to serve this worthwhile purpose. In industrialized societies the press and television are recognized as the most potent. In developing countries, illiteracy on the one hand and poverty on the other have restricted the scope of these two media, but radio and the cinema have proved quite effective as communication media.

The role of the mass media in fostering development and welfare has unfortunately not been marked. Much that is communicated is in response to factors extraneous to human well-being. On the other hand, it could be said that social welfare personnel have not made much use of the opportunities offered by the mass media. There is need to train such personnel to do this increasingly.

There are disturbing trends within the mass media, however, which need to be watched. There is a trend toward consolidation of newspapers in the hands of fewer owners. This may limit their range of representation and views. Films, too, are more and more devoted to sex and crime and violence.

Apart from the mass media, social development personnel could exploit drama, music, art, and the dance to project people's ideas, aspirations, criticisms, and commentaries on life and events, thus strengthening their self-knowledge and self-confidence.

THE ROLE OF WOMEN

The contribution of women to development is crucial both within the family and in terms of their role in development generally. The restrictions and inequalities which hamper women's full participation are still widespread despite increasingly favorable legislative measures which are often ignored or only partially implemented.

The woman is frequently unable to use or even relate to her rights, nor may she wish to do so. The restrictions and restraints that confine her need to be removed, to permit her to exercise the right of choice. As the main socializer of her children, she requires reinforcement through a variety of social welfare services aimed at increasing her competence and reducing the inordinate pressures with which she contends as mother, wife, and worker.

The nature of relationships between men and women is undergoing change in all societies, with greater stress on shared responsibility in all aspects of life and living. The right of women to develop their talents fully and to utilize them for the benefit of society and creative self-fulfillment is acknowledged. At the same time, it might legitimately be asked whether at certain stages of development the more traditional role of women in providing stability and security in the home is not the most effective protection against the confusion and turmoil that invariably accompany rapid change.

THE ROLE OF YOUTH

The phenomenon of loud and sometimes violent youth protests in recent years has alerted people to the special problems and needs of youth. It is recognized that some youth protests have also reflected adult frustrations within the society. But by and large, what youth protests and movements indicate is a desire to do something, to participate not only in nation-building, but in decision-making.

Because of the power that youth can generate, many governments are uneasy about youth generally. In many developing countries, governments try to harness the energies of youth for community programs which are sometimes voluntary, sometimes compulsory. Some try directly or indirectly to politicize and to control youth. Current youth unrest in developing countries seems to be a protest against authoritarian rule, abuse of power, and corruption.

Youth in developing countries form the majority of the population (sometimes 60 percent). Yet in many areas they are not offered meaningful opportunities for participation in development. Prospects for their education are still bleak. Only about 50 percent to 60 percent get into primary schools, and of these not more than 20 percent go beyond that level. Many face serious problems of unemployment thereafter. The majority, who have no formal education, are often completely neglected. Youth, whether educated or not, represent a tremendous resource and can make a major contribution to development.

Youth in developing countries in general do not have access to many recreational facilities to channel their energies into constructive and meaningful activity. Conventional recreational facilities available in developed countries are too expensive, although it was pointed out that even where they exist, they are not always utilized for the purpose for which they were provided. Excellent recreational activity is possible with minimal expenditures, and imaginative projects have been successfully demonstrated.

In developed countries the violent phase of youth protests seems to have abated, but nonviolent protests of various kinds continue. Many of the questions being raised relate to the issue of relevance of structure and institutions, of conventional morality and attitudes. These issues must not be shelved. Youth clearly does not intend to be left out of participation in the life of their communities. So long as the adult population is unwilling to permit youth to participate in the reshaping of society, they are likely to continue to protest. New ways that will permit youth to participate meaningfully in the life of the community have to be found. Here is an area where social development workers can play a great role in seeking to understand better youth's motivations and problems and to help them find meaningful participation in social development.

TRAINING FOR SOCIAL DEVELOPMENT WORK

The training of a social worker must reflect the changing needs of society within the broader perspective of social development. The social work function now covers a wider area of activity, from remedial welfare to community development and social development work. It is with this broader connotation that the term "social worker" is used here.

Welfare and social work thus embrace a variety of activities at different levels. Personnel in social work are equally diverse. There are full-time officials in both government and private organizations and part-time and voluntary workers, administrators, and direct-service personnel. Each type must receive training suitable to their broadened roles and responsibilities.

Among the major areas of activity in social development are:
1. Elimination of poverty in both rural and urban areas
2. Strengthening of family units and family education
3. Articulation of needs and interests of the underprivileged
4. Community education and "conscientization"
5. Organization of communities to do their own planning
6. Participation in community decisions affecting the people themselves
7. Stimulation of self-help activities where appropriate.

The dichotomy sometimes suggested between the social or welfare worker and the community development worker is a false one and not helpful. Their work entails the ability to work with people, building good social relations within the family and the community, getting people and groups to co-operate for their mutual welfare. All social workers—including community workers—must have a good understanding of the processes and techniques of social development. They should be taught to stimulate leadership in development activities, and through more self-help eventually to render remedial services largely unnecessary.

At the community level it is not uncommon for social workers who have good rapport with the people to clash with local politicians, who may see them as competing for local influence. Programs have sometimes been rendered ineffective as a result of such conflicts or misunderstandings. Social workers must be equipped to handle such delicate situations, and other situations of community conflict which may hamper collective community action.

The social worker must therefore learn how to work with the politician and the legislator, the economist and the planner. In order to increase citizen participation in community activities, he should be capable of planning outside government structures, be trained to initiate more revolutionary action and to engage in advocacy of the cause of the underprivileged. Conversely, he should be trained to inform people of their welfare rights and privileges under the law. The need for training social development planners was emphasized.

It was noted that in social work the more highly trained personnel are often assigned administrative functions, and the least trained are usually the ones in contact with the clientele. This anomaly should be corrected.

The need to reorient training of social workers imposes a need on schools of social work to retrain their staffs to perform the new functions. In some countries, teachers of social work have no laboratory. They no longer have their own clients to deal with and may be in danger of being out of touch with the current realities of the problems they want their students to handle.

Improvement of the methodology of instruction and assistance to self-learning constitute an important area of growth and change for institutions preparing people to work in social development. Student learning and evaluation must focus more on the demonstrations of performance outcomes that stimulate self-learning and realistic confidence in self.

Another important matter considered was the fact that there exists in many countries a great deal of social legislation that is not applied, either because people do not know about it or because the machinery for enforcement is weak. Social work organizations and social workers must take on the functions of helping people know their rights and entitlements and of lobbying to ensure that effective machinery is established to implement existing legislation.

RESEARCH AND EVALUATION

As social work assumes new and challenging dimensions there is need to test new concepts and theories of social welfare and social development. The type of research typically carried out by many is still largely determined by the interests and preoccupations of the funding agencies. Much social science research, especially in developing countries, is now being devoted to population and environment and general problems of social structure. Much of this is, of course, relevant to social work and social development. It is necessary, moreover, to develop research expertise in the specific field of social development with reference to the role of social work.

The nature of social work requires a problem-oriented and multidisciplinary approach. Although it is helpful for social work research dealing with social development to use tools of various disciplines, it is necessary to organize research in institutes and university departments devoted primarily to the problems of social development and methods of solving such problems.

Evaluative research of projects and experiments must not only test the cost-benefit effects usually required for convincing donors that projects are useful, but also to test client reactions to what has been provided over a period of time.

Because the results of social welfare work are not always quantifiable it is often difficult to appraise them. The development of indicators of social development has been slow and unsatisfactory. But it is both possible and sometimes appropriate to assess performance indirectly, using nonconventional and even subjective indicators. It is not always helpful to insist on quantification. Happiness, satisfaction, good health, peace of mind, good community relations—these are not readily quantifiable, but they can be perceived. At the same time, work must continue on developing more effective social indicators.

Much research data, it is known, are unutilized. It would be helpful if some national as well as international institutions were to establish social development documentation and information retrieval centers to further their use.

# Opening Address

## MZEE JOMO KENYATTA
### PRESIDENT OF KENYA

ON BEHALF of the government and people of this republic, I extend a warm welcome to all delegates to this conference. I hope you will find an opportunity to meet our people in different parts of the country, giving you a glimpse of their economic vigor and social aspirations.

Our republic is now well-launched upon its second decade of development as an independent state. We describe this as a process of nation-building, generated by a country-wide spirit of self-help and a deliberate association between the government and the people. Our culture is rooted in convictions of human dignity, the expression of talent, and a keen sense of community responsibility.

We feel that economic and social development cannot be approached in isolation, and, as I said at the time of independence, that real social progress can only spring from the determined efforts and involvement of our people.

Social welfare is no longer just an academic matter but is concerned also with the struggles, needs, and hopes of ordinary people. If asked to define the ultimate objective of any social welfare institution, we would say that the true purpose should be to help people feel that they matter and to guarantee for them a place and prospect within a society that is orderly and worthwhile.

These are the philosophies that have driven the machinery of my government in Kenya. The majority of our people live and work on the land, often in districts which are highly congested and intensively farmed. For this reason, the direction of physical and planning resources to the rural areas continues to be the strategic key to our development.

However, as in other parts of the world, we face the substantial problems of urban expansion as well. It is the belief of my government that efforts to bring about the increasing expansion of two or three cities must be switched to the more amenable development of a comparatively large number of urban centers. Only then can we harness the self-help spirit to effective allocation of resources. Just as rural life is incomplete without some access to the amenities of towns, so towns can only thrive when they have access to the countryside.

This occasion is also being celebrated in Kenya as Youth Day. The population of this republic is almost twelve million, of which about 50 percent are under fifteen years of age. Young people are energetic and adventurous by nature, but they must be armed with a clear understanding of the structure of society and all the social challenges that must be confronted. Only in this way can we ensure the involvement of youth in the efforts made today to win the social progress we hope to see tomorrow.

Ladies and gentlemen, I wish you success in your deliberations, and trust that the outcome of your studies and discussions will affirm the belief that social welfare is no longer an academic phrase, but a reflection of our national effort of working together in the spirit of "Harambee." It is on the foundation of such hopes that I have great pleasure in declaring this international conference to be formally open.

# Development and Participation:
## Operational Implications for Social Welfare

### REUBEN C. BAETZ

EXECUTIVE DIRECTOR, CANADIAN COUNCIL
ON SOCIAL DEVELOPMENT; PRESIDENT,
INTERNATIONAL COUNCIL ON SOCIAL WELFARE

DEVELOPMENT HAS been endorsed as a cornerstone of public policy by political leaders in virtually all countries of the world for more than a quarter of a century. An important underlying principle has been that all people of all nations have both the right and the capacity to develop. Specialists from a wide variety of professions and disciplines have examined in detail many aspects of the concept of development, building up a substantial body of literature on the subject. ICSW has also discussed various facets of development in every world forum since the Madras conference in 1952, and the term "development" formed part of the theme of two conferences: "Rural and Community Development," in 1962 in Brazil; and "Urban Development: Its Implications for Social Welfare," at the Washington conference in 1966.

We have not attempted until this conference, however, to approach the concept in the comprehensive and integrated way implied by the theme "Development and Participation." While this comprehensive approach will likely prove intellectually stimulating, it could lead us into a rarefied atmosphere of philosophical and abstract thought. We are indebted to Mr. Lukutati of Zambia, chairman of the Program Planning Committee, who protected us from such a "flight to the stars" by insisting that the second part of the theme be "Operational Implications for Social Welfare."

We have come here from over seventy countries and bring with us a wide range of backgrounds and disciplines: social workers, community development personnel, members of religious organizations employed in a wide range of social welfare activities, elected political leaders, administrators of public and private agencies, social planners, social scientists, university staff from many faculties, and volunteer workers. One of the things we have in common is that we are action- and service-oriented; conferences such as this are designed primarily to improve effectiveness in our operations at home as we apply some of the new concepts and broader insights we may gain here.

With this objective in mind, let me sound strongly one note of caution. Much of what we will be discussing here cannot be applied without adaptation to our various situations and programs at home. Development consists of systematically interrelated growth and change processes in human societies. These processes have many uniformities and universally predictable sequences. They also have unique characteristics in each country or society, deriving from historical patterns, cultural traits and values, territorial and population size, resources, internal class structure and power relationships, and the nation's place in the international system. Each society has its own more or less limited range of choices open to it and a more or less limited capacity to make choices. At any given time, the political capacity to make choices may or may not be compatible with the real developmental alternatives that are open to it. For example, in a political democracy in which a large middle-income group has virtual control over the political process, developmental strategies which might open new opportunities for the low-income minority are politically impossible to attain for the time being at least. Social welfare personnel returning from international conferences such as this equipped, it is to be hoped, with new insights and renewed zeal for change should be aware of these reality factors.

My observations on the operational implications for social welfare are derived from my personal interpretation of our theme. "Participation in development" refers not only to how individual members of a community are guaranteed a fair and equitable share of the benefits of development, but also to how they can be assured the opportunity of contributing—to their fullest capacity and in ways most meaningful to them—in the creation of the community's goods and services, in producing the common wealth. This view assumes that in the process of freely participating in development, both as consumer and producer, and in taking an active part in the decisions governing that development, wider avenues for full self-realization are opened and a sense of interdependence and a spirit of community are created.

While the economist sees labor primarily as a tool of production, along with land and capital in economic development, social welfare sees the individual's participation in the productive process as an avenue toward independence, interdependence, and self-realization, namely, social development. Hence, economic development and social development can be described as being the two wings of the same bird—national development.

An active interest in development and participation seen in this broader context has vast implications for social welfare. It requires at least three different types of intervention strategies and techniques, employed when and as circumstances indicate:

1. The provision of traditional personal social services to individuals and groups, particularly to the most vulnerable members of society—the aged, the handicapped, children without families, and so forth

2. Community development, "social animation" largely at a village, district, or local level

3. Formulation and promotion of social policies outside government by bodies such as national and international councils and institutes which have the capacity to direct constructive criticism at government, urge legislative reform, and help generate an informed and sympathetic public attitude.

Recognizing the need for this three-pronged approach should help settle the internecine war which has gone on at

least since the 1952 Madras conference between the advocates
of community development and casework. The simple fact of
the matter is that both are necessary.

Obviously, in many situations and especially in developing
countries, community development and the "social animation"
approach seem the most desirable; but there are many situations where the casework approach can be equally developmental by assisting individuals to participate in society. For example, casework in rehabilitation of the physically and
mentally handicapped and delinquents, aiding them to return
to a full and useful life in the mainstream of society, can claim
to be just as much a program in social development as is the
community development approach in a Third World village.

This is not to suggest that all social services can claim to be
developmental. One of the essential tests or criteria to be applied is the extent to which the service or program facilitates
greater participation by the individuals to whom the program
is directed. A service which is highly paternalistic, which
creates dependency, which isolates individuals from the mainstream of society by institutionalizing them unnecessarily, cannot claim to be fostering social development. While no doubt
many of these paternalistic programs are highly motivated,
and provide sympathetic care, they hinder rather than facilitate participation in the mainstream of society. It is little
wonder that with the urge to institutionalize our handicapped,
we have made so little effort in our public life to facilitate their
full participation. A recent City of Toronto report depicts em-
phatically how, through ignorance and thoughtlessness, we set
up obstacle courses for the handicapped in our public buildings, streets, and transportation systems.

The aged are another sector of our population whom we
tend to remove from full participation. The tendency toward
earlier retirement in industrially developed countries may be
motivated as much by a desire to make room in the labor force
for younger members as it is by a desire to remove the burden
of daily toil from the aged. Likewise, in Third World countries, the early age of retirement—in some, as low as forty-
five—can only be regarded as a cause of hidden unemploy-

ment. At any rate, forced retirement at an arbitrary age can cause hardship rather than comfort, and early retirement legislation must be watched by social welfare everywhere with a healthy skepticism.

One of the most meaningful ways, both socially and economically, for individuals to participate in development is through gainful employment. Yet in most of the world, unemployment and underemployment continue to plague people and nations. The baby explosion of the 1950s is becoming the labor explosion of the 1970s. In the Third World, the labor force is increasing two to three times faster that it ever did in the West and Japan. Moreover, industrial development in the Third World, unlike that in the West, has not grown fast enough to absorb the growing number of employable workers. More and more it is recognized that Western-style investment, which is capital-intensive rather than labor-intensive, even if it were substantially increased, could simply not absorb those able and willing to work. Each year the situation worsens a little because the machine-oriented investment pattern of the Third World does not create enough jobs to employ the annual addition to the labor force, the politically vulnerable young.

Fortunately, and of great significance to the field of social welfare, there seems to be growing emphasis, especially in rural areas, on the labor-intensive "small producer" rather than on large-scale mechanized operations. Development is thus decentralized, with more people participating in both production and the management of their own enterprise. Not only does this present all the social advantages that accompany greater participation, but statistics from countries such as the two Koreas, Taiwan, Israel, Puerto Rico, Egypt, Yugoslavia, and no doubt China, show success in strictly economic terms. Small producers, self-managed, can be high performers regardless of political systems—a fact which should both encourage and challenge us.

The shift from emphasis on massive mechanized units of production to smaller decentralized labor-intensive units has enormous implications for social welfare, especially in rural areas of the Third World. It should encourage and open up additional opportunities for a wide variety of small, innovative, self-help enterprises which can be readily sponsored by national and international, public and private social development agencies. Management and leadership, however, must come from the villages.

Helping people to find meaningful employment requires suitable training and education, along with supportive personal social services. Here again, we have reached a point where priorities, policies, and programs need alteration. For at least the last quarter of a century, more education for more people was seen as the key to national development and personal advancement and fulfillment. The benefits, of course, have been enormous, but in recent years in many countries there is a surplus of qualified men and women for the number of available jobs commensurate with training. One result is that more and more, employers are arbitrarily raising their standards; those who at one time accepted employees with elementary school education now ask for, and are able to recruit, college graduates for the same price. But the aspirations and the job expectations of the employees have not changed, and they expect jobs at the level their education would have brought them earlier. This universal dilemma was best illustrated by President Julius Nyerere of Tanzania in his Tenth Anniversary report when he said,

. . . a young man or woman with a full primary school education in 1961 regarded himself, and was regarded by others, as being educated. He expected wage employment—probably in an office. But now, with 70,000 students graduating from Standard VII this year, and an increasing number every year in the future, none of this is true. Not only is there insufficient wage employment to absorb all these people; they are needed in the *Ujamaan* villages and on the farms of our country. Nor do they have much formal education in comparison with the thousands who now graduate from secondary school every year. Yet, the expectation of these young people, and of their parents, has not changed to keep up with this development. Many still feel disappointed at what they regard as failure to get wage employment. The attitudes have not kept pace with the real changes.

The dilemma of people with levels of education and aspirations which exceed job opportunities is world-wide. Western Europe has responded by importing 7 million semi- and unskilled workers to fill jobs which would fall below the aspirations of the educated young in those countries. North America is experiencing extremely high rates (15 percent–18 percent) of unemployment among disenchanted educated youth looking for "meaningful" jobs. University graduates in Japan are driving taxis, and highly trained doctors and engineers in other parts of Asia are not practicing their professions.

What are the implications for social service agencies interested in development and participation? It is evident that counseling, retraining, and replacement services must be increased, but there is a difficult and more complex task ahead. That is to bring into greater harmony the educational system and the realities of the present and future labor market. Admittedly, preparing people for the labor market is not the only purpose of education. The task will be difficult, first, because the educational system, like all systems, finds adjustment extremely unattractive. Secondly, in many countries the educational system is an entity in itself and has been traditionally of no direct concern to social planners and social welfare professionals. Thirdly, the world is changing so rapidly that many analysts say people must prepare not just for one career or type of work in a lifetime, but for several. All of this means that effecting change in setting educational policies will be a long and difficult process, but it offers a worthwhile challenge.

What is required is a fundamental change in attitude, both in the educational system and in the labor system. We should be prepared for some restructuring of the pecking order of jobs in respect to status and accompanying salaries, and for an increasing reduction in the vast spread of incomes within and among professions. There is, after all, no logical reason why a doctor's income should exceed by ten times that of a nurse, especially if, unlike in the past, we will have a surplus of doctors.

A rapidly increasing number of women throughout the industrialized world see their entry into the labor force as the best avenue leading to greater participation in society at large. This too has major implications for social welfare, not the least of which is the vast expansion of day care services of adequate standard for children of working mothers. It is also incumbent upon social welfare to promote the cause of women—obtaining "equal pay for work of equal value."

In providing all the necessary facilities to enable mothers with dependent children to join the labor force, it would be unjust not to recognize the value to national development of mothers who stay in the home to care for their families. It is an irony of our time that we place so little value on the contribution they are making. Their work does not appear anywhere in our national accounts as part of the gross national product (GNP), and very few social services are set up for their benefit in spite of the fact that a number of studies show young mothers to be among the loneliest, most alienated members of the population. Surely here are implications for social welfare.

Gainful employment is not the only way for people to participate in society. Active voluntary participation in a host of cultural, social, and community services, both formal and informal, provides room for service, self-enrichment, and development of a community spirit. I am convinced there is a vast, untapped potential of human resources in most countries that can be translated into volunteer work with enormous benefits for all. Urbanization has given mankind many benefits, but has so far failed to provide us with the most essential ingredient of all—the sense of an integrated community life. In urban centers, for example, the integrating sinews of tribal and family life that were so evident in early rural societies have not been replaced. We have built carefully planned neighborhoods with no neighbors, and asphalt jungles in which most of us are strangers, lonely and afraid. Volunteer workers can help to create the spirit of community which is so sadly lacking. Agencies and organizations wishing to enlarge the quantity of services they provide and to maintain a high degree of personalization in delivering these services will do well to look to participation by volunteers for help in their activities.

If the goal is greater participation by individuals in development, then a powerful argument can be made that programs designed to eliminate malnutrition and starvation can also be classified as developmental. It is folly in the extreme to suppose that anyone suffering from serious, long-time malnutrition is participating in any respect in society. It is a source of universal puzzlement, and a good deal of embarrassment, that in spite of all our highly touted technological know-how we find such widespread malnutrition and, in at least two areas of the world—Bangladesh and the Sahelian area of Africa—famine.

I do not claim to know the reason for the tragedy. The experts themselves seem to be divided on whether this is a temporary phenomenon due to a series of factors, such as planned cutback in food production in the world's largest producing countries plus bad weather in others, or whether it is a chronic situation, with the world population outpacing our ability to produce.

It would seem to me incomprehensible and intolerable if we who are convened in this conference with a professed concern about human well-being and participation in development do not state our abhorrence of the situation, and press for immediate and effective help from public and private sectors, especially for the two most acutely hit areas of the world. If we are looking for operational implications for our theme, we have an obvious and urgent one at our doorstep.

Widespread malnutrition in many countries, very likely, is only the symptom of a more fundamental cause, namely, national poverty. In this regard, we should examine the report presented by Robert McNamara, president of the World Bank Group, at the Board of Governors meeting held in this magnificent Center in September, 1973. The findings show that financial aid to the developing nations has not increased sufficiently to help these countries with three major interrelated difficulties: an insufficiency of foreign exchange earnings from trade, an inadequate flow of official development assistance, and an increasingly severe burden of external debt. These difficulties cannot be dealt with overnight, but surely we can at least put pressure on our governments to increase the official development assistance. Many would argue that pressing domestic problems in the wealthier countries prevent them from sparing additional help to the developing nations. But the fact is that they are already so far ahead that their GNP will continue to grow so rapidly that they need commit only 2 percent of their future incremental income to help meet the needs of the developing countries.

In the final analysis, probably the most accurate indicator of the degree of active participation in national development is how a nation distributes its wealth. This is usually expressed in terms of income distribution. Access to income is still the crucial indicator, even though some services are also universally provided by the state. Dostoevski noted that "income is coined freedom."

Ideas of hierarchy and equity have survived together in relative peace in modern democracies. Apparently few people expect *equal* shares of the national income, but there is everywhere a strong desire for a *fair* share. And in virtually every mixed capitalist-welfare state economy there is tension due to what is regarded as an unfair spread of income. In the United States, the top one percent of the population receives as much income as the bottom 50 percent; the same distortion is evident in many other countries, including most of the Third World. A proverb of the African Hausa tribe has correctly noted that "God gives blessings to all men; if man had to distribute them, many would go without." The idea as to what is a fair share and what is equitable will vary from country to country, and it does not only—or even primarily—mean that the poorest should compare their income to that of the richest in their particular society. More significantly, it means comparing the income of one group to that of the next, either immediately above or below. The explosive relationship between the working poor and those who live on public welfare assistance is only one example of many within a nation's antagonistic groups. Public policy requires, therefore, not only an acceptable span of income between the richest and the poorest, but also an equitable share for all between the two extremes.

Traditionally, democracies, especially in industrially devel-

oped countries, have relied heavily on income-security measures—income-security programs such as old age security,
family allowances, welfare payments, and so on—to effect distribution of income to those of greater need from those finan-
cially better off. Two general observations are relevant. We
will undoubtedly see continued growth of income-security
programs, but as Richard Titmuss, whose untimely death was
such a loss, urged us at the Hague conference, we must utilize
more than ever the taxation system as the major redistributive
tool. We must also bring the tax system into greater harmony
with the income-security system. Failing to do so has resulted
in far too many countries having governments which hand out
benefits through income-security programs with one hand,
and take back with the other a disproportionate amount from
the lower income groups through the taxation system. Despite
the wide use of progressive income taxes, when all taxes are
taken into account—including sales, excise, and property
taxes—the total burden of taxation is either proportional or,
in many countries, results in the travesty of the poor carrying
relatively the heaviest burden. If our goal is to have a more
equitable distribution of income, the social welfare community
must pay far closer attention to the tax system than has traditionally been the case. And my special plea to the developing
countries who have not yet introduced social security programs is to take a good look at their tax system before doing
so, in order to determine whether it could not be used to meet
the same objectives. Existing social security systems, which
grew out of the nineteenth and twentieth centuries, may be
antiquated in many respects for the new states. They may
benefit only an insignificant number of the population and, in
fact, can result in a subsidy of the rich by the poor. Benefits
through an existing tax structure, such as tax credits and
other allowances, might avoid the need to set up cumbersome
and expensive new social security administrations.

In searching for ways to bring about a more equitable share
of income, we are now experiencing the added obstacle of
rampant world-wide inflation. The impact of inflation is
always greatest on the poorest and on those with fixed in-

comes. This applies equally whether we speak of the low-income individuals within any country or whether we think in terms of the poorest nations among the family of nations. As prices rise through inflation, those individuals who have essential goods and services to sell on the market can simply pass off the cost of inflation by raising the prices of their products. Members of powerful professional associations or trade unions demand, and get, higher wages and incomes. In both cases, they add to the inflationary force. But the poorest members of a nation, or the poorest nations, lack the necessary power to increase their income to adjust to rising costs of living. They may not possess the necessary skills, may not be members of trade unions or professional associations. Moreover, the cost of basic consumer commodities which the poor must buy tends to rise more rapidly than the cost of luxury goods.

The world-wide impact of inflation on the poor demands that we redouble our efforts to index our income-security programs, thereby guaranteeing higher benefits along with rising costs. There is a dangerous and hypocritical argument current in many countries that such measures would simply raise public expenditures, thereby feeding the flames of inflation which, in turn, would leave the poor worse off than before. There is no doubt that increased public expenditures create additional inflationary pressures, but the humane and sensible counter to that argument surely should be that expenditures for nonessential luxury goods should be curtailed rather than expenditures for basic necessities. The social welfare communities around the world must remain vigilant on this crucial point.

I have presented a sweeping view. This wide-ranging discussion has, I hope, shown the virtually endless operational implications for social welfare if we accept the broad approach to the theme "Development and Participation." I now pose the crucial question and suggest for consideration at least a partial answer: where will all our efforts for greater economic and social development likely take mankind? Evidence and forecasts pour in from all sides. Much of it is contradictory and ranges from optimism to complete despair. At the inter-country level, the pessimists believe that the developmental processes followed by the present high-income countries in the past are not open to the developing countries of the world today except possibly in a few special cases. In fact, so this argument goes, the high-income countries exploit and dominate the weak, and, under changing guises, this remains true today. Under these circumstances, the developed countries are inherently incapable of helping the others to catch up. The same pessimistic school of thought applies to the search for greater equity among citizens within any given country. The richer are richer because they exploit the poorer, and hence they cannot tolerate a changed structure.

There is, of course, ample evidence to justify both pessimism and cynicism in the search for greater equity, both within and among countries. But I suggest that we gain nothing at all and have everything to lose by adopting this defeatist attitude. I believe the world-wide social welfare community should take a stance which perhaps can best be described as one of "angry optimism" accompanied by a determination that social progress is possible, and that we can achieve greater social justice within and among nations, for these two goals go hand in hand. No nation which has a callous disregard for its own poor is likely to concern itself with the poor of other countries.

In our search we must identify the real obstacles to social progress and not look for simple solutions. The traditional villains in the piece are of course still there: the few wealthy landlords who block land reform are now joined by the greedy urban land speculators whose unearned income has skyrocketed land and housing costs beyond the reach of many; and huge multinational corporations that in their never-ending search for profit all too often exploit countries and people. But to use only these few apparent obstacles to explain lack of social progress is overly simplistic because they could be dealt with readily by the angry masses: indeed, some steps are being taken to regulate their activities for the public good. Unhappily, a far more formidable roadblock to social equity lies in the attitude and value systems of people. In some countries, the obstacle to greater equity is a majority—the so-called "middle-income" groups who constitute the majority of the population and therefore exercise great political power. Ironically, the poorest themselves in all countries often fear change in case they lose what little they have.

How do we in the social welfare field deal with these massive attitudinal roadblocks of indifference and selfishness? One thing is clear: we will achieve little by building, in the euphoria of this conference, utopian models of society which have no chance of being created anywhere. Rather, each one of us must begin "where it is at" in our own countries. We must understand and deal with reality in our own way. In some societies and nations it will require fundamental radical changes; in others, it will require amendment to the existing infrastructure.

But ultimately, we are forced to deal with the moral issues involved because the nature and extent of participation and development rest on a foundation of values and principles. Without conviction and understanding about these, it is not likely that much progress will be made. Our computer technology can produce accurate profiles on poverty and gross inequity, but unless what is reflected is considered morally offensive, the statistics remain simply statistics. It is in drawing attention to the principles involved that the social welfare community, as the social conscience of the nations, can play a unique and indispensable role. We must step up our campaigns in the national communities—and, through this council, in the global community—to remind mankind of the principles on which we stand: the inherent dignity of the individual and his need for independence and interdependence.

Man's only hope is to live interdependently with his fellow man within national communities as well as within the global community. Communities of whatever size will survive only if the spirit of interdependence, social justice, and equity flourishes. In future, this will require a narrowing of the gap in the standard of living, both within and among nations. It is morally offensive and unacceptable, for example, that 6 percent of the world's population living in one country consumes 35 percent of all resources. The disparity between many of the have nations and the have-nots is continuing to grow. We could close the gap partially without reducing the standard of living for the haves, for economic growth is likely to continue. However, since our planet's resources are not infinite, it will likely also require some reduction in consumption of luxury and nonessential goods. While this might reduce the present standard of living in strictly quantitative terms, it will not lower the quality of life, since so much consumption has been artifically induced through the mass media advertising campaigns whose expenditures in North America exceed the cost of public education.

I am deeply concerned but I do not yet despair, because although man displays selfishness and cruelty, he has repeatedly demonstrated his capacity to be altruistic and kind. Man everywhere is reluctant to change, but he is also remarkably adaptive; man can be incredibly stupid, but can also move with wisdom; man is capable of terrible destruction of life and environment, but possesses an inventive and constructive genius. The challenge for social welfare is to harness for the common good those great inherent capabilities with which man has been endowed. Barring the holocaust of nuclear warfare, development will continue to be mankind's common cause. Development is a constant, continuing unfolding, a translation into practice of man's never-ending aspirations for a better life. In the quest to attain our common objectives, the unique role of social welfare is to ensure that every individual is given the opportunity to participate fairly and equitably, even if not equally. The degree and nature of participation should so far as possible be a matter of personal and free choice, not that of the planners or even of the zealous social reformers. Social welfare, in order to carry out its role, must intervene through all its traditional methods of community development, casework, and group work. But in addition, it will be imperative in future for social welfare to initiate coalitions with other fields and disciplines, such as taxation, finance, and economics.

My sincere hope is that during this week, those of us who

are privileged to be here to consider development and participation will gain deeper insights and broader perspectives about the operational implications for social welfare. And I hope above all that we will generate a renewed commitment to carry them out, both at home and collectively on a global scale through this council.

# Participation in Development

## SUGATA DASGUPTA

DIRECTOR, GANDHIAN INSTITUTE OF STUDIES, INDIA

PARTICIPATION IS a Biblical concept. It means co-sharing; it connotes holding responsibilities together. As the principle of nonviolence originally taught by Buddha was given a new meaning in the wake of the liberation movements of our time, so has the term "participation" acquired a new connotation in the context of the development programs of the day. Sociological studies and theories of political behavior dealing with planned social change have endowed the Biblical concept with an operational significance. Social work, one of the oldest of the helping disciplines, has, however, till now been inadequately aware of the significance of the new theme. And, as with participation, social work has shown a limited understanding of some of the challenges that development [1] faces today, after a decade of its blind acceptance as the only talisman of the age.

In the Third World, poverty exists in abundance pricked by small pockets of affluence. Yet the logic contained here is equally applicable to the affluent society, where pockets of underdevelopment exist and the incidence of comparative poverty defies all measures of modernization and social service.[2]

[1] "First of all, the word 'development' has been rapidly devalued as a result of abuses done in its name. Indeed, it becomes more and more obviously true that 'development aid' for the establishment of industries or even 'development funding' results in chaining the underdeveloped peoples to foreign economies and integrating them into alienating systems and structures. Prescinding from the question of good or bad will, these systems effectively concentrate wealth and brain power to the detriment of underdeveloped countries.

"In this respect, use of the expression 'developing countries' is hypocritical and false." René Laurentin, *Liberation, Development and Salvation* (Maryknoll, N.Y.: Orbis Books).

[2] *Re* the discovery of poverty in the United States, see President Kennedy's statement in *Time*, Asia edition, May, 1960, quoted from New York *Herald Tribune*, April 8, 1960.

The main contentions of this discussion are thus of equal relevance to the North. For the incidence of dysfuntional behavior does not depend on the size of poverty. The virulence of violence, for example, can be and has been as great in affluent societies, in the past twenty years, as in the Third World.

THE MYTH OF DEVELOPMENT

The findings of the development decade,[3] the reports on the green revolution, and the spectacular growth of the affluent society in the North World [4] during the period they offered aid to the new nations have finally dashed to the ground the hope that development can help those who need it most. It is, on the other hand, a well-established proposition now that development has, over the years, brought about four tragic results:

1. It has created a global system which is a worthy successor of the imperialist world, one that the political revolutions in the countries of the Third World had once sought to defeat. Bringing great affluence in the developed countries and initiating an irreversible process of elite formation in the new nations, it has bound the elite of the Third World to those of the North in a kind of subsidiary alliance. The amalgam has naturally given shape to a new colonial relationship.

2. Development has made the masses of people of the Third World, exploited by the two elites, poorer and led to an acute realization of the bites of comparative poverty in the affluent society itself.

3. Development, uplifting the standard of living of a small coterie of elite of the developing regions, and increasing the aspirations of the masses along with it, has led to alienation of the people from the decision-makers of development. The results have been disastrous. Accordingly, what characterizes

[3] See the Organization for Economic Cooperation and Development report, 1969, which sums up the results of the first development decade.

[4] In the early 1960s the economics and foreign ministers of OECD countries established a target of 50 percent growth in the GNP in the decade 1960 to 1970. In fact, by 1970 they had achieved about 55 percent. (Alexander King, "Growing Slowly Is Preferable—Living with Limits to Growth" SE/50 Study Encounter, IX, No. 4 (1973), 5. The period mentioned is the first development decade when a rate of growth per capita in the developing countries was hardly 1 to 3.

the Third World today are "peacelessness," [5] violence, and internal clashes. A process of confrontation between the elite who have gained from development and others who have failed to do so has also become a permanent feature of the new relationship. The violence and peacelessness that thus followed development in the countries of the Third World were also reproduced in the underdeveloped areas of the developed nations in many places. It has, therefore, now become clear to all concerned that what took place during the development decade in the new nations was not development but "maldevelopment," a term recently introduced in the field of peace research in India.

This travesty of the great humanitarian effort of development was, however, due to four reasons: (1) the failure of the elitist model of development; (2) the failure of legislative reforms; (3) the failure of extension agencies and of the theory of "percolation" which had promised that the gains of development would percolate down to the poor after the rich were benefited; and (4) the fact that only a limited quantum of resources is now available for development.

Twenty-five percent of the people of the world use, according to Robert McNamara, President of the World Bank Group, 75 percent of its resources and have "secured" development.

This disproportion has in no way lessened . . . the gap has widened between the mean standard of living in North America or Europe and that in India and Brazil.

Development, as it has been realized so far, is concentrating wealth and brainpower in a kind of a metropolis-satellite structure which is profitable for the metropolis but deadly for the satellites. In this respect, underdevelopment manifests itself as a by-product of development.[6]

It is common sense, therefore, that the remaining 75 percent of the people who have access to only 25 percent of the re-

[5] For fuller treatment see Sugata Dasgupta, "Peacelessness and Maldevelopment," in *International Peace Research Association Proceedings*, Vol. II: *Development and Peace* (Netherlands: Koinklijke Van Gorcum and Co., 1968).

[6] Laurentin, *op. cit.*, Preface.

sources cannot aspire to the same standard of living [7] that obtains in the North and is called "development." Even if the
world's resources are equitably redistributed even one percent
of the people, who will be able to use only one percent of the
resources, cannot reach the standard of living which we call
"development" today. Moreover, the limitations of the total
resources available to mankind make it evident that the standard of living called "development" cannot be made available
to all and will not even be available in the future to those who
have it now! All this logic makes at least one thing clear,
namely, that the resources that a country of the Third World
has at its disposal can only lead to development for a few and
poverty for all. Alternatively, one must redefine "development" and set up practical goals which can be attained by all.
It would mean the creation of a different type of society,
where all will have just enough to live and no one will be
rich or affluent. The decision-makers of development, who
represented the interests of a few, naturally did not opt for
this society. This understanding of the inevitable destiny of
life in the Third World is surely a great discovery. It is a revolution in knowledge and is bound to change all our theories of
development and growth.

4. Added to these were the failures of the legislative measures for reform which proved that the mere enactment of
legislation does not change a society or bring social welfare to
the needy. The inability of the extension agencies to distribute
the fruits of development to the last man or to ensure that the
high standard of living acquired by a few in the early stages of
development "percolates" down to those in waiting, only
strengthened the critique of the orthodox school of development, one that harped on the hackneyed theme that development for all was a realizable goal.

The elitist model was of course at the root of it all. For it
held that the elite, the politicians, the technocrats, the indigenous leaders, knew what was best for a people; and that they
were accordingly competent to make plans for development of
all. According to this view, some people were to develop first

[7] For fuller treatment see Sugata Dasgupta, "Towards a Counter Civilization."

and the rest were to follow in the gradual process. As the theory exploded and the people in the backwaters did not see better times even where development had succeeded, the great tragedy frustrated the theoreticians of the day.

PARTICIPATION IN RESCUE

Maldevelopment, that took its stride instead, led to a bitter alienation of all those who could not be developed. In several places, it led even to confrontation, tumultous revolts, and violence. In order to counteract the situation, and to legitimize the process of elite formation, an innovation was then conceived of: the method of participation. Participation in the field of development is, however, a product of two different pulls: active catalyzation by a ruling elite and democratic pulls of the masses themselves. The two lead to contrary directions and bring to a critical impasse the clientele of development who are still in waiting.

The planners who actively catalyzed people's participation in development had a twofold purpose in view. First, since most of the countries of the Third World had limited resources at their disposal, the development plans needed access to new, hitherto untapped, indigenous resources. For people, in countries like India and China or any other agrarian society, constitute by themselves the real asset of the nation. They alone can produce by their hard labor all wealth which cannot be imported from outside. Secondly, most of these countries lacked, for want of machinery for collection of data, adequate knowledge of the resources they actually possessed. Resources, for example, that lie dormant in the hinterlands of the primary cities and in the interior rural areas could not be discovered by a distant planner or executive; only the local people could help to identify them. A survey and a mobilization of resources, and their judicious use, require active involvement of the people in the task of development. The killing of sparrows and insects in China and the construction of miles of roads and minor irrigation work in India could not have been completed without the active involvement of the people in the task.

The people are also required not only to discover their resources but to maintain them as well. The story is told of an Indian village where a road that lay unrepaired for twenty years was reconstructed in the early days of community development work. The people who lived on both sides of the road were mobilized to lay earth on it and to "achieve" a road for themselves. The road, known as a district board [8] road, was thus reconstructed by the people themselves. Soon after this was done and a heavy rain had taken place, a big, hefty, pickup van passed by. It dug into a soft spot of the road and broke away a portion of the newly constructed rural avenue. The van also got stuck. Normally, when such accidents took place, the way to rescue a car was to offer some money to the local youth who could help to pull it out of the cavern created by it. This time it did not so happen. When the village youth learned that the road was damaged, they were furious. The driver had to pay money this time too—not for rescuing the truck, but for repairing "their road." The district board road had, thanks to the magic of participation, become a people's road.

Participation is thus necessary not only to discover resources and to create assets but to maintain them as well. Helping to multiply the value of an asset created with the resources which otherwise would have remained unknown, participation becomes the *summum bonum* of development in the Third World.

In reality, however, participation did not always achieve the purpose for which it was meant. Quite often it worked in reverse gear. The greatest tragedy was that the people who were asked to participate could not become the beneficiaries of the process. The structural impediments robbed them of their due and transferred the benefits to those who did not work for it. The rural works program is a case in point. A large number of people, mostly those without land, were given work under the scheme. They were asked to build "productive" assets which were to be used, naturally, by those who owned

---

[8] A district board is a district authority constituted by the government to look after the roads (in India). This institution, that existed in the British period, has now been merged into the local self-government institutions known as *Zila Parishad*.

the land and did not work for it. The resources of the state were used, then, not for the participants but for the upper, ruling class.

What is true of rural works is also true of industrialization. Japan's plans for industrial development of Southeast Asia provide an excellent example. The industries set up in Taiwan, by Japan, for sale of goods in Thailand surely gives employment to the Taiwanese and provide consumption goods to the Thai elite; but the process also exports pollution, exploits cheap labor, and imports wealth to Japan. As with rural works, so with the program of industrialization, the real fruits of development elude the masses and lead to a new type of imperialism.

This "developmental imperialism" brings in a new type of exploitation. It is built into the structure of internal colonies of each nation of the Third World and often represents a direct venture of the indigenous elite and the outsider. People's participation, whether of the landless in the Indian rural works program or of the Taiwanese labor and the Thai masses, provides only a means for the development of a few.

PARTICIPATION AS A TOOL

This effort to use people as a tool for development and not as its decision-makers may quite often create disasters. An excellent example is provided by Dr. T. R. Batten.[9] A group of people somewhere in an African country, says Batten, were asked to bring dead rats to their public health department, which provided a rather large sum for each dead rat. The purpose was to eradicate plague, but an inquiry revealed that a group of people who were bringing increasing numbers of dead rats every day had, in fact, set up a rat-breeding farm! The vanguards of development, a small ruling elite who are also its only beneficiaries, are usually interested in using people as tools and in introducing thereby some type of "mechanical" participation as means for their own aggrandizement. This distorted strategy, this limited use of participation en-

[9] See T. R. Batten, *Communities and Their Development* (New York: Oxford University Press, 1957).

visaged by the elitist model, has often created negative results. It has made the rich richer and the poor poorer—and has brought home to the poor the doubtful values of development, making it evident that the process of enrichment of the few lay in the exploitation of the masses.

THE NEW MEANING OF PARTICIPATION

The dysfunctional use of the participatory process soon disenchanted the bulk of the people of the Third World. The growing democratic consciousness of the age added fuel to the fire. The irresistible urge for self-determination made it clear to all concerned that nobody was any longer prepared to wait for the fruits of development to reach them in a gradual manner. The other pull, the people's pull for participation, then started taking shape as opposed to the elite effort for catalyzation of participation. The feeling that everyone had equal rights in sharing the "cake" led to a new pressure. It introduced the new concept of participation and demanded that not the elite but all the clientele of development should take upon their own shoulders the onus of decision-making.

This new concept of participation is not entirely new. It has in the past been mentioned by the Balwant R. Mehta Committee (India) for democratic decentralization in the mid-fifties,[10] and in Jayaprakash Narayan's plea for the reconstruction of the Indian polity.[11] The latter was issued at the same time that the great violences took place following the scrambles for development, only to disintegrate many established nations of the Third World. The new concept of participation is, however, based on four basic principles of development:

1. Planning should reflect the need of the people in general and of those in the backwaters in particular; the designs of development should accordingly be prepared not by a small coterie of elite but by all.

2. Participation should mean control of the decision-mak-

[10] The Balwant R. Mehta Committee was appointed by the Government of India in November, 1957, for the establishment of local-level governments and submitted its report to the Government of India. The report is available for sale.
[11] For a fuller treatment of the subject see Sri Jayaprakash Narayan, "Swaraj of the People" (Rajghat, Varanasi: Sarva Seva Sangh), Introduction.

ing process and the interchangeability of roles from the top group to the rock-bottom group and vice versa.

3. Participation should not mean horizontal participation by members of the same class or strata but by all people, and especially by those who belong to the class, ethnic group, color, or race which remains submerged in poverty.

4. Decision-making for planning and its priorities is to be determined not by a political vanguard or elite sitting in a far-away place but by the local people everywhere.

"Ten people sitting at Delhi and deciding for the whole of India?" queried Gandhi in 1948, commenting on the draft constitution of India that recommended a cabinet form of government for the country. It was not what he wanted; what he wanted was that "ten people in each village of India" should decide for the village and thousands of teams of men and women for the whole of India.

The new demand for participation marks the rise of the poor and the disadvantaged, emphasizes their right to self-determination as inalienable, and represents thereby the *summum bonum* of the new concept of development. The new consciousness rocks history. It brings to the fore the need to establish two separate parliaments for Wales and Scotland, creates a Bangladesh, leads to the bifurcation of Korea, to the tragedies of Biafra, and to the emergence of new small states in Eastern India. This is a new cry. The cry today is for participation in decisions for development, as also in all matters of economic and political importance. The new concept of participation demands equality, not for a few or for the many but for all.

Even this concept is not a new one. For Gandhi's political thesis, formulated in the context of the establishment of a *swaraj* society [12] in India and his theory of *antyodaya* (uplift of the last), drawn from Ruskin's precept of "unto the last," had spelled out the new theory of participation long before the development decade had started. Yet today the new definition of

[12] *Swaraj* is a Vedic word reinterpreted by Gandhi in the context of the freedom struggle to mean self-rule and self-restraint, and the freedom from all restraint which "independence," according to Gandhi, should really mean.

participation challenges many established theories, not only of development, but also of the traditional, classical view of democracy. Most important of these is the challenge to the sanctity of the concept of majority rule. Upholding the right of the common man, of the poor, and of the disadvantaged, it no longer recognizes the right of the majority to decide for all minorities what is best for them at all times. Tolstoi, an early champion of the poor, had in fact dubbed majority rule the rule of an oligarchy, no better than that of a monarchy.[13] Gandhi had similarly called majority rule violence, articulating thereby the new urge for participation by all much before the question of development had become so important to us.

This new cry for participation was reinforced by the colonial revolutions of the 1950s. It did not, however, become loud before the 1960s, when it was aided by a new "multiplier" known today as the cross-generational revolt. The thesis of development of all, backed by the new concept of participation, however, gives a new meaning to "social development." For it emphasizes the need for co-sharing resources, for eliminating colonies, and for building a new design for development, which would lead to the type of society mentioned earlier. But how could all this be done? How could the design for development be changed and the people allowed to create the necessary infrastructure of decision-making which would put them in control of it? These are difficult questions to answer. As the people of the developing countries assert their rights and seek development for all, however, they come up, as they did in the 1960s, against heavy odds of structural and institutional obstruction. The Organization for Economic Cooperation and Development report (1969) describes the tragedy. It maintains that one of the reasons development has not succeeded in the Third World is the structural and institutional impediments that prevented participation of people in development. Here, then, lies the truth. Unless a structural reorganization of the countries of the Third World takes place, unless new institutions are built and a thorough reorientation of educational

---

[13] For a fuller treatment see Sugata Dasgupta, "Violence Development and Tensions," *International Journal of Group Tension*, I, No. 2 (1971), 114–23.

and technological plans helps promote total participation at all stages of decision-making, development is bound to remain an elitist venture. Such development will not eschew affluence; it will not divert the resources from production of consumer and luxury goods to those which satisfy the essential needs of a people and/or retard the efforts of a few to become rich at the cost of the poor. Yet one thing is clear. If the structural limitations that retard participation and prevent the new type of development from taking place are a fact of life, the urge for total participation that wishes to socialize development here and now is as much a reality. There are many proofs of it. The great upheavals in Thailand to bring about participation in the government, the slogans for boycotting consumer goods and the anti-Taiwan stand, to recount only a few examples from one single country, proves, if proof were needed, how eager the people are to change the direction of development. The two new revolutions, the colonial and the cross-generational, have indeed set fire to the ecology of the Third World and have brought it to the brink of a new breakthrough.

PROTEST IS PARTICIPATION

The type of participation that would "deliver the goods" then becomes evident; but as we have seen, it is not possible to introduce it without some basic structural and institutional changes in the society. As the way to the emergence of the new pattern thus gets blocked, the clamor for participation grows; and naturally takes a negative turn, bursting forth into a series of protest movements, both violent and nonviolent. The sit-ins in America, the civil coups against the military rule in Pakistan manifested from time to time, the nonviolent social movement in Thailand, the *gheraos* of India, the violence in South America, the appointment of a spokesman for non-violent struggle in Mexico City (1968), and the grape pickers' movement in California, all protest movements, provide a decisive plea in favor of the new mode of participation. The slogans of "nonorganization" and "nonefficiency" raised in Paris add luster to the demand. Claiming that none but man, not certainly the machine, should be put at the center of the stage of civilization, they voted for a new model of development which would be less complex and more humanistic in ethos. The New Left had similarly pushed forward the case for an anti-industrial revolution which would have paralyzed the monoliths and prevented exploitation. These struggles and slogans provide the new philosophy of development and emphasize that the fact of participation rather than what comes out of it is the real goal of development. Participation, then is no longer to be seen as a movement for an end, but as an end in itself. Revolution rather than social reform [14] for a restructuring of social relations among the various strata of society, liberation from the developmental imperialism of the day, *swaraj* for all, *antyodaya* and *ujamaa* [15] for the heralding of a new society, "conscientization" and "cultural action for freedom" could also be visualized as aims of development. They underline the case of the poor rather than that of the elite who were development's main charge in its first decade.

If the present form of development and its ideology, theory, structure, and function are products of industrial revolution, the challenges to it come from the cross-generational and the colonial revolution. While the colonial revolution brought freedom to the Third World, 75 percent of the people of the globe who were previously satisfied with their lot of misery and underdevelopment have started to assert their rights to equality. They demand that they should have not only the same standard of living which the privileged sections of their own country possess but also that which the affluent North World has achieved. The cross-generational revolution today not only questions the right of the leaders to have more privileges for themselves, but also champions the cause of the poor. Before these revolutions took place, the demand on the resources of the world was limited. But as 70 percent of the Third World and the blacks, the untouchables, the landless,

[14] As Rosa Luxemburg puts it, the kernel of the problem is that in each historic period, work for reforms is carried on only in the framework of the existing social form (*Social Reform Revolution* [London: Malin Press], p. 59)—and keeps the society intact.

[15] See Julius Nyrere, *Ujamaa* (New York: Oxford University Press).

the working class, the famished, slum dwellers, and ruralists all clamored for equality of attainment, the demand grew by leaps and bounds. Since development led to affluence and affluence meant power, the demand for an equal share of the fruits of development became all the more pressing. The people's consciousness of their rights, the struggle for self-determination, and protest movements all over the world have made it evident that the design of development has to be radically altered.

TOWARD POSITIVE PARTICIPATION

Protests, however, represent a negative type of participation. The process which could bring a qualitative change in the structure and function of development should not remain confined to them.

The protests and revolutionary slogans with their own ideology or anti-ideology of development, however, represent, according to the present writer, an important phase in the growing program of participation; and protest is participation.[16] It is an indication that the people involved in protests, unlike those who withdraw from society, have a stake in it and wish to transform its contours to save it from collapse. Those who protest, therefore, also participate in the management of the ongoing process of planned social change.

Negative participation manifested through protests can be of only limited value. What is necessary, on the other hand, is to give the new process of participation a positive, concrete shape so that a new structure of society which will not retard its fruition will grow out of it. But how can this be achieved? If development continues to nourish the elitist society, if monolithic and complex social institutions of management, technology, and administration, which can only be manipulated by a highly sophisticated elite, continue to dominate the scene, any effort for positive participation will remain an idle dream. What is necessary, therefore, is to build a new institutional structure that is conducive to participation. And negatives can

[16] For fuller treatment of the subject see Sugata Dasgupta, "Protest Is Participation," *People's Action,* November, 1973.

lead to positives, destruction to new construction. As Arne Naess says, the adoption of violent means of protest may often be a plea for nonviolence. Protests, indeed, lead to a restructuring of the society and to the establishment of a set of norms and institutions which will permit positive participation to take place. The negative results of development have, in fact, already established the case for the introduction of far-reaching structural changes so that the people as a whole may, through a new instrumentality of institutions, take part in decisions. It will also lead to a people-based, austere, modest, practicable design for development. The negative impact of the present policy has also brought out clearly the limitations of the social structure and has pointed to a set of new values, institutions, technologies, designs, and plans that may help. It is thus evident that the society which will be able to contain the growing demands of the people will not be an anonymous, mass society based on atomized relations. It must, on the other hand, be a communal society based, so far as possible, on direct, face-to-face relations.

The negatives of development and the history of the last twenty-five years also make it evident that social conditions are ripe today for the development of such a society. In the South World, headed by Yugoslavia, in Africa, and in Asia there has thus been since the 1950s a great search for the development of a new structure of social relations and political systems which would provide a stable polity for economic growth and social welfare. Although the experiments carried on in different cultures are strikingly different from one another there is a single, uniform strain common to all of them. This is now discernible and is represented by the choice made in favor of a communal system and small-sized units of decision-making as the key to the development of the society. The communes in Yugoslavia, the communes of China, the *gramdans* and *panchayats* in India, the basic democratics of Pakistan, the Commilla experiment of Bangladesh, the Sarvodaya experiment in Sri Lanka, the new experiment of Marcos in the Philippines, and the kibbutzim of Israel, however fallible they may be in their approaches, signify a definite swing in this direction.

From the mass society to the communal, from the monolithic, monopolistic structure of decision-making to small units, from the representative and oligarchic parliamentary democracies to direct communal systems, all the different designs have one thing in common. It is the new faith evident today in all of them that the old pattern of community institutions may still have a function. A finding of a seminar on participation held in Japan in 1973 was that one of the main reasons for the failure of social welfare in many Asian countries was the unqualified rejection of the traditional community which had once functioned through the instrumentality of folk institutions.

SOCIAL WELFARE IN THE INEVITABLE SOCIETY

If these contentions are valid, the structure and functions of the new society, the "inevitable" society, as I call it, will then become evident. For the new society will be agrarian in form and consist of communal institutions. Organizations, both economic and political, will be small in such a society, and technology, organization, and management of noncomplex social services, delivered through the traditional channels of the society as well as via the established institutions like family, kinship groups, religious organizations, and village institutions of different strata of societies, will make it possible for all men, or for a very great many, not only to participate in decision-making but also to reap its benefits. Backed by the indigenous infrastructure of institutions the delivery system will be of special use to the poor.

If the traditional process of development is thus on its way out, it must be clearly understood that neither social services nor development has helped the twentieth century any more than charity did the nineteenth century. A mere palliative in the new phase of developmental imperialism, social welfare, not unlike the social services of the old, has helped only to legitimize the role of the ruling elite in their unlimited urge for the development of a limited number of people. People's participation, nay, a participatory society, with a participatory structure of institutions working as a corrective to the traditional, neoimperialist design of development, will rectify the situation. It will lead the way to liberate the victims of development from the tentacles of the exploitative, developmental system. It will also mark, thereby, the final phase of social development in this century. Social welfare, if it is to be relevant to the present situation, must help the process of development of such a society in the shortest possible time and evolve methods and institutional structures required for its sustenance. The new processes of adult education, institution-building, appropriate technology, and politics may help in the process, but the real burden will have to be borne by social welfare.

The revised functions of social welfare, in the context of the changing theories of development and participation, are thus threefold. Yet before we enumerate these, it is necessary to emphasize that social welfare must realize that its tasks today are enormous, much greater than ever before. Social work's task is no longer to help a few maladjusted to conform to a process; its task is to help a great many people, the vast masses of the poor, to help themselves by dint of their own efforts. To do this, it will be necessary for social welfare to remove a number of political and economic handicaps that cripple the people everywhere and still keep them in fetters. Faulty education, traditional institutions, unwieldy political systems, unworkable organizations for social welfare, and the inability of its methods to bring structural changes are some of these. They are to be removed.

Social welfare should first introduce a number of enabling measures, such as land legislation and so on, which will remove these basic incapacities of the vast mass of its clientele and help them to assert their rights as Tagore says, "in a bolder social order." An important task of social welfare in the new context, therefore, is to evolve a radical social policy suited to the needs of the poor. Since most of the Third World live in villages and their megalopolises have been dysfunctional to development, the main emphasis of the social policy should be on rural development and the abolition of absolute poverty. To do that, the new social policy should be closely linked to the political objectives of the nation and provide for suitable enabling measures so that the disadvantaged too can participate in political decision-making. Such a social policy should, therefore, have an integrated frame of reference dovetailing with provisions for new systems of education, appropriate technologies, and small-sized economic institutions run by the average citizens of the rural society.

The new policy must, then, be the main plank of the developmental policy of the country which, in turn, is to be linked to the over-all political and economic policies of the nation. A measure of success of such social policy will be that it ensures the development of the weaker sections of the community at a rate higher than that of the rich and the advantaged.

The other tasks of social welfare are institution-building, adult education, and development of social action as a method of work. All social services, including social welfare measures, for example, have to be delivered through a series of more effective, indigenous institutions. As explained earlier, the new institutions should be community-based and small in size. They must grow out of the existing social units of the village or the town, such as the family, the caste, the tribe. Social welfare should thus rebuild the original structures in the society and ensure that the leaders of these institutions, the parents or the village leaders, for example, are fully trained to do their job.

The training program should not, however, be confined to the leaders of the institutions but must also include the vast masses of the clientele who need help. Paulo Freire's program of cultural action for adult education could provide a basis for training the clientele for direct involvement in development. If the institutional leaders are trained in techniques of social work and the masses in those of social action, it will go a long way to ensure that the services delivered to the last man reaches him in the most effective manner. Lastly, social welfare will have to reorient substantially its method of work, drawing profusely from the experiences of the social movements of the Third World. Social welfare must, thus, use the technique of direct, nonviolent, social action as its main tool for the implementation of the new social policy. For that will help. It will help to bring the enabling measures that make it

possible for the clientele to participate in developmental programs and also to reap their benefits. It will help to build up
the new community-based institutions in every village and
town. It will also enable the institutional leaders to reorganize
the social structure and to build new institutions by their own
voluntary efforts. Voluntary effort and not government control will then provide the lever for the new institutional infrastructure for delivery of services to those who need them
most.

It is evident from the above that social welfare, in the new
context, should not be target-oriented but society-based. Its
functions will not only be to help children, the retarded,
women, and the handicapped to adjust to the societal process
but to build a new society. It is then, and then only, that the
poor and the disadvantaged, the handicapped and the backward, will be able to face their problems by dint of their own
efforts and overcome the obstacles.

# The René Sand Award

HUMAN DEVELOPMENT AND THE WELFARE OF NATIONS:
THE CONTEMPORARY CHALLENGE FOR CONCERTED
INTERNATIONAL ACTION

## J. RIBY-WILLIAMS

CHIEF, HUMAN RESOURCES DEVELOPMENT DIVISION,
UNITED NATIONS ECONOMIC COMMISSION FOR AFRICA,
ETHIOPIA

IT IS with great humility that I accept this very high honor which has been conferred on me. When I agreed to receive personally the René Sand Award, I did so for three reasons.

The René Sand Award symbolizes a fitting acknowledgment of the tremendous progress which mankind has made toward a common welfare of nations. This we owe, to a very large extent, to the imaginative foresight and the pioneering work of men like the late Dr. René Sand, the founder of ICSW. In a lifetime of devoted service to humanity, such men have toiled against great odds in order to fulfill the hope that one day all peoples of the world may enjoy, in an equal manner, the benefits of a world society in which human rights are regarded as inviolable. Now we appear to be on the threshold of accepting this new philosophy of development, which seeks to protect and advance the well-being of the individual, and which acknowledges the paramountcy of human welfare in the economies of nations.

Secondly, the fact that the XVIIth Conference and the presentation of the award are taking place, *for the first time,* on African soil should indeed bring back to memory the establishment, sixteen years ago, of the Economic Commission for Africa (ECA). In the words of the late Dag Hammarskjöld, then Secretary-General of the United Nations, the establishment of ECA marked "the point at which Africa began to play its full role in world affairs." Thus, this occasion bears a forceful testimony to the sixteen years of experience and progress gained by ECA in applying a unified approach to the developmental activities of the region.

And thirdly, this auspicious occasion provides the long-sought opportunity to express appreciation for the tremendous flow of good will, encouragement, and substantial support which have stimulated our efforts in the promotion of better standards of living and general well-being for the people of this region. They have come from bilateral technical assistance agencies, from various foundations and international voluntary agencies, from the UN, which I serve, and from within the membership of ICSW itself.

THE ICSW AND AFRICA

As I look back on the many years of my association with ICSW, at least one incident stands out most prominently. Ten years ago, in 1964, in my official capacity as head of the Social Development Section of ECA, I received an invitation from Secretary-General Joe Hoffer and President Lester Granger to assist in popularizing, in the countries of Africa, the XIIth International Conference on Social Work, which was scheduled to deliberate in Athens on the theme, "Social Progress through Social Planning."

In all my earlier discussions with Lester Granger, Eugen Pusić, Joe Hoffer, and his dynamic assistant of blessed memory, the late Ruth Williams, I had stuck to the strategy of a purposeful development of African national social welfare coordinating councils. But when at Athens the decision was taken, it was *not* in favor of national councils. I was sorely disappointed then; but now, events have so proved the wisdom behind the subtle strategy which ICSW adopted that I have come before you to expound on aspects of the original theme, as stated in the 1965 Plan of Action.

In 1964 a solitary national committee from this region was accorded a provisional member status in ICSW. Within ten years, the number of active national councils affiliated with ICSW has risen sharply to twenty. What is more, a regional professional Association of Social Work Education in Africa has been established with the support of the Friedrich Ebert Foundation to promote higher standards of social work education and research. And the several regional and subregional seminars, which had been held under the joint auspices of ECA and ICSW, appropriately culminated in an All-Africa Seminar on Social Welfare, in December, 1973, in Lagos, Nigeria.

CHOICE OF TOPIC

Central to the theme of this conference are two crucial factors: one, the paramountcy of the human being, both as the prime participant and the beneficiary, in the development process; and the other, what I see as a contemporary challenge both to governments and to nongovernmental organizations (NGOs) for concerted international action in raising the levels of living of the peoples of the developing world. Behind these two crucial factors is my proposition that in contemporary development the transformation of the very life style of people should be conceived as occurring *only* through the willing cooperation and the initiative of the people themselves. If this is a valid proposition, what, then, are its operational implications for international voluntary organizations with respect to their actual participation in national development and the promotion of international understanding? It was from this introspection that I decided on the topic for my address.

INVESTMENT IN MAN

Until recently, the major drawback to economic growth was generally considered to be shortage of capital and goods. Within the past decade, however, it has increasingly been realized that national development does not begin with money or goods, but with people—their development, their education, their training, and the orientation of their attitudes and support toward national objectives and aspirations. Knowledge, skills, capacities, and motivation of people *are* the essential ingredients of any development effort. Intensive studies in the mechanics of economic growth, even in the highly developed countries of North America and Western Europe, have revealed that only a small fraction of such growth can be explained by the actual amount of investment made in physical capital. Indeed, it has been found that a considerably greater part of development can in fact be attributed to a very wide range of other factors, which include social education, vocational training, health, nutrition, social research, rational attitudes toward life and work, applied technology, organization, management, good government, and administration. With this realization, major attention is now being focused on the development of human resources and the fostering of people's capacity for development. As a direct consequence of this, the role of social scientists and social workers who normally work at the level of, and are closely in contact with, the people has become or is fast becoming an essential factor in development.

Charles Myers has written:

The notion that investment in human resources should be considered along with investment in physical capital, such as railroads, harbours, hydro-electric projects, plant and equipment, is relatively new. To be sure, such great political economists as Adam Smith and Alfred Marshall understood the significance of human resources. Marshall emphasized the importance of education "as a natural investment" and said that "the most valuable of all capital is that invested in human beings." But subsequent economists became more concerned with capital-output ratios (meaning physical capital), and [they] considered education and training as a social welfare expense, secondary to the more important physical capital investments.[1]

Oddly enough, it was somehow assumed that if hydroelectric power stations or steel mills, or even huge government ministries were constructed, there would automatically be trained people available to run them.

Many of us realize now that the pace of agricultural and industrial development is seriously hampered not so much by scarcity of capital and natural resources as by the forces of social tradition, coupled with a complex of other human fac-

[1] Charles A. Myers, "Human Resources and World Economic Development," *International Labour Review*, November, 1966.

tors. Age-long traditional social structures are not responding fast enough to the planned rapid change in the economic structure. Rigid property structures and land-tenure systems, in certain cases, are rendering futile the efforts of governments to achieve more equitable distribution of income. And inflexible customs and philosophies of traditional life continue to act as a bulwark against the introduction and acceptance of social change and modernization.

We need to admit that we who are involved in development strategies and programs have made mistakes despite our good intentions toward achieving a higher level of living for all our people. During the first development decade, in the 1960s, we emphasized industrialization; and we were preoccupied with the attainment of immediate increases in our gross national product. We thought that reaching these goals would automatically bring an overflow of higher levels of living to most of the people in our countries. But we were proved wrong on two counts. First, our goals were unrealistic and often well beyond our reach. We have now found out that to achieve industrialization, or to increase the material wealth of countries, at a time when the capacity of their human resources has not been sufficiently developed, is a painfully slow human process. Secondly, there is no built-in mechanism for ensuring that any wealth which has been created will be broadly shared. The rich may become richer, while the poor will continue to be dependent upon nature's whims, and often also increasingly dependent upon the whims and fancies of the rich.

It follows that a quick transition from an underdeveloped, dependent economy to a developed, self-sustained economy must largely depend upon a planned mobilization and the participation of both the human and the material resources toward the desired development goal. Unfortunately, mass poverty, mass illiteracy, and general underdevelopment are still being perpetuated because we have not yet cultivated our human resources: we have not properly looked after their health and nutrition; we have not educated them; above all, we have not discovered the most appropriate methods of utilizing the very human elements which could most significantly contribute to the modernization process. So long as this human capital is not fully exploited, *so long* will social and human factors militate against our greatest endeavors to survive, much less to develop.

So, in this second development decade—the 1970s—we look to greater dependence on our own resources, especially our human resources. And we are trying to make the benefits of development reach out to the majority of our people, who most often live in rural areas and who have often been left untouched by the achievements of science and technology. More than that, we are finding ways and means of stretching the benefits of development to reach a world of peoples.

THE UNIFIED APPROACH

Currently, the United Nations Research Institute for Social Development (in Geneva) is undertaking a research project entitled "Unified Approach to Development Analysis and Planning." The study is concerned with problems created by the uneven and haphazard nature of development that has been taking place in recent years and its frequent failures to involve and benefit the poorest groups in the developing countries.

In terms of basic objectives, the main factor underlying the study project is the same as that expressed in the UN "International Development Strategy for the Second Development Decade" proclaimed on October 24, 1970, that: "The ultimate objective of development must be to bring about sustained improvement in the well-being of the individual and bestow benefits on all. If undue privileges, extremes of wealth and social injustices persist, then development fails in its essential purpose."

It is needless to point out that the issue of the unified approach is of equal relevance to developed countries,

which are experiencing growing social problems as a result of a lopsided preocccupation with economic growth. Delinquency, criminality, violence and drugs, as well as continued mass poverty, increasing income differentials and growing unemployment can be regarded as direct side effects of not following a balanced development strategy.[2]

[2] *Unified Approach to Development Analysis and Planning: a Progress Report* (E/CN.14/CAP.5/7), 1974, p. 1.

I dare to suggest that, from the trends in changes of development concepts and theories which we have been witnessing since the first development decade failed us, it is not unlikely that we shall all be transported into a third development decade which maximizes the key role of human and social development. *Now* is the time for social planners and social workers to prepare for that event.

In anticipation of this new situation, ECA is doubling its efforts to avail itself of facilities and technical support for social welfare programs available from bilateral voluntary (international) sources. A significant proportion of such aid is already being channeled through ECA; and our social development section maintains direct relations with various international nongovernmental organizations which are actively engaged in social welfare activities in Africa, and whose professional advice and other forms of assistance we utilize and extend to countries in the region where they are needed.

ACTIVITIES OF VOLUNTARY AGENCIES

In trying to establish working contacts with international voluntary agencies, the UN system seeks to emphasize the fact that there is a considerable amount of waste of valuable human resources in the underutilization of manpower, particularly in the subsistence economies of the vast rural areas of the developing world. Programs of international voluntary agencies have concentrated, for example, on the provision of water for human consumption and agriculture; health and sanitation projects, with special reference to nutrition and child care; the introduction of simple but modern agricultural techniques, the encouragement of cooperatives, self-help groups, and more effective marketing schemes; and the setting up of loans or credit societies. In most areas where these organizations operate, schools and training institutions have been established to meet the needs of farmers and agricultural technicians; short courses have been organized for farmers, and service facilities have been provided.

One advantage of the pioneering work of the voluntary organizations is that their activities can be performed with the full participation of the villagers and the local communities themselves. Not only do these developments start from the grass roots but they also foster self-reliance and self-respect.

From the very systems and methods of operation of voluntary agencies, one could discern a number of significant characteristics which ensure their success in situations where other technical assistance agencies fail. They have a high degree of policy discretion to suit their program to local needs; they are largely self-administering and can buy what they can afford, without filling in forms; their field agents are usually imbued with the idea that development work at the rural level must bring imperceptible changes to the countryside and permanent improvement in the earnings of its farmers; and they often undertake projects which benefit the greatest possible number of the country's population. They are, also, of necessity, restricted to simple and inexpensive methods and investment, whether they are working in an urban slum or providing a small clinic or dispensary in a remote village.

In many instances, NGOs have initiated new programs before government is able to undertake them; they have experimented with programs that may have risks attached to them; and they have provided expertise to government and UN agencies. Some NGOs have assisted in promoting public understanding and public participation with respect to specific development programs; and they have contributed significantly to national, regional, and international seminars and training courses. When there is a national disaster, they are usually the first to enter the scene and arrange for emergency relief services. We have seen this in Bangladesh, and we are currently seeing it in the parts of Africa that have been devastated by severe droughts.

We do realize, of course, that there are differences among NGOs, both their fields of interest and in their methods of programming and operation. From the report of a recent workshop sponsored by the NGO committee on the United Nations Children's Emergency Fund (UNICEF) in cooperation with UNICEF and the United Nations Development Program (UNDP), we learn that some NGOs are primarily informational and educational; and "their main role is to assist local peoples to adapt to the changes that development brings, and to encourage them to join their country's overall development drive." Others are active in professional and technical assistance, bringing in experience, experts, and goods and services on programs which often open opportunities for nationals to involve themselves directly in the development effort. Still others are primarily concerned with the transfer of resources of money and materials to meet emergency situations.

### HOW IT ALL STARTED

But, we ask ourselves, how did all this start? According to Frederick Lees of the British Voluntary Committee on Overseas Aid and Development, the religious pressure groups which agitated for the abolition of slavery at the end of the eighteenth century were closely associated with the movement which established the various missionary societies in Asia, Africa, and Latin America. He points out that,

the initial preoccupation and the motivating factors of these missionary societies were the same: they were all filled with the commitment and the enthusiasm to look for the world's newly discovered pagans [and to convert them to the ways of Christianity].

Each missionary society tended to specialize in a particular region of the world and many took a part of Africa as their own special concern. The exploration by Europeans of the interior of Africa was in large measure associated with the humanitarian ideals of the anti-slavery movement. It was as a missionary that Livingstone sought to develop his countrymen's enthusiasm for the advancement of the Christianity and commerce which would relieve the Africans from ignorance, famine and disease.[3]

Before the last quarter of the nineteenth century it was the view of many people—mistaken, as it turned out—that the activities of the missionaries, associated as they were with humanitarian intentions, would in due course lead to the emergence of modern states, just as the activities of Christian missionaries in the Dark Ages outside the bounds of the former Roman Empire had led to the development of more civilized societies in Europe. Of course, this was not ac-

[3] Frederick Lees, *Africa in the 1970s,* published by the Royal African Society.

complished by them but by the colonial powers, after their division of Africa. But they leaned heavily on the work of the missionaries, particularly in the educational and medical fields.

In the postwar period, just as the colonial governments in the last years of their lives were beginning to give attention to the problems of economic development, so too, the voluntary bodies began to extend their interests beyond the fields of education and health, to the problem of hunger and hence to the problems of economic development. But by now there were differences in approach, reflected in the emergence of new forms of international voluntary agency.

NGOS AND THE UN

So far, we have seen how the abolition of the slave trade helped to stimulate the rise of transfer of certain types of resources—mainly humanistic and religious services—from international voluntary agencies in Western Europe to overseas national and local groups. We have also seen how the nature of these services gradually assumed a developmental role during the span of the two world wars.

My studies lead me further to suggest that what the slave trade and the two world wars together inspired by way of international voluntary activity, the UN has endeavored to mobilize, consolidate, and direct into purposeful development goals.

It is, of course, well-known that the history of the involvement of NGOs in development activities of the UN is as old as the UN itself. Article 71 of the 1945 Charter of the UN provides, *inter alia,* that the Economic and Social Council may make suitable arrangements for consultation with nongovernmental organizations which are concerned with matters within its competence, with respect to economic, social, cultural, educational, health, and related matters and to questions of human rights.

Since 1946 various arrangements for consultation with NGOs and for their progressive participation in the work of the UN system as a whole have been adopted by both

ECOSOC and the General Assembly. Originally, so far as ECOSOC was concerned, these arrangements for consultation merely boiled down to securing expert information and advice, and enabling the organizations which represented important elements of public opinion to express their views. With the appointment, in 1946, of a standing committee on NGOs, whose main task was to submit recommendations for registration of NGOs, for consultation, there was practically not very much else expected from the accredited NGOs. Recognition was (and is still) accorded to NGOs, depending on the extent and nature of their respective fields of interest and activities, in relation to the work of ECOSOC.

Organizations accorded the first category of consultative status are those which have a basic interest in most of the activities of ECOSOC, and which are closely linked with the economic and social life of the areas which they represent. The second category of organizations is expected to have special competence and to be concerned with only a few of the fields of activity covered by ECOSOC. The last category consists of those primarily concerned with the development of public opinion and with the dissemination of information.

It is interesting to note that in 1946, organizations holding consultative status with ECOSOC numbered only three: the World Federation of Trade Unions, the International Cooperative Alliance, and the American Federation of Labor. In contrast, the nongovernmental organizations in consultative status as of June 15, 1973, totaled 589.

*The changing role of NGOs.* It is an undisputed fact that the role and influence of NGOs associated with the UN have in recent years changed significantly; but the question may still be asked as to whether their separate and collective impact on development and welfare of nations has likewise increased. Considering that organizations accorded Category I status may send observers to all public meetings of ECOSOC and its committees; may circulate to members of ECOSOC written statements or communications; may be invited by the Council to consult with any standing committee; are entitled to receive provisional agenda of the Council at the same time as

ECOSOC members; may even propose through the Council Committee on NGOs items of special interest to be placed on the provisional agenda of ECOSOC; may be invited to undertake specific studies or investigations, or prepare specific papers for commissions of ECOSOC; and may be invited to participate in conferences convened by ECOSOC, could we really testify, (*a*) that these several roles and facilities were being effectively fulfilled and adequately utilized; and (*b*) that there was no room for a greater contribution to the decision-making of the UN, and the implementation of the development goals and targets set by the UN?

Apparently, the answer should be in the negative; for in 1971, under ECOSOC resolution 1580(L), the Committee on Nongovernmental Organizations was specifically requested to submit to the Council, at its 54th session, recommendations on ways of improving the contribution of NGOs to the implementation of the goals of the international development strategy as regards: mobilization of public opinion and political will; substantive contributions of NGOs through the consultative process; and relations at the field level in technical cooperation and material assistance activities.

Both in the UN system and in the community of NGOs, this ECOSOC resolution of May 20, 1971, sparked off a whole series of agitated activity in which various agencies of the UN system endeavored to discover the existence of NGOs, as if they had never been there before. NGOs, on their part, intensified their consultations and search both among themselves and with the UN agencies as to how best they could be of mutual assistance. And there was a flurry of consultations between the NGOs and representatives of member states on ways and means of increasing contact with member states and of maximizing impact on their national development programs.

ECA AND NGOS

I must probably be biased, but it is my view that the first credit should go to the Regional Commission for Africa. At the Commission's ninth session in 1969 it had adopted a resolution which, *inter alia,* requested its secretariat:

ects of FAO's Freedom from Hunger Campaign, which was undertaken under the leadership of Professor Pensioen of The Hague's Institute of Social Studies, between 1967 and 1969.

The other was a preliminary study undertaken in 1972-73 by a private, independent, nonprofit American consulting firm—Polit-Econ Services—on the role and problems of voluntary agencies in African development under the sponsorship of the Bureau for Africa of the United States Agency for International Development.

PROBLEMS CONFRONTING NGOS

The various consultations, field studies, symposia, and workshops appear to have fairly well succeeded in bringing to light certain problems and deficiencies which at present act as serious constraints on the endeavors being made by NGOs to contribute more fully and meaningfully to the implementation of the international development strategy. We must look on these constraints as the contemporary challenge, requiring concerted international actions for their solution. I shall give some leadership in their identification and examination, and I shall also endeavor to draw attention to specific methods and strategies for meeting the challenge; but we should expect the commission of ICSW which has special responsibility for assessing the role of NGOs and governments in development to finish the job.

*Housekeeping problems of management and administration.* The delegates who attended the NGOs symposium at Addis Ababa in 1971 recounted the following problems and shortcomings inherent in the structures, management, and field operations of some NGOs:

1. Often, projects of voluntary agencies had been mounted without pre-investment studies. Field management of ongoing projects was often defective, and generally no attempt was made to evaluate such projects. Some agencies had been insufficiently interested in how their own efforts, related to development efforts in general projects, were often so isolated and far between that their benefits were subsequently lost. Agen-

cies sometimes failed to transfer expertise to indigenous staff. The operational directory of one major agency had shown an unevenness in distribution of projects, both geographically and by function; historical considerations (and some times former colonial associations) had tended to be important factors in influencing the pattern of allocation of expenditure.

2. Because of the absence of centralized records, experience which might have been used elsewhere was often lost, and there was need for some *structural* integration of the efforts of governmental agencies, UN specialized agencies, and voluntary agencies, as well as for integration of rural development projects in national development planning.

3. The symposium realized that governments were sometimes aware of the work of voluntary agencies, but would like to see this awareness expressed in willingness to collaborate more actively with voluntary agencies.

*Problems arising from lack of information or communication.* According to the UNDP field inquiry, lack of information about one another's activities seemed to be one of the main barriers to increased collaboration. It also appeared that there was lack of cooperation among NGOs themselves as well as, often, between their headquarters staff and their professional experts working in the field.

The workshop sponsored by the NGO Committee on UNICEF confirmed that one of the major deterrents to cooperation was lack of communication between NGOs and the UN agencies, especially at the field level, and that this was mainly due to negligence. In the words of Kate Katzki, who contributed to the debate:

We find Governments highly organized, we find United Nations agencies highly structured and organized, and we find that the non-governmental or voluntary agencies are somewhat nebulous. They are much less structured and organized. . . . [however] We find NGOs with excellent structures, excellent programmes who manage to keep it either a secret or have not succeeded in any way of letting the other NGOs know who are their members, where they are and what they are doing. We haven't found ways to share this material with each other. Surely, it is important that this kind of information be made available internationally.[5]

[5] *Companions in Country Programming,* pp. 24, 27.

*Conflicts in motivation.* The studies which were undertaken by the American consulting firm in 1972-73 have also shown up a number of other problems facing voluntary agencies. These include conflicts in motivation, arising from new socioeconomic pressures, and dilemmas in determining the right developmental approach to adopt. There were also many problems brought out relating to the appropriate institutional roles of the voluntary organizations.

*The crucial problem of cooperation.* In our study of the role of NGOs we have attempted to analyze the crucial problem of cooperation at all levels of operation, in terms of cooperation among the NGOs themselves as well as with governments and with the UN system as a whole. In this regard, the 1971 ECA symposium felt that now that the magnitude of the contributions of the voluntary agencies was being recognized by officialdom, and by the agencies themselves, organizations involved in development could hardly afford to be indifferent to the way in which such sums were being applied, especially if they were not being applied wisely, even if they were being spent honestly.

Basic to the issue is cooperation among the NGOs themselves, both at the local project level and at the national and international levels. Operational and administrative problems of the NGOs, coupled with the widely differing and peculiar systems, which make communication difficult, largely account for the problems in achieving the desired cooperation.

Governments are in a sense intermediaries between the voluntary agencies, which operate with governments' approval, and the UN agencies, which operate at the governments' request. It is my firm conviction that cooperation among NGOs, within the individual countries where they operate, could be fostered either through existing national councils of social service or through their own associations or committees. This should facilitate regular contact with government as well as exchange of experience, plans, and expertise among the NGOs themselves.

It has been suggested that there is an urgent need for some structural integration of governments, UN agencies, and the efforts of NGOs, in planning, execution, field management, and evaluation. Furthermore, three forms of integration have been suggested: integration of objectives, integration of financial resources, and integration of agencies participating in a given project. I am positively unhappy about such rigid structural integration. For one thing, it cannot meaningfully take place between NGOs and the UN agencies at global headquarters level; and for another, it is not what was anticipated by ECOSOC in its resolution 1580(L) of 1971.

Furthermore, it is not my view that the call to international voluntary agencies for a greater participation in the strategy for the second development decade should be taken to mean an imposition of preconceived ideas and of prescribed roles and structures. Rather, it is to encourage them to enhance their comprehension of the reality in which they operate and to increase their motivation and capacity to act as better agents of development. We must realize that conceptions of what development is and how it should be approached are constantly evolving, resulting in the establishment of new priorities and demanding the adoption of new approaches.

In short, what the situation demands of each international voluntary organization is *not* necessarily that it should change its conceptual framework and operational modalities, but rather that its policy objectives be consistent with contemporary concepts of development; and that it decide what particular competence and assistance it can offer, what particular development area is most suitable for its operational objectives, and the minimum acceptable terms under which it can cooperate with its affinity groups, host governments, and the UN system.

ACHIEVING BETTER COORDINATION

I have referred to the crucial problem of cooperation at all levels of operation in terms of cooperation among the NGOs themselves, cooperation with host governments, and cooperation with the UN system as a whole. On the basis of certain recommendations made by the ECOSOC Committee on NGOs, steps are currently being taken by the Secretary-General of the UN:

1. To improve coordination with NGOs within the entire UN system so as to achieve the most appropriate relationships which can best contribute to the goals and objectives of the international development strategy
2. To develop various forms of relations with NGOs at the regional and national levels through the regional economic commissions, the UN information centers, and the offices of the UNDP resident representatives
3. To facilitate liaison between the UN system as a whole and NGOs so as to rationalize and coordinate the efforts of the UN system in mobilizing public opinion in favor of the goals and objectives of the international development strategy for the second development decade.

However, the achievement of an effective and concerted international action would require many more specific obligations on the part of the UN system as a whole, member states, and the international voluntary organizations. Many of these obligations have been indicated in the consultations, field studies, symposia, and workshops which have so far been undertaken on the subject.

# Reaction of Participants to the Conference Theme

## EVA SCHINDLER-RAINMAN

### ICSW CONSULTANT

"WE WANT to listen and ask questions." "We want to be heard." "We'd like to help make decisions." "We are interested, we are here." "We want to communicate across cultures." No matter what tongue we speak, we have ideals, resources, experiences, and ideas for action to share. So spoke approximately 2,000 participants at a plenary session of the XVIIth International Conference on Social Welfare.

These participants, seated in small discussion groups of ten in three language sections, French, English, and Spanish, had an opportunity to help evaluate this conference, and give ideas for the next one. One hundred and seventy-eight groups discussed, ideated, and reported their deliberations both on large sheets of paper and verbally over a microphone at this meeting. Another 150 persons handed in individual evaluation sheets. All of these were read and analyzed.

What were the major ideas and recommendations? They fall into the following categories:

### PREPARATION

There were strong recommendations that speakers, resource persons, and participants need more material about the conference before the conference, so that they will really understand how and when to participate. Suggestions varied from providing an explanation of the schedule and the purposes of the various groupings (commissions, exchange

THIS PLENARY session gave participants the opportunity to react to the conference theme. The meeting was chaired by R. Bwembya Lukutati, Zambia. The subject was introduced by Manuel Perez Olea, Spain, and Jules A. Ahouzi, Ivory Coast, who presented their reactions to the conference program and discussions.

groups, committee meetings) to make substantive papers available early so that participants can take part knowledgeably in the various sessions. It was indicated that many of the resource persons could be better prepared and organized to lead their sessions. Also that help to speakers and resource people is needed so that those who attend are encouraged to participate.

Perhaps there could be more orientation meetings at different times held in separate language groupings at the beginning of the conference. These could be divided, so that participants and speakers meet separately and get their own appropriate instructions.

GROUPINGS

There was an almost unanimous suggestion that there be more small groups discussing the same topic, and then opportunities for reporting to each other. It was felt there were too many groups meeting at the same time with too many topics from which to choose. Perhaps some reports could be a part of the *Daily Bulletin,* or at least be available on a daily basis. Also, there was much value in groups that met on a continuous basis, like the commissions, so that participants, resource persons, and speakers could have interactions with one another, and get to know each other rather well.

There were many suggestions that seating at plenary sessions be in small groups so that participants can discuss or formulate questions for the speaker or panelists. The respondents liked sitting in small groups within their own language choice at the closing plenary session.

It was further suggested that there be more opportunity for geographic regional groups to meet to discuss common interests, needs, and ways to support one another.

All the language groups requested more simultaneous translations in small group meetings. Perhaps there could be a group of volunteer translators available for such meetings. Some of the participants indicated their willingness to sign up for such volunteer service.

The groupings liked best were the commission meetings.

There were many favorable comments about both the valuable content and the warm atmosphere of many of these meetings.

COMMUNICATIONS

Is there a way to insure more mixed representation at exchange group and commission meetings? This was asked, because participants felt they learned most in small groups in which many different countries were represented.

It was felt that most lectures were too long and too nonparticipative. Perhaps if lecturers used visual aids, and/or broke their presentations into several parts with discussion in between, these meetings would be more fruitful. Also it was suggested that a straight lecture, whether at the plenary sessions or at smaller meetings, just is not an interesting or inviting format. "More imagination in the design of plenary sessions is needed" said several groups.

Suggestions also included pleas for shorter introductions with the idea that the program participants' résumés could be available in printed form. Perhaps each program participant could prepare a paragraph on his or her background, and these could be put together alphabetically in a booklet or as part of the program. Persons who arrive late or who do not meet the deadline could bring their own materials. There were many comments requesting that less time be spent on "protocol" and more on substantive matters.

This leads to the suggestions that there be fewer large social occasions and more opportunity for participants to socialize in smaller groups during their free time. It was felt that the large receptions diminish rather than enhance communication between individuals. There is need to decrease the distance between the decision-makers of ICSW and the participants. Many persons felt that there was no opportunity to communicate with the "heads of the conference." There was a strong wish to be able to have more opportunities to influence ICSW planning and decision-making.

The *Daily Bulletin* was much appreciated and applauded, with just one major suggestion for improvement, namely, that the *Bulletin* appear more regularly at more places so it can be easily picked up.

Many comments were made about language, simultaneous translation, and some language groupings. But the strongest suggestion for the next conference was that Spanish be one of the official languages. Participants were aware that if groupings would have many countries represented, there would be language problems unless enough translators could be recruited.

It seems that the best communication took place at the commission meetings, at the multitable plenary session, and at some of the exchange groups, including those on aging, new approaches to delinquency, and new towns. High ratings, too, were given to two presentations: Reuben Baetz's presidential address and Sugata Dasgupta's discussion of community development.

FOLLOW-UP

Participants recommended that a follow-up evaluation system be designed to ascertain the value of this kind of conference to individual participants, and the impact, if any, on social welfare services in the participating countries. Strong feelings were expressed that this large conference of persons engaged in human and community services should make a difference in such specific areas as health care, alleviating poverty, increasing the participation of recipients, and developing appropriate alternative strategies for development and participation.

Such follow-up material might be sent to participants several months after the conference is over, or/and the Secretary-General and other decision-makers who travel could conduct group and/or individual interviews in the areas they visit, to ascertain what difference ICSW conference participation has made. Also, they could gather additional suggestions for the next conference.

SPECIFIC RECOMMENDATIONS FOR THE XVIIITH
ICSW CONFERENCE

1. That youth participate in the next conference
2. That more persons in the local area be involved
3. That the subject matter deal with poverty and hunger and how to ameliorate these human sufferings
4. That there be more discussions around the changing role of women throughout the world
5. That there be an emphasis on alternative *action* strategies appropriate for different cultures and countries—not just philosophy
6. That persons with different views be invited to discuss the same subject matter
7. That regional meetings be part of the total conference design
8. That leaders, speakers, and resource persons have an opportunity to participate in some orientation training sessions on how to involve participants in the deliberations in both small and large group meetings
9. That developing nations have even more opportunities to learn from the less developed countries (It was felt that one of the big learnings at this conference was by participants from developed countries from participants from less developed countries.)
10. That there be additional opportunities for participants to take part in ICSW committee meetings
11. That agency tours be more carefully supervised and organized
12. That consideration be given to limiting the number of participants from any one country. (The suggested limits on the number of delegates per country ranged from two to ten.)

It was heartening that persons at this plenary session participated so fully. Indeed, it was felt by some that this session should have been lengthened so that all reporters could have had a chance to speak. "You did not hear *us*—what do you know about participation?" was the note on one written report.

There is much we do not yet know, but we are very clear that those who attended the XVIIth International Conference on Social Welfare mirror the trends of our world—to get into the action, to speak up, to be heard, to influence planning, problem-solving, and decision-making.

The voices of the participants request "participant power," and this request must be further reflected in the design, the format and the content of the XVIIIth ICSW Conference in Mexico City in 1976.

# Summary and Review of the XVIIth International Conference on Social Welfare

## CHARLES I. SCHOTTLAND

PROFESSOR, FLORENCE HELLER SCHOOL FOR ADVANCED
STUDIES IN SOCIAL WELFARE, BRANDEIS UNIVERSITY,
UNITED STATES

THE XVIITH International Conference on Social Welfare is now drawing to a close, and I have been assigned the almost impossible task of summarizing the discussions of the past several days—discussions involving 2,000 delegates from 85 countries who engaged in approximately 150 or more meetings and sessions exclusive of informal meetings, and who listened to remarks or papers from more than 200 persons, as well as to the comments of hundreds of delegates in meetings, commissions, and various groups.

How does one summarize the excellent national reports from many of our seventy-three nation members, the report of the Conference Working Party, the seven plenary sessions, the sixteen general meetings, the forty exchange groups, a number of special-interest groups, regional meetings, meetings of other organizations, such as the International Federation of Social Workers and the International Congress of Schools of Social Work, the films and exhibits, the agency visits, and the informal gatherings from which some of us learned more than we did in the formal parts of the program?

An important and significant factor influencing our sessions was the locale in which they were held. It was our first African conference, and the delegates could not fail to be aware of the fact that we were in a unique setting. Some forty-five or more countries on the African continent, where man probably originated, present great contrasts: deserts lead into tropical jungles; equatorial Africa also has perpetual snow; the superb hotels of Nairobi stand in marked contrast to the villages of rural Africa. On this exciting continent, variety is the predominant note. Its 237,000,000 people represent almost every population group in the world—black and white and yellow races; Christian, Moslem, Jew, Coptic, and other religious groups; sophisticated urbanites and rural peoples still unrelated to the complexities of the 1970s—all of these move in the African culture, speaking Arabic, French, English, Swahili, Portuguese, Spanish, Amharic, Italian, German, Kinyarwanda, Hausa, Bantu, and other local tongues.

Those of us who have visited Africa for the first time and who studied this continent in preparation for the conference have been impressed with its vitality; with its large number of countries, some old, some newly formed; with its great natural resources; with its diversity of government. We have been interested in some of the new approaches to development as we heard about the Lushoto integrated development project in Tanzania, the Mwea irrigation settlement scheme in Kenya, and numerous settlement schemes in Malawi and Zambia—to mention only a few.

But the outstanding impressions I shall take away are personal rather than professional. The hospitality of our Kenya hosts shall never be forgotten; and the optimism and faith of our African friends in the future development of their countries, in their economic growth, in the ever-rising level of living, and their conviction that out of the current striving, turmoil, and problems will emerge new and just societies, have inspired us all.

This optimism expressed itself early in our meetings and at many sessions as speakers noted the world-wide progress over the past several years: man's increasing conquest of nature and disease, the demise of colonialism, the increase of the gross national product (GNP) in the developing countries, the lessening of international tensions.

But many delegates looked at the world through pessimistically colored glasses as they noted that the increase in the GNP did little to raise the level of living of the poorest groups; that the first stages of industrialization in developing countries frequently cause greater poverty, dislocation, and family disorganization; that many of the "developing" nations were showing little development and that in some countries, the current economic status is worse than that of previous years; that the political instability of major countries made international relations uncertain and insecure; that the world-wide migration from the countryside to the cities aggravated the most serious problems of our societies; that intolerance of other classes, races, religions, political philosophies, nationalities, and ways of life continues and in some areas has intensified; that drought and famine plague Africa and other areas of the world.

PRESIDENT'S ADDRESS

The conference began with the opening statement of Reuben C. Baetz of Canada. From his rich background as Director of the Canadian Council on Social Development, from his various experiences in countries around the world and as President of ICSW for the past two years, he spoke on the theme of the conference. His wide-ranging comments covered almost all the major subjects considered during the subsequent six days. He emphasized the differences in background of the countries represented at this conference; asserted that all nations have an inherent right to develop and that development has been a theme in ICSW conferences for many years. He cautioned the delegates that they need to apply what they learned here in Nairobi with full realization of the specific realities in their home countries. Participation, President Baetz maintained, means not only participation in the benefits made available by society, but in the basic decisions that establish and implement those benefits. Such participation will open up avenues for greater self-realization.

In emphasizing the contributions of the individual to social development, he touched upon problems of the handicapped, the aged, unemployment, education, volunteers, income redistribution, poverty, inflation, income security, and other subjects. Maintaining that the movement of women into the labor force meant a greater avenue for participation in society at large, he urged equal pay for equal work.

Pointing to the attitude of defeatism of many people, he urged an attitude of "angry optimism" as he proclaimed that "progress is possible." And so our President set the stage for the most exciting, significant, and challenging discussions that I have experienced in twenty years of attendance at ICSW conferences.

WORKING PARTY REPORT

The challenge to deal with fundamental solutions and not palliative measures was issued in the report of the Conference Working Party which was given to each delegate and presented at the second plenary session by its able chairman, Zena Harman of Israel. This session opened with a choral group singing a song with a line which proclaimed, "Let the needs of the nations be known."

Mrs. Harman let these needs be known. The Working Party's report was a significant statement, controversial but never dull, raised fundamental and challenging questions. Consensus was not achieved during the sessions, nor was it even considered desirable. Differences of opinion cropped up between those who claimed to be practical and those who felt that a new vision and a new horizon are needed if we are to solve our fundamental problems. The practice-oriented felt that some members were too theoretical, that they ignored the gains achieved through practical social action; while the more theoretically oriented felt that "being practical" meant slow progress in solving the problems of poverty, disease, maldistribution of wealth, and other tragic and unacceptable global conditions.

Mrs. Harman reported that the Working Party was unique in several ways. Never before did such an undertaking have a rapporteur from each region to synthesize the national reports. Likewise, the group decided not to follow the headings given for the national reports in order that discussions might not be inhibited by a rigid outline. To quote Mrs. Harman, the report sought to raise the curtain on a new script; new challenges need new approaches; 1974 is not the time for equanimity but for decisive action if we are to mitigate the suffering of millions who are experiencing hunger, poverty, unemployment, and the other social ills familiar to all.

The Working Party offered no single definition of development, and Mrs. Harman pointed out that some common terms had different meanings in different countries. She urged ICSW to attempt to formulate some common definitions of terms.

The report covered many areas and furnished the basis for many exciting discussions at a number of meetings. It was a catalytic agent in stimulating consideration of fundamental questions and was used as a guide by many delegates. Discussing development, participation, economic growth, poverty, education, women, youth, training, research, and other subjects, it touched upon most of the major themes of the conference. The report challenged traditional attitudes and the conventional wisdom; it attempted to place social work into the context of a rapidly changing society with new institutions and new values. If social work is to play a key role in our changing world, social workers must have greater functions in development programs; all social workers must have an understanding of development techniques and methods of social action; and Mrs. Harman called for change in the training of social workers.

The report emphasized poverty and maintained that unless the problem of poverty is attacked systematically, there cannot be adequate welfare programs for all. It set forth ten conditions or points to redress the inequality of incomes and other social requirements—a model or charter for the just society. It recognized that to achieve the goals set forth, some people will have to sacrifice material comforts and make adjustments in their way of life. It was, indeed, a sobering message.

In conclusion, Mrs. Harman challenged the conference to explore further the questions and challenges set forth by the Conference Working Party and the conference did.

The report met with general approval although there were some minor disagreements on some points. Some delegates felt that the emphasis on poverty was not the best way to promote social services, that experience has shown that services geared primarily to the poor resulted in poor services; and those who felt this way preferred the statement in point nine of the Working Party's ten points which emphasized that "resource allocation should be directed first and foremost toward meeting the needs of all the people."

OFFICIAL OPENING

The "official" opening of the conference took place on July 16. We shall never forget the greeting by His Excellency Mzee Jomo Kenyatta, President of the Republic of Kenya, a national leader revered and loved by his people and renowned throughout the world.

Welcomed in accordance with Kenya custom by national choirs, President Kenyatta officially opened the meeting with a statement which covered many of the problems with which the conference was wrestling. Maintaining that social welfare is no longer academic but is concerned with the needs and struggles of ordinary people, he asserted that the true purpose of social welfare is to have people feel that they are part of a just and orderly society. Referring to Kenya, the President pointed out that the majority of the people work on the land, and therefore the rural areas are a key to development. But Kenya must face also the problem of urban expansion. Development must involve the youth, and 50 percent of the population of Kenya is under fifteen years of age. It was indeed an impressive message from an impressive leader.

President Kenyatta was thanked by Reuben C. Baetz, who hailed the President not only as the head of a state but as the father of a nation.

From the opening of this historic meeting by Jimmy Verjee, chairman of the Organizing Committee, to the final gesture of President Kenyatta with his world-renowned flyswitch, it was a period and an event we shall all remember.

CONFERENCE THEME

The theme of the conference was chosen after intensive consideration by the Program Committee and other committees and officers of ICSW. Expressed as "development and participation—operational implications for social welfare," it was broad enough to enable delegates to discuss almost anything they wished, and pointed enough to emphasize two basic concepts sweeping the world today: "development" and "participation." To direct the delegates to practical considerations, the theme added "operational implications for social welfare." The concept of development was, of course, the overriding and dominant theme, and the word "development" appeared in most of the 150 meetings. The Program Committee viewed development as a balanced and integrated process. Throughout the conference, economic growth and the gross national product were attacked as unsatisfactory goals for development.

The Working Party, acknowledging that no one definition of development will fit all circumstances, emphasized that it is a process that enhances the long-run capacity of a society to function for the well-being of all its members; it should mean a better standard of life, involving moral concepts, and at the same time should be the basis for political action.

*Population growth.* Four main subjects in addition to development seemed to crop up repeatedly during this week. Population growth, a favorite topic, was the major focus of a general meeting and surfaced in many discussions. Yet it seems to me that many discussions still fail to recognize that unbridled population growth is the gravest danger to social progress and social development. A few figures can put this into context. Ten thousand years ago, the population of the world is estimated to have been about ten million people. It took from the dawn of civilization to the year 1825 to produce one billion people simultaneously alive; it took only 105 years to produce the second billion—in 1930 there were two billion people in the world; it took only thirty years to produce the third billion—in 1960 there were three billion; it will take only seventeen years for the fourth billion, which we shall reach by 1977; only ten years for the fifth billion by 1987; and eight years for the sixth billion by 1995. (These are neither the high nor the low estimates.)

This dramatic rise in population is the result of modern public health education, better nutrition, and rising levels of living, and this increase aggravates many of the social problems with which we deal—poverty, housing, overcrowding, unemployment, and so on.

Because of the seriousness of the population problem, many delegates reported on their country's work in family planning. Some have been successful; some, unsuccessful. Thus, Japan has been able to slow the population increase but India has not. One study in Canquenes, Chile, revealed that the birth rate was in direct proportion to the level of education. In families where the mother had no formal education, the number of births per couple was 4.86; where the mother had some primary school education, the number of births was 3.40; where the mother completed primary school, the births dropped to 1.21, just one quarter of the number for those without any formal education.[1] Will education, then, solve our population problem? As I reviewed various discussions it seemed to me that a consensus was expressed in the words of Y. F. Hui of Hong Kong in a general meeting who mentioned that all nations have a concern over population growth, but the concern is not the same in all countries. Many do not have a population policy. He emphasized the concept that a population policy is a policy of means and not of ends; such policy is an instrument for other ends—economic, political, environmental, social—but is aimed at improving the quality of life.

*Poverty.* A second prominent subject, poverty, dominated many sessions. Plenary session speakers opened the subject, which was mentioned by President Baetz. It constituted a major thrust of the report of the Working Party and was an important concept in Professor Dasgupta's presentation. The general meetings also recognized its overriding impact on the

[1] Carmen Miro and Walter Mertens, "Influence Affecting Fertility in Urban and Rural Latin America," *Milkbank Memorial Fund Quarterly,* July, 1968, p. 105.

conference theme. A general meeting under the chairmanship of Mme. Andrée Audibert of France devoted its considerations to the maldistribution of wealth; another general meeting saw poverty as a major problem of urbanization; exchange groups, discussing employment of youth, recognized the relation of jobs to poverty. There was an exchange group on public assistance; one on disadvantaged minority groups; and a group on social security in developing countries—all these and many others found the poverty theme a core consideration in their deliberations.

The all-too-easy answers appeared at several sessions, and I would like to comment on them and place the poverty question in some type of perspective.

The poor form the majority of the world's population, and they are concentrated in the developing countries. In 1970 the developing areas of the world had a population of 2,542,000,000 as opposed to 1,090,000,000 in the industrial areas. The poorer the population, the higher the birth rate. In 1970, there were 785 million children in countries where the per capita income was $100 or under $100; 210 million children in countries where the per capita income was $101 to $300; and 70 million children where the per capita income was between $301 and $500.

Just ten years ago most "experts" predicted that the increase in the GNP would provide employment and reduce poverty. It has not worked that way. The unprecedented increases in output of the past ten years have failed to trickle down to the poorest majority of the people.

The elation and enthusiasm which greeted the first UN development decade have been replaced by sober stocktaking. It was evident that economic growth frequently worsened the distribution of income. In some countries the income of the poorest in the population has deteriorated even in absolute terms.[2]

Examples are gleaned from country reports, discussions of the past few days, and my own research.

[2] Irma Adelman and Cynthia Morris, "An Anatomy of Income Distribution Patterns in Developing Nations," *Development Digest,* October, 1971, p. 37.

Although Pakistan's economy grew at a healthy rate in the 1960s, unemployment increased, real wages in the industrial sector declined by one third, and in 1968 when the GNP was at its peak, the government collapsed under the strain of social and economic pressures. Mauritius shows an increase in its GNP, but the ICSW report indicates an unemployment rate of 27 percent. Mexico has had a dramatic increase in its GNP, but the report of the Mexican committee to ICSW indicates widespread unemployment in rural areas, causing migration to cities where rural workers do not find jobs. Brazil is a brilliant example of economic growth, but a large portion of the population has not benefited from the impressive increase in production, and the share of national income received by the poorest 40 percent of the population declined from 10 percent in 1960 to an estimated 8 percent in 1970, whereas the share of the richest 5 percent grew from 29 percent to 38 percent during the same period. In the Philippines, the distribution of income appears to have worsened in the past twenty years, and in India the real income of the poorest 10 percent of the population (50 million people) appears to have declined during a decade in which the GNP increased by 50 percent. One study estimated that in Pakistan, Ceylon, Malaysia, the Philippines, Bangladesh, and other countries, 15 percent or more of the labor force is unemployed.[3]

Poverty in developing countries is in large measure a problem of rural poverty. To some extent this is due to obsolete methods of agriculture. In many countries a farmer produces only enough food for himself and six or fewer persons, whereas in highly developed agriculture a farmer can produce enough food for himself and thirty or more other persons.

If, in the early stages of economic growth, inequality of income increases, as appears to be the case, what is the answer? Some answers came out of this conference. The Singapore report stressed the role of social welfare in seeking answers. Social welfare programs, Singapore reported, provide a safeguard for the hazards of modern life. So long as the poor trail

---

[3] Taken from various sources, including William Rich, *Smaller Families through Social and Economic Progress* (Washington, D.C.: Overseas Development Council, 1973).

behind in the economic growth of the country, such growth is jeopardized. Two strategies received attention. One has been hailed as a "new strategy." The new strategy shifts the emphasis from economic growth and the GNP to the immediate, concrete, and critical needs of people. We used to say, "Increase the GNP and the needs of people will take care of themselves." We now know this has not worked. The new strategy says just the opposite: "Concentrate on participation of people and make available education, jobs, health services, better housing, and a variety of human services and the GNP will take care of itself." A planner in Pakistan puts the new strategy clearly:

Development goals must be defined in terms of progressive reduction and eventual elimination of malnutrition, disease, illiteracy, squalor, unemployment, and inequalities. We were taught to take care of our GNP as this will take care of poverty. Let us reverse this and take care of poverty as this will take care of the GNP.

*Development strategies.* There is growing evidence that policies designed to raise the income of the poorest half of the population can actually accelerate, not hinder, growth.

Those of us engaged in social welfare need not be intimidated by the esoteric language of the economists and other GNP enthusiasts. Our obligation is to people, to programs that will meet their needs and services which they themselves help design to enable them to reach the better life.

This is the essence of the new development strategy, implicit in the theme of this conference. The most important feature of the new strategy is that it shifts attention away from the high generalities of economic growth to the immediate, concrete, and critical needs of human beings for income, jobs, housing, medical care, and other services. This is not to diminish the importance of economic growth. Without more economic resources, productivity, power, food, and so forth, only misery lies ahead. But the new strategy involves the people who do the bulk of the work and gives them the highest incentive—the hope of sharing in the fruit of their labor.

A second strategy discussed tries to reconcile economic development and social welfare goals. The national report of the Republic of China sets forth this goal in its opening sentence:

The purpose of economic development is to increase the nation's over-all production power while the promotion of social welfare from the standpoint of humanity and justice ought to enable all of the components of society to share the fruit of economic development and, in particular, help the weaker ones cultivate their latent faculties so that they may work out their salvation by their own efforts.

But this reconciliation of economic and social welfare goals is encountering difficulties in the current political arenas. As P. N. Luthra, Secretary of the Department of Social Welfare of India, remarked at a meeting of the Committee of Representatives, in this period of economic distress in developing countries, with inflation and the rising cost of living, with the oil shortage which has had catastrophic effects on some economies, with drought and famine in many countries, it is inevitable that economic factors should predominate and that in such a climate it is difficult to impress policy-makers with the importance of social factors which seem less likely to solve the immediate distress. Although some disagreed on the emphasis to be given to poverty programs, all agreed that there can be no just society until poverty is banished from the earth. In the developed countries poverty is immoral; most developed countries can abolish poverty readily by a redistribution of resources. When will we reach the point where we decide that it is not necessary to spend billions on weapons and armaments to kill our fellow men but decide instead to abolish poverty, hunger, and disease? For developing countries, the problem is a more long-range and serious one. But people are people wherever they may be, and many sessions stressed the elimination of poverty throughout the world as an indispensable goal of a just society.

*Urbanization.* A third subject was prominent. Everywhere at this conference three words surfaced: "migration," "industrialization," "urbanization." Millions of rural dwellers are moving to the cities, leaving farms untended, leaving the old behind, and creating great problems for the cities to which they go. Many examples were presented. To cite one, in Egypt people have been moving from rural areas to cities at an alarmingly rapid rate. Cairo alone, with a population of about 6.5 million, contains more than a third of Egypt's urban families and is growing at a rate of a million people every four years.

Although urbanization is a world-wide phenomenon, it is particularly serious in the developing countries. It seems as though modernization and industrialization almost automatically mean urbanization. Very few countries have been able to stem the tide of rural folk flooding into cities and metropolitan areas. This recurring theme was presented vividly by Harold H. C. Ho of Hong Kong, who reported that the lure of city lights has attracted young people. Even in Communist China the movement to require young intellectuals to return to the farm is dreaded by the youth who defect to Hong Kong.

Delegate after delegate commented on the social problems caused by urban growth. Yet it is interesting to note that urbanization is a relatively new phenomenon. Prior to 1850, no society or country could be described as predominantly urban, and by 1900, only one—Great Britain—could be so regarded. Today, all industrial nations are highly urbanized and urbanization is world-wide, increasing in developing countries even faster than in developed ones.

In the United States less than 7 percent of the work force are farmers. When developing countries reach this state of affairs, how much more serious will the problem be? In the next ten years, the United States will add probably 40 million people to its population, and almost all will become city-dwellers.

*Approaches to the problem.* What is the answer? Three general approaches came out of the conference. One centered on "keeping them down on the farm." Yugoslavia appears to have had some success in this. Apparently in Slovenia they have experienced modernization and industrialization without urbanization. In Slovenia, 42 percent of the work force are in industry and related occupations—more than twice that in agriculture; 59 percent of the nonagricultural labor force live outside urban communities. Perhaps this is due to the Yugoslav policy of decentralizing industry. Nevertheless, the Yugoslav report confirmed a substantial movement to cities, particularly of young people. For most countries, the reports were dismal. In the developing countries, 70 percent to 80 percent of the population live in rural villages, and most of them are farmers. And they are flocking to the city.

A second proposal which received attention was population control. Many tie the population explosion to the migration to the city and feel that stopping urban growth must involve effective population control.

Other country reports stated the stark facts. In Mauritius 37 percent of the labor force are wholly unemployed; 70 percent live in rural areas, and they are moving to the city. The Swedish report described succinctly the decline in population, the increasing percentage of older people left in rural areas, lack of jobs, increase in service costs in cities, and other factors familiar throughout the world. The Japanese reported that from 1960 to 1970 the number of agricultural workers was reduced by 29.5 percent and that only 8.7 percent of male and 2.1 percent of female graduates of junior and senior high school entered agricultural work. Since the Japanese farmer obtains less than half of his livelihood from agriculture, it is common for all members of the family to seek outside employment.

Mexico reported that the country is changing from a predominantly rural to an urban civilization. Indonesia echoed the reports from many developing countries: 80 percent of the population is rural; they are flocking to the cities; and the measures taken by government and voluntary agencies have not been able to curtail this urban migration.

One of the few countries where the national report indicated this was not a problem was the Netherlands. This report indicated that urbanization was far advanced; there are no "typical" rural areas as there are in other countries; and the rural areas may be termed "urbanized rural areas." Will all countries reach this stage in the years to come?

A third proposal or series of proposals emerged. Let us recognize the inevitable. The future is paved with city asphalt, so let us make life more livable in the cities and tackle our problems there. Do cities hold the means for doing this? One study of urbanization maintains that urbanization increases political participation and that this development is far-reaching in developing countries.[4] Let us hope that this is one positive factor in urbanization, because many experts believe that although the world is not yet fully urbanized, it soon will be.[5]

*Participation.* The fourth and overriding subject of the conference was "participation," a favorite topic of the country reports. The Israeli report asserted that it was difficult to find a clear and concise definition of citizen participation, but other national reports adopted their own definitions. Denmark and Australia both pointed out the importance of funding. Denmark asserted that citizens' participation needs money support if it is to be effective. The Hong Kong report explored quantitative indicators to evaluate participation. The report of International Social Service asserted that social workers can stimulate participation because of their "skills, training, and experience," while the International Federation of Settlements and Neighborhood Centers maintained that the most basic principle of community work is the participation of people at all levels in society in all the stages of development and in the implementation of social policy. The Canadian report, emphasizing the concept of values, maintained that participation is one of the newer values in our society.

The excellent report from Australia was entitled, "Participation in Australia." It is one of the best statements on participation I have seen. The report states unequivocally that it is committed to the philosophy that participation of people in decisions that directly affect them is a *right*. This clear assertion is in contrast to the vague generalities which frequently surround the subject of participation. The report explores the

---

[4] Irma Adelman and Cynthis Morris, *Economic Growth and Social Equity in Developing Countries* (Stanford, Calif.: Stanford University Press, 1973), pp. 21–22.

[5] Kingsley Davis, "The Urbanization of the Human Revolution," in Sylvia Feis Fava, ed., *Urbanism in World Perspective: a Reader* (New York: Thomas Y. Crowell Co., 1968), pp. 23–45.

different areas in which participation may operate and the methods of participation.

The Conference Working Party saw participation as an essential element of development, as an end as well as a means. It stipulated certain conditions for effective participation: access to information, knowledge to be able to participate meaningfully, the will to give time and energy, and an attitude of mind promoting personal service. The report argued for new approaches to participation.

Plenary session speakers expounded on this theme. President Baetz, Sugata Dasgupta, and others touched upon this significant subject which was a popular area for debate at many sessions.

Several general meetings also expanded the theme. One discussed participation of youth; another, under the leadership of Mme. Andrée Audibert of France, maintained that participation is hampered by the maldistribution of economic resources; another meeting discussed the contribution of the role of volunteers; the role of the family was examined under the presiding officer, Yohana Issaya Shekiffu of Tanzania; and the role of the elderly, in a general meeting presided over by Dr. Alois Stacher of Austria; and other general meetings and exchange groups touched upon the participation theme.

PLENARY SESSIONS

*Address by Sugata Dasgupta.* The plenary session addressed by Sugata Dasgupta of India was, to use an American expression, a blockbluster. Logically reasoned and dramatically presented, it met with both enthusiastic approval and violent disagreement. It is difficult to do justice to Professor Dasgupta's closely reasoned thesis in a few lines. He attacked some of the most cherished beliefs and fondest hopes of world and national leaders as he maintained that "development" has not worked. The rich nations and the rich in the poor nations have become richer, and the masses of the people in the Third World have become poorer.

Likewise, he maintained, "participation" has also failed. The elite used people as a tool, to develop resources utilized more

by the elite than by those who produced them. The time has come, he argued, for a new vision and a new society. People are simply not going to wait for the fruits of development to reach them in a gradual manner. There is a new cry for participation which demands equality, not only equality of opportunity but equality of attainment; and not for a few or for many, but for all. The processes of development and participation as we have known them over the past many years are on the way out; there must be a new society, national economic policies must be replaced by community economic policies, and the main emphasis should be on rural development and on the abolition of absolute poverty. This new society will be one "where all will have just enough to live and no one will be rich or affluent."

It was inevitable that these ideas would stimulate discussion. Professor Dasgupta's comment about taking away the Rolls Royces from ambassadors did not cause controversy, but almost every other major proposal did. In the halls and in meetings many questions were raised. The new society, some maintained, was utopian but was it practical? Where were the specifics and detailed description of this new society? Was the abolition of a national economic policy and substitution of a community economic policy a way to avoid national responsibility, to "pass the buck" to local communities which simply could not have the resources to solve the problems of a technologically advancing world society? One delegate even asked whether the proposals would not result in institutionalizing and hiding poverty. Another felt that the proposals were based on a pessimistic view of the potential of new technologies to abolish poverty. What were the implications of this new society, another asked, for national programs of health, welfare, education, and related services?

But there was general agreement on several of Professor Dasgupta's basic ideas, namely, the failure of many programs of development, the need for a new concept of participation, and new approaches if we are to tackle the basic problems of development and participation successfully. Whatever position an individual may take in this controversy, this was the kind of address which makes the ICSW forum vital and exciting.

*The René Sand Award.* The fourth plenary session was a gala affair as eighty-five nations answered the roll call of nations. The ICSW distinguished service award was presented to Manoel Francisco Lopes Meirelles of Brazil by President Baetz. In his acceptance speech Mr. Meirelles recalled his work with many distinguished personalities connected with ICSW. President Baetz then presented the coveted René Sand Award to J. Riby-Williams, Chief, Human Resources Development Division, United Nations Economic Commission for Africa. Mr. Riby-Williams's acceptance address on "our contemporary challenge for concerted international action of nongovernmental organizations" presented an historical account of the development of welfare councils in Africa and the role of nongovernmental organizations (NGOs) of the UN.

Mr. Riby-Williams emphasized that change can occur only by the wish of the people themselves; that today it is the human resources that we recognize as the key to development; that traditions sometimes block progress and change; that we still have not discovered the best way to use human capital; that countries which have emphasized physical and industrial growth have paid a heavy price in the creation of social problems; that for the next development decade a more meaningful and effective relationship must exist between and among NGOs, governments, and the UN, and if NGOs make their works consistent with development goals and UN objectives they can make a major contribution.

Responding on behalf of ICSW, Robert Leaper, Vice President for Europe, stated that international solidarity requires long and patient work and that the way had been shown in Mr. Riby-Williams's review of NGOs and government and UN relationships.

GENERAL MEETINGS

There were other dramatic moments also, so many, in fact, that I cannot present them all. For example, at a general meeting, Jean Vanier of Canada and France, discussing the contribution to development by the physically and mentally handicapped, brought tears to the eyes of many delegates as he urged taking the mentally handicapped out of institutitons.

Such persons have a contribution to make, he stated; they have experienced suffering and they can extend sympathy and compassion.

One of the exciting experiences at these conferences is learning about new developments around the world. We heard numerous stories of successes and failures; of new approaches and experiments: how land reform and community development in Bolivia were assisted by four international organizations—the International Labour Organization, the Food and Agriculture Organization, the United Nations Educational, Scientific, and Cultural Organization, and the World Health Organization; the success of rural cooperatives in Costa Rica; the resettlement of new lands in Nigeria; the changes in the kibbutzim in Israel; the continuing experiences in the new towns of Great Britain and Finland; new initiatives in rural developments in Pakistan; the success of family planning in Japan and Taiwan; the overwhelming problems faced by Rio de Janeiro as thousands of rural dwellers leave the farm for the city; the upgrading of the villages in the Philippines; the experiences of countries hit by the worst drought in decades, causing famine, migration, and the establishment of refugee camps—almost 300,000 persons were in camps in Nigeria, 5,000 in Mali; in Ethiopia scores of thatched huts have become desperate, dependent suburbs; in Chad the four million residents, hard hit by drought, have only forty-four doctors; and some estimate that at least 100,000 persons have perished from the drought in Africa alone. ICSW through its Executive Committee has taken note of this situation, and appropriate representations will be made to responsible bodies.

Throughout the conference many contradictory and opposite points of view were expressed in the free-wheeling, free-speech tradition of the conference, and many speakers found their opinions challenged.

*Aging.* At the general meeting on aging, presided over by Bernard Nash of the United States, delegates were moved by the discussion and asked for consultation and advice so that they might organize societies for the aged in their respective countries.

Three excellent papers gave an overview of the problems and of programs for the aging: in a developing country (Christopher Sipanga of Kenya); in two industrial countries (David Hobman presenting the English experience); and in Japan with Datsaki Maeda presenting the situation and reporting on the emergence of "old people's power" as the aged increase their participation in community and political activities.

The conference also became aware of the emergence of the International Federation on Ageing as an important organization in the international social welfare arena. The Federation presented a symposium on world action on aging. Other meetings discussed the subject also, recognizing that the percentage of older persons in the population is steadily increasing due to a variety of reasons: the growing conquest of disease, lower fertility rates, and the rise in the level of living. But with this increase in the aged many problems emerge. How can the experience and talents of older people be used? Must they be forced to retire at what for many may be a very young age? Do the health problems of the aged demand special health programs?

*Youth.* The subject of youth received prominent attention at the conference. It was discussed by President Kenyatta, President Baetz, and the Working Party. Mrs. Harman discussed the massive problems of youth unemployment and the unschooled and unskilled and asserted that youth constitutes a tremendous resource for development. One general meeting on participation of youth in development involved delegates from eleven countries. There was agreement on the importance of youth participating in development; some disagreement as to whether countries should have a "youth policy," or a "people's policy" and not separate out youth; disagreement also as to whether youth are revolutionary, in that they initiate violent protest, or more often are used by radical adults.

*The family.* Another subject which surfaced at many meetings was the family, and it was the primary subject of a general meeting presided over by Yohana Issaya Shekiffu of Tanzania. Several papers gave views on the family, and one

speaker, Catherine Chilman of the United States, raised many
disturbing questions about the institution of the family—an institution that we have assumed for centuries is the backbone of
our society. She asserted that the power of the family declines
in a mass industrial society as other power systems—industry,
government services, and so forth—gain power: divorce rates
continue to rise; out-of-wedlock birth rates become higher.
But there was optimism expressed as the speaker stated that
out of this decay of the family may be born new social guidelines for living, new life styles, and perhaps in the long run,
changes for the better.

*Housing.* The subject of housing received attention in a
number of meetings and was the major subject of an exchange
group. If I could sum up in one sentence the various reports
on the subject of housing I would say that there was agreement that more important than the germs he encounters or
the genes he inherits is where a man lives and to whom he
speaks.

COMMISSIONS

The commissions did a herculean job in examining in depth
many of the issues of the conference.

Commission I, discussing the role of social welfare in economic and social development, targets and programming,
touched upon many of the major topics discussed in the conference: population explosion, development, participation, social research, social welfare, terminology. It was evident in the
discussions that there are great differences among countries,
that these differences—economic, cultural, political—result in
different approaches. The commission proclaimed that a social worker protecting the *status quo* against needed change
"betrays" his profession.

Commission II explored the role of government and nongovernmental organizations in development and how to encourage this participation as partners in development. Taken
together with the address by J. Riby-Williams, this subject received thorough exploration. Commission II concluded that
the relationship between governmental and nongovernmental

organizations, which should represent the interests of all the people, must be balanced, supplementary, and complementary. Partnership, with a degree of productive conflict, is an important ingredient in this relationship. Goals and priorities should always be developed through active participation of all organizations concerned.

The Israeli national report reminded us that a most important voluntary organization is the political party. Those of us interested in change had better consider our roles in political parties if we are to be effective.

Commission III discussed ways and means of encouraging participation of local communities and individuals in development. This same theme was discussed in two sections and added to the intensive consideration of the subject throughout the conference.

The French section discussed alternative ways in which participation at the local level might be achieved. It stressed training for participation, beginning with the family and occurring at all levels; it regarded research as essential to participation; and asserted that professional personnel must be capable of interdisciplinary cooperation.

The Spanish-speaking section emphasized participation as a right—a theme set forth in the Australian national report. Participation was also looked upon as a value and a good for a meaningful life.

Commission IV concentrated on the subject of participation. Discussing participation in the promotion and delivery of services, it was agreed that the test of participation is the opportunity people have to participate in the design and implementation of schemes which affect their lives. Each country, even community, must find the particular combination of governmental, private, and voluntary organizations which suits its cultural and social-economic stages of development. There must be a structure for two-way communication which permits people at the local level to express their needs, aspirations, and plans for effecting them, and for the national aspirations and plans to be conveyed to the people. At all intermediate levels planning and appropriate bodies should determine relationships, the relevancy of the two sets of aspirations and plans, and the extent to which support can be given to the self-help efforts of the communities. Considerable attention was given to the importance of values and the necessity for education for integrity, honesty, and altruism.

Commission V considered the implications for training and education in the encouragement of participation in development. The commission recognized that progress in development depends upon participation by people and that such participation if it is to be meaningful, depends upon education. The commission urged ICSW to encourage educational institutions to enhance student participation and prepare students for participation in social development; and further, to stimulate pilot studies in participation. The commission urged that greater emphasis be given to the mass media in promoting participation.

Commission VI turned its attention to planning and utilization of research information in development. The commission concluded that the specific national conditions that contribute to economic growth, the elimination of poverty, and the participation of individuals and groups in the processes of national development must be understood and analyzed in the context of the "real" resources available to a given nation.

Research can be used as a tool to provide planners with information designed to reduce the risks associated with the decisions they must make. Planners and researchers alike must not expect research to do more than clarify available alternatives: decisions are made, after all, on the basis of a value belief. National resources should be allocated so that social development research is clearly a high priority. The commission recognized that the comment in the national report of Mauritius, that research has barely begun, applies to a large number of countries.

Commission VII examined a subject which concerned many at this conference, namely, the essential problems of urban and industrial pressures on rural societies. There is little doubt that urbanization is resulting in great upheaval in rural areas. Unless this upheaval can be "managed," the problems of migration to the city will multiply. The commission urged that the social costs of industrial development be presented vigorously to the governments concerned.

EXCHANGE GROUPS

In the exchange groups, which many found matched their professional interests in their daily practice, present and traditional subjects intermingled with some new approaches: racial discrimination, employment, aging, youth, social legislation, housing, new towns, social indicators, leisure time, adoptions. These and many other subjects were examined, discussed, argued about, and country experiences were exchanged.

One exchange group discussed the creation of employment opportunities for young people in rural areas. Presided over by Harriet Kawala Kagwa of Uganda, this was but one of the many enthusiastic exchange groups where delegates could exchange experiences. The group outlined steps to create employment for rural youth and to overcome resistance to change.

Another exchange group, under the chairmanship of Joe Hoffer of the United States, discussed "councils of social agencies—partners in development." The general feeling was that voluntarism is on the downgrade and that voluntary agencies must provide useful services to survive. There was consensus that government must assume the major role in promoting and financing social development because it is the only instrument that can command the necessary resources.

Local and central planning councils under nongovernmental auspices both in so-called "developing" countries and in developed countries can play an important role in such areas as supplementing and complementing governmental programs and especially in monitoring these programs. They must, however, enlarge their horizons beyond merely social planning and include economic and physical planning within their functions. Finally, planning councils can provide channels for increased participation and input from technical experts through selected educational, planning, and legislative activities related to social development.

The role of social welfare-oriented personnel in high policy-making positions was discussed in several sessions. Jamaica reported that "there is a lack of social welfare personnel in policy positions," and this was reported also by other countries. However, in conversation many delegates reported that in many countries, particularly some in Latin America, social workers are being utilized increasingly in top planning roles. Numerous other reports indicated that social welfare personnel are achieving a higher status in many countries than they had a decade ago.

An enthusiastic meeting of an exchange group on "racial discrimination—a hindrance to development," composed of approximately a hundred delegates, considered this important topic. The group recognized that racialism is an international problem which is usually seen as discrimination due to color, physical features, attitudes, or culture. It stated that in fact the root cause of racialism anywhere is economic exploitation. The group expressed firm opposition to political systems which legitimize economic exploitation. Among the recommendations were:

1. That the oppression of people become the theme of the XVIIIth ICSW
2. That a more vigorous action be taken to strengthen the ICSW consultative status with the UN and with other affiliated bodies within ICSW dealing with human rights.

SPECIAL MEETINGS

A special meeting on new approaches to development in the village and poor community saw the necessity for long- and short-term strategies against poverty. In the long run, a fundamental restructuring of society is necessary in the immediate future; it is urgent that programs to help the poor community be given the highest priority. The group recommended that a continuing ICSW committee be set up to work, through correspondence if necessary, for a study of definitions of social development, social welfare, and social work in the light of new concepts emerging and new social horizons, to constitute a new kind of continuing program for ICSW.

In 1962, in Athens, the ICSW went on record as favoring a world-wide meeting of Ministers charged with responsibility for social welfare programs. A number of governments supported this proposal, and in 1968 the UN called such a meeting. An exciting meeting, it was attended by the top Ministers of most of the countries of the world, and its deliberations were indeed significant.

At this 1974 conference in Nairobi, the Ministers or their chief deputies of social welfare held a very important session. These top government officials insisted that social welfare programs must be interested in the "whole man," in the "whole human being," and not just in his health, or his education, or his job. Man is the center of government and society concern.

Let us hope that the Ministers will carry on in this spirit and that their views will prevail in their respective countries in the years ahead. ICSW hopes that at our 1976 conference in Mexico, we may have an even larger number of Ministers. In a very real sense these top officials hold in their hands the well-being of millions of people.

INTERNATIONAL CONGRESS OF SCHOOLS OF SOCIAL WORK

The XVIIth International Congress of Schools of Social Work was an eventful experience both for the organizers and for the participants. All but one of the speakers and a majority of the participants were from the developing countries of Africa, Asia, and Latin America.

In response to the theme of "Education for Social Change, Human Development, and National Progress," the educators projected a new look in social work education, with enthusiasm and confidence in the ability of the profession to educate for social change.

INTERNATIONAL FEDERATION OF SOCIAL WORKERS

The symposium of the International Federation of Social Workers centered on three topics:

1. The philosophical content of "social worker"
2. The goals, objectives, and functions of social workers
3. The means to achieve the goals.

And so this summary comes to an end. It may be somewhat scattered and uncoordinated, but I have tried to record some of the specifics as well as the general trends of conference discussions. I ask understanding for the omission of some country reports, and the reports of some 150 meetings. The spirit was willing, but the capacity to grasp and interpret this huge forum and the hundreds of thousands of words spoken and written here in Nairobi is limited.

It has been a grand conference. Under the able leadership of Reuben Baetz of Canada, our President, and with Kate Katzki at the administrative helm, the sessions have gone well. I express the thanks of all of us for their work. Our thanks and appreciation also must go to Jimmy Verjee, who first invited ICSW to Africa and who has guided much of the preparation for the conference; to Mrs. Dorcas Luseno, Assistant Secretary-General for Africa, who handled much of the preparatory work; to the numerous volunteers who made the conference run smoothly; and to many others—Yohannes Gerima, Vice-President for Africa; our assistant secretary-generals; our advisor on protocol, ICSW history, and all other matters, Ginette d'Autheville. Special thanks go to Bwembya Lukutati of Zambia, chairman of the Program Committee, for producing a magnificent program; to the choral groups; and finally to all others, too numerous to mention, who made this meeting a success. The beautiful conference center has also added to the success of our conference.

We have made new friends here at this XVIIth meeting of ICSW, and this meeting in Africa now makes it possible for us to say that we have met on every continent and have forwarded many of the important by-products of these meetings; better communication among social welfare communities all over the world; and better understanding of our cultural, political, language, and other differences.

We have found some answers at this XVIIth conference of ICSW. We hope we shall be able to make progress in the coming years in solving some of the problems with which social welfare is concerned. The challenge before us was set forth in the report of the United States Committee, which quoted a revered poet, Walt Whitman: "Now understand me well—it is provided in the essence of things, that from any fruition of success, no matter what, shall come forth something to make a greater struggle necessary."

As I listened to the various plans of the country members of ICSW as reported here in Nairobi, I thought that perhaps our plans can never be finished in a world that is ever-changing and difficult to understand. Or perhaps we must come soon to the realization that world-wide problems cannot be solved by nations acting individually.

I guess I am an incurable optimist but I believe that in spite of wars, internal strife, the slow development of some countries, the future looks brighter than it appeared at many of our sessions. When people all over the world become well-fed—as surely they will be in our world of the future; when all persons become literate—as surely they will be; when many become interested in change and a better life, many of the problems we examined at this conference will be on the way to solution, and perhaps the nations of the world will adopt the law from the earliest legal codes of Rome which in Latin reads *salus populi suprema lex esto* and which translated proclaims that "the welfare of the people shall be the supreme law" (of the land).

# Urban Problems—Today and Tomorrow

## HAROLD H. C. HO

ADMINISTRATIVE CHAIRMAN, BOARD OF STUDIES
IN SOCIAL WORK, CHINESE UNIVERSITY
OF HONG KONG

URBAN PROBLEMS are not new. What is new is the pace at which the future is engulfing cities throughout the world. The phenomenon of urbanization appears to be a world-wide problem. The rate of growth is as significant and potentially disastrous in Nairobi as in Hong Kong, in Lima as in Tokyo, in Sydney as in Los Angeles. In urban society today man faces not only an uncertain future but a whole spectrum of possible consequences and therefore constant conflict over desirable changes. The future of the city and its problems vary from one society to another and relate to resources and cultures with particular reference to traditional value systems and their vulnerability to change.

In this context we are particularly concerned with Asian urban problems, principally in Southeast Asia. Population explosion and transitional difficulties from agrarian societies to industrialized societies will focalize the source of urban problems. It seems essential to outline some general conditions of Asia if we are to understand the problems in their proper perspectives.

Politically, Asian countries are torn between two political blocs, and the increasing influence of China has made substantial changes in the political attitude here. Premier Lee Kuan-yew of Singapore remarked recently that Asian countries should learn how to live with China. In fact, political alignment with either the Russian or the American bloc seems less palatable a solution than "peaceful coexistence" and neutrality.

The economic policies of Asian countries vary widely: North Vietnam's socialist planning contrasts sharply with capitalist Malaysia and the Philippines. Though there was little development of major industry during the region's colonial era, Asian countries have been striving to correct the unbalanced economy by emphasizing industrialization.

Asia is a land of extreme diversity in its political, social, cultural, and religious institutions; these diverse factors have an important bearing on determining the degree of progress to be achieved and on national building. In Vietnam, for example, the mountain tribes have differing cultures and value systems quite distinct from those of the rest of the Vietnamese, making integration difficult. Likewise, the Hoa-Hao, Buddhists, Catholics, and Protestants have great difficulty in getting along with one another. Needless to say, the antagonism between North and South Vietnam is equally disastrous for sound nation-building. The existence of a large group of people of Chinese descent in most Asian countries and their dominance in the urban economic scene have created anti-Chinese sentiments and racial riots. The conflict between Muslims and Christians has resulted in internal upheavals of immense proportions. Racial imbalance and differences in political, cultural, and religious persuasions highlight some of the more important problems of urban societies in Asia.

POPULATION EXPLOSION

Assuming no change in growth rate, it was estimated in 1973 that the world population would double in thirty-five years, while Asia, with a population of 2,204 millions in 1973, will only take thirty years to double its population.[1] In fact, we need not wait till then: the population pressure is felt right now in food shortages, unemployment, the energy crisis, inadequate social services, and a rising crime rate as well as increased alienation.

Though population is a global concern, nowhere has its adverse effect been felt so deeply as in Asian countries. Feeding a large population is an insurmountable task. We are familiar

[1] Information obtained from Population Reference Bureau, Inc., Washington, D.C.

with Malthus's warning of the unequal race between the rate of population growth and the means of subsistence. Fortunately, up to now, this has not been true for most Asian countries, except Indonesia and Pakistan [2] where food production really lags behind population. Despite this, all Asian countries face a common nutritional problem. The calory and protein intake is unsatisfactory, and malnutrition leads either to infant mortality or to physical and mental deficiencies in later years.

In addition to food and nutritional deficiencies, Asian rural-urban migration has created high-density agglomerations in the region, with poor housing conditions. Slum settlements are characteristic of most Asian cities. According to a UN report, the housing problem is deteriorating in Asia except in Hong Kong and Singapore.[3] In these two cities, notable government action in the face of a housing shortage can best be illustrated by the low-cost housing policy of both Singapore and Hong Kong. The Housing and Development Board of Singapore has admirable housing projects which other Asian countries have tried to emulate; the Hong Kong Housing Department has also been demonstrating a gigantic effort in providing accommodation for more than one million people, about one quarter of her total population.

Population explosion not only causes food and housing shortages, it also creates a labor problem. As yet the use of manpower in agricultural and industrial sectors is not balanced. As a whole, Asians engaging in foodstuff production amount to about three quarters of the total population. In large cities, however, unemployment and underemployment are commonplace. It is not that industry is unable to absorb a proportion of the unemployed, but that the lack of training and the increasing influx of rural migrants have combined to worsen the situation.

"Overtertialization" is a growing urban problem in Asia: the employment of nearly two thirds of the working population in

[2] United Nations, *Asian Population Studies Series; Population Aspects of Social Development* (E/CN 11/1049), Bangkok, 1972, p. 76.
[3] *Ibid.*, p. 41.

the service sector, government departments, and commercial firms is alarming.[4] Hawking as a form of employment is peculiar to Asia, and this urban phenomenon brings with it social problems of a significant nature. It was estimated that in the late 1960s hawkers numbered 61,000 in Greater Bangkok, 4,500 in Kuala Lumpur, 25,000 in Singapore, 100,000–200,000 in Greater Djakarta, and 92,000 in Hong Kong.[5] Hawkers obstruct traffic and are a hazard to public health. They also drain off a substantial number of men who would otherwise be employed in industry or other productive activities. Regulating and controlling hawkers becomes a difficult and delicate task for the administration in most Asian countries.

TRANSITIONAL DIFFICULTIES

In Asia, agriculture continues to dominate the economy, and in the wake of industrialization Asian countries are gradually departing from the traditional mode of livelihood: from subsistence farming to the modern market-oriented and profit-making forms of economic enterprises.[6] In places like Singapore and Hong Kong where there are no natural resources, there is little choice but to adopt commerce and industry as the chief means of economic development. One significant aspect of transitional difficulty is the rural-urban migration, which is one of the factors influencing the population size and consequently is very important in determining the socioeconomic growth of any country. The main reasons for rural-urban migration are rural poverty and the attraction of urban life. Life in the village is hard and often unpromising, especially for the younger members. At times, the land they cultivate may even fail to feed them. The city seems to offer attractive housing, improved living standards, and better prospects for social and economic advancement.

Though urban areas may, in fact, not necessarily offer bet-

[4] T. G. McGee, *The Southeast Asian City* (London: G. Bell and Sons, Ltd., 1967), p. 88.

[5] T. G. McGee, "Scourge or Blessing," *Far East Economic Review* (Hong Kong), July 23, 1970, p. 26.

[6] Gunnar Myrdal, *Asian Drama* (New York: Pantheon Books, 1968), p. 466.

ter prospects, the lure of bright lights has attracted many young people to the cities. Even in China the dialectic of the movement which requires young intellectuals to return to the farm is much dreaded by the youth, who often defect to Hong Kong. These illegal immigrants have high hopes of a better life, greater freedom, and rewarding employment. Sad to note, the harsh reality is soon unveiled, resulting in bitter frustration and disillusionment.

IMPACT OF RURAL-URBAN MIGRATION

The consequences of migration are far-reaching. First, the urban agglomerations abound in slums and mass poverty. For example, Calcutta, with a population of over eight million, is one of the largest urban agglomerations in the world. With the poor living conditions and squalor, it has become a "disaster city" in Asia.

Secondly, the primate-city effect as a result of rural-urban migration has been evident in many large cities of Asia. The overpopulated primate city has made it impossible for any other town to stand on its own feet economically and politically.

Thirdly, the rise of a number of new towns to offset the overconcentration and diffuse the rural exodus seems at first a plausible answer to the problem. However, the heavy funding to install local mechanisms of administration (new town councils, for instance) and other amenities is burdensome to the central government.

Fourthly, the increase of population by intake of migrants is disruptive to social planning and adds uncertainty to demographic projection. Social welfare services, health facilities, employment and training opportunities as well as educational programs become less and less adequate. In other words, the administration is at a loss trying to keep pace with the population influx in providing adequate transport, communication, water, power, education, and other community facilities.

SOME SOLUTIONS TO THE URBAN PROBLEMS

It is futile to look for short-cut solutions to urban problems because of the diversities of human cultures and needs in

Asia. The following steps seem logical to me in attempting to solve some of the difficulties experienced by most Asian countries, and some of these measures have been adopted already.

The first step is population control as a national policy. In this respect Asian countries have made tremendous progress in the past decade. Population control is considered basic to the solution of urban problems, be they economic or political. Except for Burma, Cambodia, North Korea, Saudi Arabia, Syria, and Yemen all Asian countries have either an official policy or official support of family-planning programs.[7] While it is very encouraging to see a decrease in the birth rate, there is always the need continually to inform and educate the public about family life education in order to bring about a better quality of life in the not-too-distant future.

The second step is regionalization and the balancing of agricultural and industrial activities. New industrial centers need to be established to offset the effects of rural-urban migration and to avoid overconcentration in the main cities. The rural working force retained in this way will help develop local industry and relieve cities of population pressure. On the other hand, it is imperative for careful planning to strike a balance between agricultural and industrial development; the two are closely interrelated, and undue concentration in either area will have serious consequences. Despite the need for industrialization, agriculture should receive its rightful share of planning priority through mechanization and adoption of high-yielding food crops; measures such as these will help overcome the nutrition deficiency which is so common in this region.

The third step is the development of top and middle management in public bodies. With the departure of colonial rulers from most of Asia, local people assume leadership readily. Some leaders are exceptionally capable, partly because of their personal attributes and partly because they were previously the elite cadres educated and trained in Western countries. This form of "technocrat" leadership has proved extremely successful in some Asian countries, notably India and

[7] The Family Planning Association of Hong Kong, "Population Policy: a Survey of 27 Countries in Asia" (Hong Kong, 1974).

Singapore. Training and using professionals in government administration is the surest sign of progress. The abolition of red tape and excessive control by the central government will help boost innovation. The concept of management should be introduced to the bureaucratized governmental mechanism to allow flexibility and growth on local levels.[8]

The fourth step is to maximize participation in local affairs politically and economically. Active participation in political activities is a rarity for Asian people. Despite the existence of a democratic atmosphere, apathy and passivity still prevail. A writer remarked once that "a hungry man . . . . has no interest in democracy." [9] The discrepancy between potential and actual political participation may be illustrated by the Hong Kong Chinese. Despite the introduction of a new electoral ordinance which opened up twenty-three categories of persons, the voting rate was only 39 percent in 1967 and 26.7 percent in 1971.[10] While Hong Kong has a unique place in Asia, it can still reflect by and large the passivity of Asian people. Participation in the Asian context is more talk than deed. Evidently the development of a political alertness among the population is essential for sound nation-building and social development. The younger generation, especially student groups, should be given active encouragement and support to engage in positive and constructive political activities.

The heterogeneity of Asian countries calls for no simple answer to their problems. The glaring difference between rich and poor often calls for a redistribution of wealth, which forms the basis of many a land reform program in Asia. Economic hardship, in varying degrees, was given as the main reason for practically all migration, and the problems of Asian cities are the result of a growth that does not take place around a well-organized nucleus, socially and physically. The growth of heterogeneous agglomerations as part of the colonial laissez-faire legacy is understandable because the colonial

[8] M. Graves, "Developing Countries, Ltd.," *The New Internationalist* (London, Wallingford: 1974), p. 20.
[9] *Asian Magazine* (Hong Kong), April 19, 1974, Publisher's note.
[10] J. S. Hoadley, "Political Participation of Hong Kong Chinese: Patterns and Trends," *Asian Survey*, XIII (1973), 614.

government in the past was only interested in extracting raw materials and the entrepôt trade and had little interest in planned social and economic development.

This brief résumé of present-day Asian problems also sheds some lights on our future problems. In essence, the problems of today will persist in tomorrow's Asia. Population explosion with its host of attendant problems will continue to be our major concern. There will be few new problems in tomorrow's Asia, but alienation, moral degradation, and other deficiencies will emerge more fully and demand more of our attention. We can therefore look for tomorrow's problems amid the present-day ones; they are certainly related and vary only in their gravity.

Solutions to these problems, then, must be based on a realistic appraisal of any given city as a reflection of indigenous culture and as an important component in the "global village." It has long been recognized that "no man is an island unto himself." It should be equally clear today that no culture, no city, is an island unto itself. Agreement on principles of urban development and preferred futures reached in this conference could affect cities in Asia and Africa, and indeed throughout the world.

# The Role of Social Welfare—an Integrated Approach to Development

## PART I

## DOUGLAS GLASGOW

DEAN, SCHOOL OF SOCIAL WORK
HOWARD UNIVERSITY, UNITED STATES

NO MORE timely theme could have been chosen for the first International Conference on Social Welfare held on African soil than participation and development. Clearly, these two activities are essential components in the human equation of man and his society. Participation, when applied to citizen involvement in the activities of the local and national community, speaks to the basic ingredient of a strong, democratic, and healthy society. It is the organizing medium through which each citizen can engage in the tasks necessary to establish the community's social goals, to develop society's organizational format, and to implement the desired objectives.

Despite the complexity introduced into social organization by the participatory roles of citizens, history has demonstrated that there is no substitute for people's involvement in charting and implementing the goals of their society. In addition to the ideology undergirding social work's concerns with the social rationale of citizen participation, there are other derivatives of this activity. Social scientists have long sought to isolate those factors which determine variations in the individual's capacity to structure his environment.

An increasing body of knowledge supports the notion that a close link exists between human psychological growth and participation. Studies by Commings, Maxwell Jones, and Stanton and Schwartz have documented the health-producing effects gained from persons' involvement in pursuits directed at organizing their environment. Such social roles can allow for reality-testing, can strengthen ego functioning and capacity, and can also enhance the sense of belonging and attachment. These are all needed elements of positive social functioning.

Aside from the social and personal gains arising from participation, of uppermost importance to developing nations is the fact that participation by citizens can result in structural and social change. What is more essential than goal-directed action to enhance the social organization of living? The developing of education, of housing, of functional communities, both in rural and in urban areas is imperative. These changes cannot occur in most cases without the involvement and, yes, the investment of the local citizen in the change process.

The dialectic of the process of change is that structural change produces the need for ongoing activity by the individual in response to the new social context of social organization, a continuance of the activities to order the environment. In theory, one can project a continuum of human activity over a period of time, achieving a higher order of complexity, responding to new and more complex systems of social organization. These activities are engaged in by man as he seeks to create an environment which fulfills the needs of man. Thus the social work role in encouraging citizen participation has social value and personal therapeutic value and can serve to bring about social change in the structure relations in society.

In the literature of social work there is much greater clarity regarding the goals and objectives of participation. There is much less elaboration on the question of development. What, then, are we as social workers referring to when we speak of development? In a paper given at this conference Dr. Tlambo referred to development in terms of human growth. In a most scholarly manner he examined the human developmental processes, the organism's adaptability to genetic and sociocultural factors, the function of natural selection in the survival of organisms, the function of energy as a factor influencing capacity, to name only a few concerns. In the end, he concluded, "it is now apparent that a more balanced consideration of biological and social and cultural aspects of human development is needed."

It is to the social and cultural factors abetting human development that we as social workers need to address ourselves; that is, giving attention to the living environment of people. It is clear that participatory activity can enhance human growth and development. However, it does appear remiss to avoid the fact that this very same activity can produce structural change, and it is this which may be the primary goal in encouraging participation. This is no small or secondary issue. In fact, not to argue which has primacy, but depending upon goals and the objective for change, the reorganization of the social context may hold primary focus in social work actions. It is this order that is suggested in the primary goal of community development. Community development is directed at planful activity to reorder and to rearrange the social context of living so that it will serve the needs of people.

Early themes of community organization dealt with the activities of social services coordination, although there were concurrent efforts to define the community development process. In the United States, particularly in the 1960s, community organization expanded its perimeters to incorporate social movements concerned with people's rights and to encourage the involvement of people in the amelioration of their problems.

The community organization works of Haggstrom, Orlansky, and Ross articulated the methods of involving people, of mobilizing people in behalf of securing their own rights, and of encouraging activities toward self-determination, all as a means to bring about change in their life situation. However, community development involves an extended dimension as it is concerned with structuring the living environment. It is concerned with planning for communities—the living space and its use; providing adequate human services—hospitals, medical care, schools; with appropriations for adequate housing; and ultimately with having available to community residents enterprises and industry for securing incomes. Essentially, community development is directed at providing a social environment which enhances the quality of life. This may involve reallocation and redistribution of various forms for the creative use of resources. In all, the objective is, through a planful process, to create the interrelated patterns of social institutions which serve to maximize the social functional capacity of people.

For the social work profession, community development holds extreme importance. Within this province new issues emerge for our professional examination. Let us for a moment assess the dynamics potentially involved in community development. It has already been suggested that citizen participation is a crucial component in any developmental activity. It has further been suggested that participatory activity can have both a personal and a therapeutic effect upon the individuals so involved, and can also produce change in the social conditions of life.

In these areas the professionals have had little difficulty in accepting or acting upon these theoretical assumptions. However, in moving to the next level of social and community development, there is need for a new knowledge and skills base to support the appropriate professional behavior. It will not suffice to depend on the knowledge of the positive mental health aspects of participation for the individual or of the concomitant benefits toward the realization of democratic societies.

Each process—participation and development—is important in its own right and, as has been argued above, is interrelated. However, there may be an even more important factor of social work concern, and that pertains to the right to "opportunity." If as social workers we seek to encourage citizens to participate, to engage in the activities of development, we must also take on the responsibility for assuring that there is opportunity for change, growth, and unabridged functioning resulting from participation. Participation without the concomitant right to equal opportunity negates the effectiveness of the participatory role. "Opportunity" as used here refers to having access to available openings to already existing routes to the opportunity system of society. If social workers are to encourage participation, then there should be opportunity for mobility and for movement growing out of participation. For if there is no structural change which affords new opportunity for those who have been actively engaged, then assuredly this can result in (*a*) withdrawal, alienation, defeatist and retreating behavior; or (*b*) confrontation, conflictual and aggressive manipulation of society.

Alerted to the resultant behavior of those deterred from acquiring the fruits of the system, we need to be equally alerted to the specific advocacy roles to be performed by the profession in order to expedite the structural changes needed to legitimize the stimulation of participation in development efforts. For example, vigorous campaigns for economic growth, acceptable rates of unemployment, locating and developing industrial sites, and for arranging transportation patterns should be mounted in order to safeguard the interests of those who participate in community-building activity. Councils of social advisors to government continue to be as vitally needed as the existing Council of Economic Advisors. There is an urgent need for broader inclusion of social work practitioners in the policy streams which severely impinge upon areas of opportunity. Community development is not really so radical an idea or departure from traditional social work focus. It has always been apparent that there is a close correlation between poverty and severely disadvantaged living conditions and limited and abridged social functioning. It has also been abundantly clear through practice and experience that much of our therapeutic work with people is rendered ineffective by the social conditions which surround them. Community development only more immediately dictates that in certain conditions a different modality of intervention should be employed, one which concentrates on social reorganization as a primary target for change. The real challenge is to provide the skilled manpower for this manner of professional work.

A false notion persists that community development as a modality of intervention has limited use in the more industrialized nations. Incorrectly, it is viewed as having wide applicability only to severely underdeveloped communities, or to developing nations. Despite the variations in the etiology of the problems, which has produced retarded development, the science of community development is universal. If one examines the characteristics of underdevelopment, whether in highly industrialized nations or in developing nations, one will find, in the main, common factors: poverty, overpopulation, inadequate or absent utilities; limited systems or institutions of human services under the control of the indigenous population; low-level incomes; under- and unemployment and a low level of available skills. The causes for the existence of this human misery may vary from nation to nation: unplanned development; religious, racial, or national persecution; special geographical conditions. However, the etiology of the condition in no way lessens the vitality of a professional modality of planned intervention to bring about change. It is suggested that irrespective of the apparently common characteristics of underdevelopment, the strategies for change will often differ significantly from nation to nation and from situation to situation. For in developing strategies for change, such factors as national ethics, mores, cultural practices, resources, level of technology, and readiness of the indigenous population will affect the social work intervention role. Possibly above all else, as a factor determining change, may be the national will to see change occur. Social work as a method of intervention and of providing social services has wide prominence in the United States and, too, its validity has encountered severe testing as it has sought to frame its programs and techniques and to alter the quality of service to meet the multivarious needs of a very complex society. (Currently, there are some 208 million people in the United States; about 67 percent—75 percent of the population live in urban areas, with some 80 million persons living in only thirty-four metropolitan areas. Equally significant, the citizenry of the nation is made up of many racial, ethnic, religious, and geosubcultural groups. This provides much diversity and enrichment, as well as strains in the social organization of daily life.)

At the same time, members of some of these sub-groups are burdened with a disproportionately large share of the hardships of life in comparison with other Americans—an inequality which is not due to chance factors alone. This is particularly true of the American Indian, the Chicano, the Puerto Rican, the American Black, and, to a somewhat lesser extent, the Asian-American.[1]

Best estimates currently place the black population of the United States at 35 million. The experience of social work in ethnic minority communities in the United States holds great importance for countries and program areas currently undergoing development.

In the summer of 1965, the United States and the world were struck by reports that black citizens of the Watts community in Los Angeles had taken to the streets, burning property, seizing goods from stores, confronting police, and in every manner seemingly rejecting traditional forms of protest to which the nation and its people had grown accustomed. Examination of the causes for the community explosions pointed to some common underlying factors:

1. The people were from lower income groups.

2. The participants were persons who had aspirations but who failed to achieve them.

3. The population showed high incidence of alienation from the traditional ethics of society.

4. Most had migrated from rural areas to the city with hopes and aspirations for upward mobility.

Although examination of the participants' involvement in the explosions was important in understanding human behavior and dynamics, of equal importance, although given much less attention, were the outcomes of these community rebellions, and the role of social work in these developments.

More recently, there has been increased concern with documenting the trends of development emerging over the past years. In an incomplete study some factors have already become evident. Since 1965 two major trends have begun to emerge. One involves the response of indigenous citizens in undertaking self-help actions through programs and community activity, with an increasingly dramatic shift of attention to

---

[1] John B. Turner, "Development and Participation: Operational Implications for Social Workers," U.S. Committee Report, ICSW, 1974, p. 12.

construction of institutions. These have principally involved community-generated activity. On the other hand, the official government response has been activity generated initially to quell community explosions, while initiating programs designed to encourage local citizen participation in the activities of community building, ultimately providing resources to the local community through traditionally existing structures of local municipal and state government.

It is quite clear that in the almost ten-year period since 1965 there have taken place in this community some limited, though significant changes. From the activities initiated in 1965, which were directed at establishing community facilities, upgrading the quality of services to the community, creating specialized programs to aid children in school, and setting up various programs to provide needed social avenues for the youth of the community, there emerged a new impetus directed not only at building programs but at constructing community institutions. Through coalition and self-supportive activity, blacks with skills were enticed to become part of the community's thrust for development and self-reliance.

In the same period, various institutions, particularly those providing human services, have been established. Health centers, medical and psychiatric services, and locally sponsored housing reflect the independent initiatives on a community level. These institutions are not only permanent fixtures in the community but now provide human services, employment for both professionals and nonprofessionals, and opportunity for new and skilled ethnic leadership to manifest control of programs.

In contrast, the federally sponsored programs placed great emphasis on citizen participation. This democratic ideal was strongly supported, for in addition to encouraging citizen participation it provided a channel for potentially healthy activity for human development. Some have argued that it also served to keep many members of the restive population engaged in legitimate activities, thereby lessening their time and energies for other concerns. Irrespective of the reason, this program although stimulating wide involvement by community citizens.

has done little to bring about basic change. In part this is because effective participation was negated by traditional practices. One was the practice of transmitting resources for community programs through standard local government apparatus, thereby forcing local and indigenous organizations to conform to traditional practice in order to be eligible for resources. Also the practice of involving a limited number of indigenous persons on the decision- and policy-making boards of traditional organizations was ineffective because these representatives usually were co-opted or used confrontation tactics to enforce their will. Most apparent, representing the failure of these efforts, was the absence of any significant institutional system created as a result of the years of activity.

Notwithstanding, social work was instrumental in both the community self-determinative actions and in the federally sponsored programs. In the community programs where there was greater indigenous control, the social work function was found in large proportion noninstitutionalized, and indigenous social work activity and its role were adjunctive, supportive, and ancillary to the community's actions. In the federally sponsored poverty programs, the social work role was much more administrative, and authoritarianly directive. It is important to note, even with the distinction in roles, that at no point did social workers have the role of policy-makers, and only in small measure that of planners.

Critical analysis of federal intervention would point to a dangerous practice which encouraged participation by citizens, while failing to assure that opportunity for fundamental change in the conditions of the entire community was possible. In fact, despite the gains which have occurred for some select individuals, for the large majority of the community's population little signifcant change in their abject condition has taken place. Underemployment, limited housing, low-level skills still prevail, and the opportunity system, curtailed by racism, has not been effectively opened up. This becomes most evident where people are stimulated to participate, and are motivated to seek viable roles without the concurrent opportunities to achieve a fundamentally new existence in sociality resulting from their activities. Such an occurrence has the potential to deepen alienation, or it can encourage a more intense adaptation of dependence upon secondary systems of support and survival.

The lesson of the ten years has done much to stimulate new thinking among black scholars and social scientists concerned with breaking encapsulation, confinement, and ghettoization. Increasingly, there has emerged thinking and strategies for change which rely on independent and self-generative activity. In the United States and particularly among ethnic minorities who have been maintained in underdevelopment due to social racism, the strategy of development of "independent inclusion" is gaining wider audience. The essentials of this strategy call for self-determined actions to build community institutions, to coalesce power from a community base, and to develop the organizations and modalities which strengthen the family as an institute of socialization. Actually, self-dependent development is viewed as the lever to more adequate interaction with the broader society from a more equitable position. Further, as a strategy it recognizes that highly industrialized societies function from various loci of power, and without such a base, effective communication, exchange, or negotiation is not possible.

The purpose in sharing this abbreviated information was to demonstrate that:

1. Community development as a strategy of change is viable in Western industrialized nations.

2. There are often variations and differences in the goals of local and national efforts toward development.

3. There is a social work role, and it can vary.

4. Ultimately, the strategies for change adopted will vary significantly depending upon the availability of supports, resources, and the community's perspective for development.

Some special obligations seem to accrue to the profession immediately as a result of adopting community development as a focus of professional activity. One is the professional responsibility to provide expertise. This demands that the educational wing of our professsion develop a curriculum which will provide manpower with the skills of planning, administration, and policy.

It further suggests that the concept of social workers as receivers of the wretched of the earth and of injured societies be updated to identify the profession (growing out of its factual roles) with a planful developmental role in national activity. The profession should continue to produce clinicians, to respond to individual needs; however, a priority in manpower development should be established in those areas undergoing development.

It further suggests that there are ethical considerations we need to examine. It is surely time that we as profession cease to perform those roles which we as experts know are antithetical to people's healthy growth and development. If we are to use our skills in motivating people's engagment and participation, then as a profession we have the obligation to assure that there is opportunity for change or, at best, to share with those with whom we work our knowledge and belief that there may not exist real opportunity growing out of the activity.

Further, and as earlier suggested, the processes of development are varied and are influenced by many unique factors. As is apparent from this discussion, when developmental needs arise in a nonsupportive environment the strategies of development and the targets of development may change and reflect different goals. On the other hand, when there is conformity between the national goal and the goals of the population undergoing change, a whole new host of dynamics can potentially enter the developmental process. It does appear that today in the developing nations there is real opportunity to launch into community development activity in unique and different ways. The activities of nations like Tanzania, Ghana, Nigeria, and Kenya attest to the diverse strategies. However, one common element is the recognized need of the developing nations to attack the problems of housing, population growth, illiteracy and education, health, employment, and, at the same time, economic development.

Social work in the developing areas has a unique opportunity to contribute to the speedy emergence of nations, to become a helpful and planful arm in national and community development. It need not replicate the history of social work in Western societies. The emergence of social work in the Western nations occurred in distinctly different times and conditions, and social work was early conceived to perform different roles in that social context. The definitions of social work in developing nations need not replicate those of the West. There is the potential for the professional to become the arm of government in planful social development. Social workers are still close to the people, and may not wish to develop irrevocable structures and institutions which screen them from those who seek to help.

The social work community, in further refining understanding of community development as a means to further society and human development, enters into an important phase of growth. Community development as a professional strategy for improving the quality of life of people may represent a new and significant posture of the profession as it aligns itself with the pressing task of mankind, controlling and making the environment serve human need.

PART II

# DANIEL S. SANDERS

ACTING DEAN AND DIRECTOR OF INTERNATIONAL PROGRAMS, SCHOOL OF SOCIAL WORK, UNIVERSITY OF HAWAII

ANY DISCUSSION of the role of social welfare—especially in the African, Asian, and Latin American countries—has to be in the context of over-all national development. We have come to a recognition—the hard way—that social and economic development are closely related and that national development plans should take into consideration both the social and the

economic factors in planning, policy-determining, and allocation of resources.

In the past there has been a somewhat narrow approach to
development due to an almost exclusive emphasis on the economic aspect. Distinct lines were drawn between "economic"
and "social" factors, and there was a tendency to view them as
being in opposition to one another. The consequence of such
nearly exclusive emphasis on economic development has been
the neglect of the important human dimensions of development.

Economic development and increasing productivity hold the
promise of increased wealth and improved standards of living
for people. But to what extent is this increased wealth shared
by all segments of society? Increase in productivity does not
necessarily imply moves in the direction of greater distributive
justice. There is also considerable difficulty—with serious adverse implications for the future—when economic policies are
pursued without due consideration of their social impact,
especially on groups that are already socially disadvantaged.[1]

In this context, the positive role of social welfare would be
to ensure the development of human resources, to work toward changes in unjust structures, and to redress inequities in
the distribution of wealth and power. Such a developmental
and change role seems particularly necessary in countries that
have been subject to centuries of colonial rule with glaring
inequalities and conditions of extreme need and human misery. The UN second development decade, for example, in
emphasizing a unified approach to development states in its
objectives that "it cannot be overemphasized that what development implies for the developing countries is not simply an
increase in productive capacity, but major transformations in
their social and economic structures." [2]

DIVERSE ROLES OF SOCIAL WELFARE

The role of social welfare varies from country to country
and is influenced by a particular country's political philosophy,

[1] Daniel S. Sanders, "Social Aspects of Economic Policy and Development," *International Social Work.* Vol. XV, No. 3 (1972), 27.
[2] United Nations, *Towards Accelerated Development; Proposals for the Second United Nations Development Decade,* 1970, p. 5.

social thought, culture, socioeconomic system, and patterns of development. The place assigned to social welfare in a particular country could be at some point in a continuum ranging from a marginal to a central role.

The marginal role stems from the "residual welfare model," which is a limited and narrow approach to social welfare.[3] Social welfare is viewed more or less as an adjunct of the economy, there is minimal or no provision for the consequences of social change, and the beneficiaries of social welfare are seen as being mainly the poor and the dependent who are categorized as problems.

In contrast to the marginal role assigned to social welfare in the residual welfare model is the situation where social welfare assumes a central role based on the institutional-redistributive model. In this model social welfare is seen as a "positive and dynamic agent of change" and has important developmental and change roles. Positive steps are taken to promote "integrative values," to prevent "diswelfare," and to apply social welfare objectives to economic policies, with a view to ensuring distributive justice.

The developmental and change roles based on the institutional-redistributive model point to a newer conception of social welfare as social development. These newer roles and the conception of social welfare as social development have the potential of contributing to an integrated approach to development that seems urgent. It is interesting to note that the fifth ICSW-sponsored seminar on the role of social welfare services in rural development, held in Lusaka (1972), recommended and advocated the use of the term "social development worker" instead of the traditional term "social welfare worker." [4]

Likewise, a UN report of an expert group meeting on social policy and planning about the time of the launching of the

[3] See Richard M. Titmuss, "Developing Social Policy in Conditions of Rapid Change: the Role of Social Welfare," in *Developing Social Policy in Conditions of Rapid Change,* Proceedings of the XVIth International Conference on Social Welfare (New York: International Council on Social Welfare, 1973), pp. 38–41; John M. Romanyshyn, *Social Welfare: Charity to Justice* (New York: Random House, 1971), pp. 33–34.

[4] J. Riby-Williams, "The Emerging Nations—What Is the Place of Social Welfare?" in *Developing Social Policy in Conditions of Rapid Change,* Proceedings of XVIth International Conference on Social Welfare, pp. 88–89.

second development decade, in stressing the need for a social development emphasis within a unified approach to development, states that "the time has come when the economic approach to development analysis and planning has to be integrated with a social approach which is different in nature and would be more relevant to the problems of developing countries in the coming decade." [5]

SOCIAL WELFARE AND DEVELOPMENT IN THE ASIAN CONTEXT

When we consider the mass-scale socioeconomic problems in the Asian region, the conditions that determine social and economic stratifications, and the continuing inequalities in the midst of extreme poverty and human misery, the need for an integrated approach to development and an emphasis on developmental and change roles in social welfare becomes urgent.

The following extract on the nature of development from the preliminary report of a symposium of representatives of national councils of social welfare in the Asian and Western Pacific region is indicative of the approaches and thinking in the region in regard to development:

Development is seen as a balanced and integrated process with targets derived from the aspirations of people for themselves and for their society. Economic growth alone is not a satisfactory objective, although for many people it is an indispensable part of development. Development also implies a greater command over goods and services by more people. In many societies this means a more equitable distribution of purchasing power among the population and an increasing capacity on the part of more people to know how to use and benefit from the resources of the community. It means also equal access to basic social services (health, education and housing); adequate provision of and preparation for employment; and increased ability to choices and to assist in reaching decisions. [6]

There is increasing realization that economic development however important is not to be pursued in isolation. Provision

[5] United Nations, *Report of the Expert Group Meeting on Social Policy and Planning*, Commission for Social Development, Twenty-first Session, Geneva, March 4–10, 1970.

[6] United Nations, Economic Commission for Asia and the Far East, Social Development Division, Bangkok, *Newsletter*, December, 1973, pp. 10–11.

is also to be made for social development, with social welfare assuming a developmental and change role. This would, in addition to providing important human resources, help to focus on distributive justice and facilitate structural changes that encourage citizen participation in new economic, social, and political roles.

The need for a more integrated development and for greater emphasis on developmental and change roles in social welfare becomes very evident when we look at some of the major problems in the Asian region, especially the population problem, the system of land ownership, the educational problem, and the restlessness and frustration experienced by the youth. It is evident that these social and economic problems are closely interrelated, and a basic prerequisite for dealing with them effectively is the needed change in institutions and structures that contribute to social and economic inequality.

Gunnar Myrdal, commenting on the interrelation between economic and social factors and the developmental process, states:

My main thesis is that development should be defined as a movement upward of a whole system of interdependent conditions, of which "economic growth" . . . is only one of several categories of causally interrelated conditions. A halt to improvement of other conditions, usually called "social conditions," and still more an actual deterioration of them, will cause a trend toward disintegration of these newly founded national communities. Sooner or later if present trends are permitted to continue, it will bring the whole development process to a grinding lame walk and, finally, general retrogression.[7]

The value of an integrated approach to development is seen, for example, in dealing with the population problem. There are important social and economic goals with potential for improving standards of living and the quality of life that need to be pursued in a planned way. Family planning can contribute to quality family life, to more stable families, and to a happier and more stable work force. In so far as it contributes to

[7] Gunnar Myrdal, *The Challenge of World Poverty: a World Anti-Poverty Program in Outline* (New York: Pantheon Books, 1970), p. 408.

limiting the size of the population, it also contributes to higher standards of living.

Developmental and change efforts in regard to one area such as the population problem and the measure of success or failure achieved have implications for related problems in areas such as land ownership, education, and youth unrest. Myrdal points out that if there is no appreciable progress, for example, in land reform in the Asian region, there is the danger of other institutional reforms such as community development, credit cooperation, and agricultural extension being perverted to serve the interests of the wealthier and the more privileged groups.[8] Social welfare has to focus increasingly on social objectives of economic development and ensure measures in the direction of equality of opportunity and adequate participation of the people in influencing policy decisions, allocating resources, and developing programs.

Social welfare could contribute to over-all development, an improved quality of life, and social justice in at least two specific ways: (a) by developing social policies and social conditions that are ends in themselves, such as ensuring basic human rights and adequate standards of health, education, and housing; (b) by developing social policies and conditions that are instrumental to the attainment of other ends, especially economic development and distributive justice. This would include activities such as mobilizing human resources for development, instituting structural and policy changes in the direction of greater equality, and providing health and educational services to meet economic needs.[9]

In all these efforts toward an integrated approach to development the role of planning cannot be minimized. In the West, planning followed industrialization and the ensuing social and economic changes. It has developed piecemeal and in a pragmatic way. In the Asian context, Myrdal points out, planning is not so much a consequence of development as an important precondition to development.[10] The very condi-

[8] *Ibid.*, p. 401.

[9] United Nations, *Reappraisal of the Role of the Social Commission: Report of the Secretary General* (New York: UNESCO, 1966), pp. 10–11.

[10] Gunnar Myrdal, *An Approach to the Asian Drama: Methodological and Theoretical* (New York: Vintage Books, 1970), pp. 738–39.

tions demand that planning be coordinated and comprehensive.

Finally, the goal of all development, social and economic, should be the development of the total person, of all persons, and the provision of opportunities for attaining our highest potentialities as human beings.

PART III

# CHARLES SCHAEFER

DIRECTOR, HOSPICE GENERAL OF GENEVA, SWITZERLAND

NOTIONS OF social welfare and development frequently go hand in hand with other more or less connected ideas, such as unified development, social development, economic or social growth, social or economic planning, unified approach, social progress, and so on. This multitude of nomenclatures is indicative of the difficulty of grasping reality satisfactorily, for reality is complex, susceptible to examination from so many viewpoints.

I am a practitioner and not a theoretician, but I would remind you that the phenomenon of social and economic integration is a matter of concern to everyone, from the social worker in the field to the philosopher. I think this is important, because one persistent impression I gain from my reading is that there is a marked gap between the theoretical constructions emerging from a certain type of literature current since around 1969 and their coherent application in practice.

THEORETICAL ASPECTS OF THE PROBLEM

*What about social welfare?* Even inside a single country, definitions of social welfare differ widely, both in theory and in practice; and this is still more noticeable from one country to another. We may therefore say that any definition will be arbitrary and open to criticism. Two conceptions, however, tend to appear with the greatest frequency:

1. The conception which sees social welfare as a group of activities devoted to the improvement of the living conditions of individuals, families, and groups in society

These activities are not conceived as including, and this is the important point for certain countries, either health services or education systems.

2. The conception which includes in the category of social welfare practically everything touching upon the population's well-being, without any limitation on the sectors of activity taken into consideration.

It is here that we come across social welfare defined as "organized social measures having as their prime object human welfare considered in its social aspects." It will be understood that this includes all those persons and services variously involved in the multifarious aspects of people's lives: income, security, health, housing, education, leisure, culture, and so on.

This vision is sometimes nuanced. Thus, for example, here and there one comes across the notion of *protection* of persons with a view to improving the functioning of the social system. This kind of terminology should be seen as the residue of a period when social welfare was conceived chiefly as a means of assisting marginal members of society—the aged, disturbed children, all kinds of asocial people, and, generally, the economically weak. This concept seems outmoded today.

I propose adoption of the definition suggested by the Interuniversity European Institute for Social Welfare:

By social welfare we normally mean the action of social services and bodies set up to satisfy material, psychological and cultural needs of the persons and groups that go to make up society, with a view to improving the functioning of the social system and of social relations at all levels.

Like all definitions, this one is imperfect. For example, what is meant here by "levels" in social relations? One would prefer "social organization" to "social system" and, likewise, "human relations" instead of "social relations."

*What about the notion of development?* Here we come to a

rather more delicate matter: this is a highly divisive notion for many reasons while at the same time it involves people's fundamental thinking.

It is worth rereading the very important text of the Declaration on Social Progress and Development adopted in Resolution 2542 of the United Nations General Assembly, in 1969. In these few extracts the very notion of "integrated development" is mentioned expressly almost for the first time:

> The General Assembly . . . :
> —concludes that peace and international solidarity on the one hand, and social progress and economic development on the other, are narrowly interdependent and influence each other mutually;
> —persuaded that peaceful coexistence, friendly relations and co-operation between States having different social, economic or political systems, can help promote social development;
> —emphasizing the interdependence of economic development and social development within the broader framework of the process of growth and evolution, as well as the importance of an integrated development strategy taking full account, at all stages, of the social aspects of this development:
>
> . . .
> Solemnly proclaims the present Declaration . . .

The text of the Declaration itself contains passages expressing ideas developed barely five years ago, of which I quote only one: "The rapid rise in the national income and wealth and their equitable distribution among all members of society must constitute the basis of all social progress and should therefore be at the forefront of preoccupations." This restrictive view of the mechanisms of development cannot hide the fact that the Declaration constitutes an important methodological backing for the cause of balanced global development. It emphasizes the need to provide budgetary guarantees or other resources for financing the social aspects of development, but above all it proposes that we envisage "the adoption of measures aimed at increasing people's participation in the economic, social, cultural and political life of each country."

Whether we call it integrated, unified, or even unified approach, the identification of development with economic growth has more or less been abandoned: there is no longer even any need to criticize it. There can be no doubt, however, that it still exercises some obscure influence and that it has certain implications for national planning in the industrial countries. It is now more or less accepted, also, that development is ineluctably a societal process even if, for the purpose of analysis, it is broken down into its economic, social, and political aspects.

Development is generally considered as occurring on two undoubtedly complementary levels. One is the global level, where all notions of compartmentalization have to be abandoned, and where the notion of an integrated strategy comes into its own. This is the meaning given to it by the Declaration on progress; this is the balanced global development to which it alludes. The notion of world development involves taking the broadest possible view, especially where relations between industrial and other countries are concerned. My intention here being rather more concrete, I shall confine myself to trying to understand what goes on at the other, the regional, level.

Thus, for example, in various texts emanating from the UN or the Council of Europe, remarks and suggestions are found concerning the emergence of a specifically European unified conception of development which, if some people are to be believed, even consecrates the tangible embryo of a European reality. There can be no doubt that each specific situation demands a specifically adapted response. Europe's high level of economic development and the rapidity of its technological evolution raise the problem of unified development in special terms. Technological hyperspecialization and social over-organization force us to admit that development can have no meaning unless it is considered differently from one region to the next and unless decision-making processes are adapted to this situation.

Theoretically speaking—as we have seen in the text of the Declaration on Social Progress—reference is frequently made to people's participation in the work of development. Without drawing any premature conclusions, we can say that this concern for people's participation could well constitute a field of particular interest for people concerned with social welfare.

Despite the fact that many people are still of the opinion that the social needs of the population are best satisfied by the rapid development of national economies, it is becoming increasingly evident that humanist considerations must be included in this development. This evolution in conceptions is having a great deal of difficulty breaking through, given the considerable obstacles still standing in the way of change, whether technological or, above all, in values.

True, from time to time we see movements of opinion which give rise to a certain optimism; take, for example, the rapidity with which "quality-of-life" considerations have imposed themselves within the space of a few years. Today, in the West, it is not really possible to back the unified conception of development with absolutely convincing scientific arguments. It is still the subject of too many passions and opinions differ too widely; for we still lack even the basis necessary for a scientific study of development, as is the case, moreover, with social indicators that permit us to keep track of socioeconomic development step by step. If a definition of a better society is ever to emerge, it can only do so through confrontations between those principally concerned, that is, the citizens involved in the process.

The theoretical studies mentioned are not without impact on decision-making. We can see this reflected here and there in the concern to improve well-being, which has become a kind of leitmotiv of legislative bodies in most Western countries, even if this is somewhat tainted with demagogy on occasion.

To sum up, we may note, finally, the existence of a new conception of development in which social aspects are neither subordinated to, nor juxtaposed with, economic ones, but in which the two are integrated. As a result, development is no longer seen as a juxtaposition of plans for each sector but as an over-all plan incorporating sectoral actions into the original perspective of a new social system whose fundamental values will have to be revised.

THE MORE PRACTICAL ASPECTS OF THE PROBLEM

In the first place, we cannot fail to notice that planners often tend to seek compatible social and economic profiles. But this kind of study concerning the unity of the socioeconomic system frequently hides the fact that social policy in industrial countries is, essentially, subject to the concept of the primacy of economic growth. This is a way of avoiding the real problem, which is that of describing what has to be changed in society or what lies above and beyond growth. We have to recognize the existence of a major obstacle to acceptance of a satisfactorily integrated system of development: this is the general resistance to the idea of paying the price for such a system. Furthermore, the allocation of large sums or investments in the economy and in social welfare demands a high degree of solidarity; it throws a new light on the attitudes of the citizen toward the consumer society. A recent international report mentioned the need to adopt in future an attitude of "sharing frugal comfort." In the West, unfortunately, few people seem ready to accept such self-limitation, although this attitude does seem to be spreading, especially among the young.

Social welfare can blame itself for having refused to assess its own effectiveness for so long. The idea that social progress could be achieved economically has only recently begun to emerge. Apart from the genuine difficulty of developing adequate tools for assessment one has to admit that very little effort has been devoted to the search for optimal yield in the field of social welfare.

Certainly, social welfare has acquired an image of good will, but at the same time this has been accompanied by a picture of amateurism which has tended to prejudice its relations with the economic sector. Voluntary and private activities have doubtless on occasion perturbed the discussions of economists or financiers by the multiplicity of the approaches to social life proposed. After all, these economists and financiers are accustomed to certain types of reasoning and to strictly quantifiable results.

We may note that if these various mechanisms have led to incontestable progress in certain areas, a number of factors prevent us from considering that progress has been truly positive on all fronts. We would nevertheless not go as far as some people have in holding that there has been virtually no social progress in the world. But it would be fair to observe that most of the time we are dealing more with an *impression* of social progress than with social progress, properly speaking.

Whether explicitly or otherwise, the question of social development is often treated as a concern of secondary importance. Thus, mechanisms that are in reality economic are often treated as more or less social ones. When one speaks of social protection, and when one speaks in particular of education or curative public health, one is merely indulging in wordplay. It is a kind of papering over of cracks to calm troubled consciences; but at no time does a change in vocabulary produce any profound change in the goals and the plans called for by a balanced global development.

By organizing itself primarily with a view to assisting marginal and underprivileged sections of the community, Western social welfare has neglected large classes of the population and has ill-perceived certain needs. In certain cases, through the relatively easy development of social insurance, Western social welfare can even be said to have masked some of the most crying needs. Finally, the most important problem remains, namely, that of man's adaptation to his environment.

A certain number of obstacles still stand in the way of the harmonization and sometimes even the clear perception of development goals:

1. Take, for example, the notion of inadaptability. If people are prepared to accept more or less unanimously that society is an evolving entity, they ought to be able to accept that the notion of inadaptability itself can vary from one society to another and even from one social group to another. And yet, people often retain a rigid conception of inadaptability. This is one cause of conflict between adults and young. Thus, over and above the notion of inadaptability, divergences concerning the philosophy of life itself emerge.

2. Another obstacle is the spirit of categorization on the basis of the degree of delinquency, marginalization, age, and so on. This categorization, while undeniably practical, leads to the specialization of social welfare work, with each specialist body tending to justify its existence by its development. When abused, the spirit of specialization can be highly prejudicial, screening out the real needs of people.

3. Many people still have difficulty accepting the need for as global an approach as possible to the problems of the inadapted and the adapted at one and the same time. This raises the fundamental problem of the future of classical social welfare work; it may be that some day this will have to give way to less conventional types of welfare activities. Still, we should beware of simply handing the inadapted person back to society as a whole without any form of supporting action.

4. As Philippe de Seynes has put it, the West is experiencing a veritable spiral of rising expectations. Mass communications have made everyone aware that individual fulfillment should take priority over all else; and yet this overrapid maturing of ideas has led to ill-formulated demands, some of them inacceptable or considered dangerous by others. Individual communication, moreover, is worse than ever before, and many Westerners suffer sharply from a feeling of rootlessness. We are also currently observing a malaise in contemporary democracy, where the individual often feels that he is incapable of having any real influence on events, thus giving rise to lack of interest, abstentionism, or, conversely, to exclusively political attitudes to the detriment of the human element.

To remedy this, and so that each individual can rediscover the possibility of participating in the collective enterprise, we must attempt to recreate genuine communities whose size and organization will generate more favorable conditions. Then will the individual feel once more that he has a place among his own people. This is precisely the idea underlying community development: development because each individual will be able to participate in the definition of needs and in collective advantages. But this is only possible through the medium of a living community, with the major emphasis being on individual relationships.

5. A further obstacle is the type of training that practitioners are now receiving. A social system can only evolve if social training is oriented toward the future. In addition, an imbalance between theoretical and practical experience—this last generally being neglected—is unfavorable to evolution of any kind.

6. Finally, and in many parts of our provinces, social welfare personnel, considered in the widest possible framework, still has only a slight influence on the decision-making centers which define development investment priorities. Some go so far as to think that the object of social welfare work should be, not the individual himself, but solely the social structures within which he lives. I think this is going a little too far and ignores the democratic instruments now available to the Westerner even if, as we have pointed out, one hopes these instruments will be perfected actively.

What, then, will be the main lines of development toward a better future, and what will be the place of social welfare in this future?

It would appear that the chief task of social welfare in the development process ought to be to enable citizens to enhance their community-oriented sensitivity. In other words, both professional and voluntary social workers are going to have to revise and broaden their objectives.

Thus, it does not seem exaggerated to say that living social welfare work is a congruent form of unified development. It will be so by its concern to harmonize and to spread social well-being in its diverse forms and could well be the expression of man's highest aspirations and of the idea of unified development through the medium of specific persons and structures. To this end:

It will concern itself with broadening and humanizing personnel training.

It will actively promote the role of professional and voluntary workers in the process of objective conscientization of the masses.

It will encourage citizens to participate in their own economic, social, and cultural prospects and future.

It will attempt to orient higher decision-making bodies in the direction of the harmonious development of society, with prevention taking precedence over cure.

We dream, too, of a social welfare that would permit men to play a creative role in their lives, at all levels. For we are convinced that it is by creating that man finds a meaning in his life; he is stronger, better able to assume his responsibilities. Society as a whole wins out in the end, for the power of the imagination is undeniable.

In this way, social welfare work could serve as the laboratory whence a new society will emerge, but only if, from today onward, it arms itself with the necessary humility.

# The Defense of the Aging

## DAVID HOBMAN

DIRECTOR, AGE CONCERN ENGLAND; VICE-PRESIDENT,
INTERNATIONAL FEDERATION ON AGEING

ALTHOUGH ALL societies have contained a few people of extreme old age, the possibility that about one person in five of the population would be retired and every hundredth person would be over eighty-five before the end of this century would have been unthinkable not so very long ago. In my country, however, this is now a reality, as it is in many other industrialized societies. In the past, those who did achieve such considerable age would probably have had their needs met within their own domestic circle, something which is now no longer possible for many.

In this sector of the community in Great Britain two million (or one in five) live in single-person households and have no immediate or extended families to support them. This may be because they did not marry and have children; because their partner is dead; because their children, if any, are no longer young and active; or in many cases, because in a mobile society separation of the generations is now the rule rather than the exception in relation to employment demands or promotion opportunities.

Apart from mobility during employment there is now the added dimension in Western Europe and North America of substantial migration upon retirement by middle-income families to coastal regions and temperate climates. Here the retirement population may comprise 50 percent or more of the total in highly concentrated single-generation communities in which serious socioeconomic problems are beginning to emerge, leading to major problems for those responsible for the planning and delivery of support services.

But the needs for services are not based simply on the numbers of people who may be assumed to require them because of their age, health, or capacities. They are related to a whole range of other factors, such as shopping facilities, transportation, the organization of medical care, the provision of suitable housing, and, in addition, the available supply of younger people from whom staff as well as voluntary workers for the caring professions must be recruited.

I referred to the increasingly high proportion of single-person households in the United Kingdom. Although there are particular historic and social reasons for this situation, my investigations suggest that the statistics have sufficiently similar characteristics elsewhere to argue that the same pattern may be expected to emerge in due course.

But there are other factors which need to be taken into account in relation to the physical, mental, and social well-being of the elderly. Here again, I believe that the statistics from our country, which confirm that 70 percent of the registered disabled, 45 percent of psychiatric patients, and 35 percent of all hospital bed occupancy are accounted for by those over retirement age, may be reflected elsewhere.

The question which must, therefore, be answered relates to the sufficiency of services offered as well as to their relevance and acceptability to those who will almost certainly suffer from multiple disabilities: those who, on the whole, have lower expectations than members of younger generations; who are often less well-informed about their eligibility, and who may prefer not to use the system, even when it is adequate, because of misconceptions about its nature and the terms on which help is provided. As a group they also lack the cohesive force of organized labor to influence policy-makers and providers of care about the special characteristics of their needs.

Clearly, our starting point has to be legislative action. Here I would issue one warning note. While governments can and do legislate some services which are mandatory, with defined and enforceable minimum standards, much legislation is permissive and open to a wide variety of interpretation by state, regional, and local government agencies. However, it is possible to identify general principles on which defense systems for the elderly could be established, and to discuss some philosophies which could be interpreted and acceptable in the majority of communities, if not all.

I therefore submit nine headings for consideration: accommodations, health, personal social services, occupation, nutrition, transportation, income maintenance, the family, and the community. At first glance they may appear to differ so widely in character as to make any form of relationship impossible. However, I believe that on analysis their interdependence becomes clear. For example, the amount of specially designed or suitable accommodations for the elderly will have a direct bearing on the need for social services; the use of well-equipped health centers is dependent upon linked public transportation systems; the need for domiciliary feeding services will be partly affected by shopping facilities; and the recruitment of home-helps (home aids) will be influenced by alternative employment facilities in the locality for married women. But perhaps the most important factor for consideration is the extent to which preventive services and early identification of those at risk can reduce the need for subsequent treatment and care.

ACCOMMODATIONS

Under this heading is included the whole range of provisions offered by the public, voluntary, and (in some countries) private sectors, spanning from independent living to full residential care and hospitalization. I should like to advocate certain principles based on the right of the individual to live in accommodations which are suitable to his need, which reflect his own preference, and which maintain the maximum degree of independence, privacy, and self-determination. This is too often missing from the lives of the elderly when either a shortage of suitable accommodations or the needs of the providers take precedence over those of the consumers.

For this reason, all specially designed units for the elderly, whether in open or sheltered housing or in residential care, should be provided in single units rather than in multiple or dormitory accommodations unless this is expressly required. All housing and residences for the elderly should be designed to make it possible for them to bring a number of their own possessions with them.

When the elderly are admitted to special and sheltered housing with supportive services, or to full residential care (but not hospital), the terms on which they may remain should be stated at the outset, and whenever possible they should be encouraged and assisted to stay for as long as they wish and are capable of supporting themselves. Even in those countries where a wide range of residential provisions exists, there is still too much evidence of the elderly being required to move on from one form to another, in itself a destructive process.

Because the total stock of purpose-built housing of all kinds can never be expected to meet demands, there should be substantial investment in the conversion of existing accommodations and the methods of adapting premises occupied by the elderly with special reference to ease of access, aids to safety, and, in colder climates, the adequacy and cost of heating—a matter of particular importance to those who are most vulnerable to hypothermia (low body temperature). All special housing for the elderly or disabled should be included in mixed development schemes wherever possible and should be within easy access of public amenities, cultural facilities, shops, and places of worship.

Opinions vary about the degree of concentration which is desirable, but a balance must be preserved between the need to provide sufficient units to justify the cost of administering a network of support services, and the creation of isolated enclaves divorced from the mainstream of community life, except in those cases where the elderly have expressly desired a life surrounded by their own generation.

Where small units prevent younger families from providing accommodations for elderly relatives, linked units should be developed. All housing or residential units designed for the elderly or disabled should be protected against use by other age groups, unless there is clear proof of a surplus beyond requirements.

HEALTH SERVICES

Although the organization of the health services in respect to preventive medicine, treatment, and rehabilitation varies widely between countries with a national health service and those which substantially rely on private medicine, or combine the two elements, there are areas of common concern in relation to the development of geriatric services and the role of community medicine.

While increasing age may intensify certain medical conditions, a number of diseases are associated with the aging process itself, and the elderly are more likely to suffer from multiple health problems, some of which are difficult to diagnose and many of which are disguised by serious overprescription of drugs. Opinion about the precise function of geriatric medicine and the practice of segregating elderly patients by placing them in what are, in effect, units of containment rather than cure in preparation for discharge is very divided. Where the practice of providing large and often overcrowded geriatric wards is adopted, it is more likely to be the result of inadequate community resources than a reflection of the philosophy of practitioners of geriatric medicine.

Where special hospitals for the elderly exist or have been adapted from older institutions they are often, in common with many psychiatric units, the least attractive and most institutionalized units, in poor buildings cut off from more recent developments and often isolated from the communities from which their patients are drawn. This trend should be reversed.

Investment in research in the diseases of aging and their treatment is often relatively modest in comparison to that in most other disciplines and in new surgical techniques. There has also been an overemphasis on clinical and biological study, with insufficient attention to the sociomedical factors on which continued functioning depends. Geriatric medicine and nursing are, in general, much less attractive to student nurses and doctors than are other specialties, although those who do practice in this field are often highly motivated and display a considerable degree of compassion, tolerance, and understanding. Major recruitment programs are required, and in many cases the working conditions and terms of service for their doctors and nurses should be improved, together with the status and prospects of physiotherapists, occupational therapists, chiropodists, and members of other professions allied to medicine on which the welfare of the elderly often depend. The training of doctors and nurses should pay greater attention to the medical and social needs of the elderly, and refresher courses should be regularly available for general practitioners.

Anxieties about admission to hospital and problems related to readjustment on discharge as well as those that arise during hospitalization itself involve far greater use of the skills and time of the medical social worker, and the need to ensure continuity and the mobilization of community resources on discharge from hospital demand close integration between social work support services and the hospital and agencies within the community to avoid the trauma of sudden and unprepared discharge.

Volunteers should be encouraged to visit elderly patients and to provide supporting services in hospitals where these will enhance the quality of life for long-stay patients, without putting the work of nonprofessional staff at risk or confusing roles with professional workers.

In the field of community medicine, physicians should increasingly be associated with primary care teams of social workers, nurses, health visitors, home-help organizers, and others who will among them be able to sustain an integrated system of personal contact with elderly patients who may be unable or unwilling to visit surgeries or health centers. Community medicine must be more closely linked with hospital care where the two systems operate in isolation with little personal contact between general physicians and consultants, and through day hospitals with a range of therapeutic and rehabilitation services for those who can be supported at home as an alternative to admission to hospital.

In this connection, it is also essential to set up systems for lending aids to mobility and special equipment for home nursing, laundry services, optical and dental services, and controlled supplies of drugs which do not involve constantly repeated visits for prescription. Adequate methods of communication for elderly patients and the installation of telephones or emergency call systems are also important factors in sustaining health or providing rapid response to calls for assistance. Loss of hearing as well as failing eyesight, common features of advancing age, require extensive and readily available services.

Clinics for monitoring the health of the elderly and early identification of those who are at risk represent a form of preventive medicine which needs to be instituted where it does not yet exist as an extension of a practice now widely adopted in maternal and child care services, as well as in relation to high-risk occupations.

Because the administration of many medical services is largely controlled by professional practitioners, steps should be taken to involve consumers with special knowledge of the sociomedical problems of the elderly. A development introduced in my own country following reorganization of the National Health Service with the establishment of community health councils in each Health Authority Area linked to a national hospital complaints and advisory service holds hopes for the future. Where medicine and nursing home facilities for the elderly are offered through the private sector, rigid registration, inspection, and controls should be exercised by public authorities.

THE PERSONAL SOCIAL SERVICES

These services require social workers, welfare officers, and auxiliaries with special interest in, and knowledge of, the needs of the elderly, whether they are provided by generic or specialized agencies. In the case of the former, control systems should ensure that disproportionate resources are not allocated to other groups.

Many elderly people and their families require social work, psychiatric, and allied professional skills in relation to problems stemming from isolation, alienation, delusions, anxieties pertaining to death and bereavement, depressive illnesses, as well as in regard to practical services and knowledge of the range of financial or other benefits about which many elderly people are ignorant or ambivalent. Studies in various countries clearly indicate that there can be continued social functioning of elderly people, often in extreme old age, when social work is fully effective and its practitioners display a high degree of motivation and sensitivity. But there is depressing evidence of a preference among social workers to work with young families rather than with the elderly, where they fail to see an equally creative role for themselves.

However, many elderly people do not require the services of a psychotherapist in order to adjust to changing circumstances. Their problems stem from purely practical difficulties rather than from personal relationships. The assistance they require may be of a practical nature, and in this connection probably one of the most significant services is the provision of home-helps who can, in many cases, enable those with quite severe disabilities to function independently.

The personal or community social services must, therefore, be in a position to offer a wide diversity of linked provisions in both domiciliary and institutional settings, including day centers, luncheon facilities, therapeutic services, and practical aids. These must be closely integrated with the provisions of health services and housing to reduce the number of agencies with different policies and possibly differing criteria in assessing need and dealing with the individual in what can become confusing and counterproductive.

The emergence of social casework as an identifiable profession with acknowledged standards of training and practice has been one of the most welcome features of the past half century. However, this has in some cases led to an exclusive attitude on the part of social workers which has denied the crucial role of many other disciplines and occupations whose practical help may be equally important to those suffering from social, cultural or economic deprivation. Social workers also need to match their interest in personal development with an interest in social advocacy and policy-making, an area in which they have not yet made the significant contribution which the nature of their work and knowledge of their clients suggest is not only possible but essential, and one which community workers have been readier to grasp.

## OCCUPATION

In many ways, problems of the elderly which lead to breakdown and the accelerated need for services stem from apathy, boredom, and a lack of sense of purpose or role. While some pensioners with limited incomes require part-time occupation to augment their financial resources, many are looking for interests which the demands of employment, a reluctance to face the realities of retirement, and insufficient preparation have not made possible without external stimuli. There is, therefore, an urgent need for major programs of education or reeducation as a part of the preretirement process.

The learning speed of the elderly may be slower than that of the young, and new concepts may be more difficult to grasp or accept as the years pass, especially when they challenge previous knowledge and experience. Nevertheless, there is no evidence to suggest that aging militates against the learning process itself, although many of the current generation of retired people suffer from educational shortcomings in their youth.

Many countries offer extensive cultural and educational opportunities through educational agencies, community development programs, radio and television teaching, correspondence courses, and centers of education. Too frequently, these are offered at places which are inaccessible for the elderly, at times which are inconvenient, and by tutors who lack sensitivity to the special learning processes which must be used with mature students.

Some elderly people will wish to occupy themselves with activities exclusively related to self-fulfillment, while others may be better assisted through sheltered workshops. There should also be further investigation into, and development of mutual-aid employment schemes organized by and for the elderly whereby they can continue to exercise old skills and learn new ones.

## NUTRITION

Nutrition is important for a variety of reasons. First is the disincentive to prepare adequate meals when one lives alone (often following the loss of a partner), or the inability to do so on the part of men who may have relied upon their wives and who did not come from this emancipated age which increasingly witnesses the sharing of household and domestic tasks. Added to this are the difficulties of shopping in terms of access and the size of packaging in relation to a diminishing income. This may, in fact, coincide with the need for more carefully balanced selective diets as digestive systems deteriorate.

Here the delivery of meals on wheels; good neighbor schemes, in which a young person is prepared to cook, on payment, for those who live nearby; and luncheon clubs, which may be established in special centers or associated with industrial canteens, all have a critical part to play. But there are still a number of important questions to be asked regarding the major service of meals delivered to the homes of the housebound and frail in relation to their social function, cost-effectiveness, the number of days on which they need to be delivered each week, and their acceptability. However nutritionally balanced they may be, if the meals do not reflect the recipient's personal taste and normal eating habits they will often be discarded.

## TRANSPORTATION

The adequacy of transportation is a critical matter in the continued functioning of the elderly, and in the maintenance of social contacts at a time when their frequencey will be lessening but their importance increasing. As private ownership of cars mounts, fast commuter service and intercity and intercontinental travel systems become more sophisticated. Thus the difficulties of many elderly people become more acute, because a preoccupation with major traffic flows and the fundamental selfishness of the private motorist are fast removing many local public bus services on which the elderly depend. In addition, many cannot afford the escalating fares, and concessionary schemes are by no means universal or acceptable when they are selective and introduce a voucher system as an alternative to disposable income. Design features of buses and trains often make alighting and leaving impossible for the elderly, fast or erratic driving makes any attempt to use public transportation too hazardous or frightening for many elderly people to contemplate.

INCOME MAINTENANCE

Income maintenance is a basic defense for the elderly which has a bearing on the need for other services.

THE FAMILY

The family, when one exists, is pivotal to the defense of the elderly. When they are willing and able to provide sustained support, their needs too should be acknowledged. However caring the members of the family may be, stresses and strains will often manifest themselves, and the resources of the social services should be supportive for those who are supporting the elderly or disabled, both in the interpretation and the resolution of interpersonal relationships and in practical ways. For example, there should be provision for short-stay accommodations to allow young families to refresh and reestablish themselves while at the same time giving the elderly a change of environment.

Families often give devoted and unstinting care because they believe it is their responsibility and duty, or because external pressures and guilt feelings appear to offer no alternative. This is especially evident with unmarried daughters who frequently devote a substantial portion of their active middle life to elderly parents, largely draining their own vitality in the process and cutting themselves off from the pursuit of their own interests. In some countries (including my own), the responsibilities they accept have not been fully recognized through fiscal policies and relief of taxation or allowances for those who work during the day time and require domestic or other help to enable them to assume the dual responsibility of earning a living and caring for an elderly parent or parents.

In spite of the growing number of unsupported or single-person households of elderly people, the contribution of the family still represents a significant factor in relation to the provision of domiciliary services and residential care, which would otherwise have to be funded from community resources and at far greater expense.

## THE COMMUNITY

The community itself has to assume the major responsibility for the care of the elderly. This may manifest itself through taxation to finance social support systems, but it is equally crucial in terms of organized voluntary services or spontaneous acts of good neighborliness. Administrations which equate or justify voluntary service as an inexpensive alternative to statutory provision are mistaken in misunderstanding its essential essence.

A recent reference work in England listed more than a hundred tasks being performed through voluntary action. It is too long to repeat but ranges from sustained and highly skilled visiting and counseling to providing meals, social centers, auxiliary nursing, night sitting, entertainment, therapy, escorting, transportation, advocacy, gardening, shopping, decorating, vacation schemes, and many others. In one large day center for the elderly administered by a local authority over five hundred volunteers give their services each week. Without their help it would be a hollow shell.

In a large industrial city, the public authority social services with an annual budget of many millions of pounds employs 1,700 paid staff members. The voluntary Age Concern (National Old People's Welfare Council) involves 3,000 volunteers at a total administrative cost of little more than £ 10,000 per year. And this is but one specialized agency among many. Although these volunteers may be able to give only a few hours a week to the welfare of the elderly, their regular, sustained service is a critical factor.

The voluntary sector involves a multiplicity of roles, sometimes as provider, sometimes as critic. It may function in direct cooperation with the services of public authorities and with trained professionals, but it is in essence the expression of consumer involvement. By its nature it is flexible and able to innovate, to pioneer, and to experiment—features with which it has been traditionally associated, although it has to avoid the danger of becoming institutionalized and of seeking to retain services which can be better provided by alternative methods. It can draw upon all the skills and resources of its community. It can and should involve the elderly themselves as well as the middle-aged, and the young who have a close affinity with their grandparents' generation, devoid of some of the tensions and responsibilities inherent in the parent-child relationship. Volunteers engaging in community enterprises will identify with groups sharing common interests and ideals—religious bodies, voluntary societies—and now increasingly in an indirect relationship with public authorities that employ or sponsor community organizers.

The voluntary sector should not be seen as peripheral. It brings two unique gifts which no professional authority can offer: time and the expression of a caring community. However, if community service is to be effective, systems have to be devised to widen the area of recruitment, to evolve more effective methods of preparation and support as well as education of the professional. The professional must not feel threatened and must learn better how to relate to volunteers, who, for their part, must understand their own limitations as well as their potential. Too, volunteers must acknowledge the mutuality of the relationship in which the giver of service and the recipient are both contributors to the satisfaction of the other.

I conclude with five final points.

I believe all these factors are of some importance to the defense of the elderly. But there are many more. However, although there may be many different ways of approaching problems in view of the particular social conditions and cultural backgrounds of different communities which will relate to social and political philosophies, I believe there are sufficient common factors and relevant solutions to justify a continuing dialogue so that we can draw what is appropriate from experience elsewhere to adapt and apply in our own situations.

Secondly, I suggest that until we are in a position to offer services and a standard of provision to other people which we should find acceptable for ourselves, we have no right to feel any sense of satisfaction or complacency.

Thirdly, even where the range of services is adequate, systems of information must be employed which can be absorbed by the elderly in a language they can understand, taking into account their remoteness, possible deficiencies in sight and hearing, and limited reading skills. This will often require the transmission of social messages on a one-to-one basis. Providers of care in both the public and the voluntary sector must also avoid the danger of creating false expectations and the impression that there are definitive solutions which can be universally applied.

Fourthly, we must learn how to distinguish short-term expediencies and crisis intervention from long-term planning and solutions.

Lastly, in all that we do we should acknowledge that the process of aging, by its nature, erodes personal choice and that our unremitting task should be to devise ways of keeping the options open so that the elderly can continue to enjoy life on their terms, at their own pace. We should make it possible for those who wish to participate to do so, and for those who wish to withdraw to have that privilege without external pressures and well-meaning but misguided coercion by those who believe they know better, but who have experienced less than the people they seek to serve.

PART II

# DAISAKU MAEDA

CHIEF, SOCIAL WELFARE SECTION, TOKYO METROPOLITAN
INSTITUTE OF GERONTOLOGY, JAPAN

SELF-DEFENSE OF THE AGED is rather a new concept, at least in Japan, not only for the elderly themselves, but also for the professional people working in the field. Until very recently the culture of elderly people in Japan was not very aggressive. In Japan, old age used to be described as the age of *inkyo,* whose literal translation is "to be in hiding." The connotation is that old age is to be spent free from worldly cares by giving up the headship of a family and living in quiet, dignified retirement. Such culture still continues in many aspects and for most people the expected role of the elderly is to lead a quiet, retired life.

Today we have over 90,000 local associations of the elderly themselves, which are called old people's clubs. These clubs are generally looked upon as social clubs. Few members would say that self-defense is one of the major purposes of their association. However, as I examine their development I realize that the very existence of these local associations and their federations attracted the attention of the public to the problems of the aging and, in turn, has had profound effects on the development of our social policy and services for the elderly.

Organizations of the elderly themselves exist in many countries. So far as I know, the United States and France have very influential organizations of this sort. In West Germany, I hear, they are in the process of development. Needless to say, the organizations in respective countries have characteristics of their own. I hope this discussion of Japanese old people's clubs will be of some interest in making cross-cultural comparisons.

## SOCIAL AND HISTORICAL BACKGROUND

An association of old people is not a new idea in Japan. From the very early ages, old people were organized into small community groups by Buddhist temples. The purpose of these groups was to offer regular worship to Buddha, to hear sermons, and to talk together about Buddha and his teachings. But after the meetings, members were relaxed and enjoyed recreational and social activities. As time went on, this social contact became more important for many members.

In addition, in almost any Japanese community, there was a custom of holding a ceremonial assembly to which all the elderly members of the community were invited. Such an assembly was named "Respect-for-the-aged Meeting," in literal translation. It was held once or twice a year, and the elders were offered respect from the leaders and members of the community with a good feast and congratulatory gifts. Both in the religious groups and in the community assembly for the aged, the old people themselves could play only a very limited active role. In the former, the leadership was taken by the temple priests; in the latter, by the community leaders of the younger generations. Therefore, it can hardly be said that they were channels for participation by the elderly.

The idea of the modern old people's clubs was introduced to Japan from England at the beginning of the 1950s. It caught the imagination of the leaders of social welfare. As a result, some of the local governments began to provide places where old people could get together very often. Such places were called "*Rojin*-clubs," that is, "old people's clubs." In other words, "the club" at that time meant a facility and not an organized group of members. It was hoped that in such clubs old people could enjoy social contact with people of the same generation, and engage in meaningful leisure-time activities. Some clubs emphasized educational programs. The number of clubs rapidly grew, because the idea was also welcomed by old people themselves. In fact, the club was meeting various needs of the elderly in the rapidly changing Japanese society after the Second World War. With the increasing emphasis on the right of the individual, many old people felt that they lost their position as heads of their households and their status was unstable. They needed to support each other, and to learn new social attitudes. In addition, especially in urban areas, because of the shortage of adequate housing, many old people could not have their own rooms or even corners in their houses. So they enjoyed coming to the clubs.

According to the survey made in 1954, over a hundred old people's clubs were opened throughout Japan. But soon we faced several hard obstacles against further development of this type of club. As the clubs spread throughout the country, it was found rather difficult in many communities to secure a suitable building with space that could be regularly opened for old people. It was also very difficult to provide workers to administer the facility and help with the club activities.

As a result, the idea of an old people's club not as a facility but as a group of the aged themselves gradually emerged. In fact, most of the old people's clubs started in the late 1950s did not have any meeting places of their own. Accordingly, they met in some public buildings only a couple of times a month. (By the way, the first type of old people's clubs, that is, a community facility for old people, began to expand again recently.)

Owing to the financial and other assistance of local and prefectural governments, the old people's club as a group of the elderly themselves developed very rapidly. According to the survey in 1960, the total number of old people's clubs was about 5,000 throughout Japan. This meant that there was at least one such club in every city, town, and village. The number continued to grow, and in 1963 when the national government started to subsidize the clubs on a matching basis, the total reached about 36,000. This means that they increased more than seven times in the short period of three years.

One of the reasons for their rapid development was that we had the traditional, community-based, religious groups of the elderly. To many Japanese old people this type of club was quite natural and acceptable. But this does not necessarily mean that the clubs were accepted and developed only as a social group of the aged members of the community. The role of the club as an important channel of participation and of social action was also increasingly recognized by some leaders. It is this expected role that gave an impetus to the birth of prefectural and national federations whose main purpose was to represent the needs of the members of the local old people's clubs to the society, especially to the government.

PRESENT SITUATION

According to recent research, almost half of old people sixty years of age and over are now participating in local clubs. The 90,000 local clubs are organized into about 2,500 local federations which, in turn, are organized into federations at prefectural and national levels.

Almost all local clubs receive public grants under the national government program. In addition, many prefectural and local governments have their own programs for the promotion of old people's clubs through financial and other assistance.

ACTIVITIES

What are the programs of the local old people's clubs? They can be classified into five types of activities:
1. Learning through discussions, lectures, outings, and so on
2. Recreational activities, like games, dances, arts and crafts, trips, picnics, and so forth
3. Activities to earn pocket money by selling small products like bamboo crafts and others that are taken up as a club project
4. Activities to maintain and promote health
5. Activities of community service, especially for other elderly people who cannot join club activities because of their physical condition. Recently the importance of this type of activity has been stressed, and many local clubs

are engaged in the friendly visiting of homebound or bedfast old people in the community.

Very few local clubs are directly engaged in social-action activities. However, as I mentioned, federations of these clubs have been promoting various social-action programs in these ten years. Of course, the goals of social action vary from federation to federation. So far, the actions of the federations on the whole have had an impact on expanding community facilities for the aged, creating free medical care programs, and improving and expanding public comprehensive pension programs. The organized actions like holding conferences, demonstrations, and handing out petitions are well reported by the mass communications, and catch the attention of the general public.

PROBLEMS

From the social work viewpoint, we are aware of a number of problems in running and promoting the old people's clubs:

1. Most of the clubs meet only once or twice a month. Therefore, the members' sense of belonging to the club is rather weak.

2. More middle-class people are registered than those of higher and lower classes. The lack of participation of lower-class people should be offset by other social services.

3. The programs of most clubs are concentrated on recreational activities, and give inadequate consideration to the need for effective participation of the members in community affairs.

4. The rate of registration is much lower in urban areas, where the elderly tend to be more alienated from the mainstream of family and community life.

5. Few club members take active roles in running the club. In many clubs, leadership positions are rather fixed. Because of our cultural trait of dependency on outside authority, many old people lack the sense of mutual responsibility for maintaining and developing their own organizations. Most of them think and act like invited guests in the club. Another reason for the lack of leadership is old people's value of patience and

self-control. They easily suppress their feelings and make little demand for improving the policies of the club. Moreover, there is a group pressure to conform to this culture, which helps the club divide into two fixed subgroups, the leaders and the followers.

6. To promote the members' democratic participation and help the members' personal growth through group experiences, we need to provide the clubs with competent professional social workers, especially those trained in group work methods. Yet, it is extremely difficult to do so, because of the lack of trained workers as well as the lack of funds to employ them.

RECENT DEVELOPMENTS

There are two noteworthy recent developments. The organizations of the elderly people themselves are certainly very important in the industrialized society. But old people's clubs as a facility where they can go whenever they want and where they can meet their friends are also very important. As Japan recovered from the economic and social turbulence resulting from the Second World War, and as other acute needs of the society were met, the importance of community welfare centers for the aged was gradually recognized. So in the last ten years such centers, large and small, were increasingly built in many communities. In most cases a large one is called an Old People's Welfare Center. The national government has been encouraging this service by providing subsidies and loans to the local governments. At present there are about 350 large-scale, well-equipped centers throughout Japan. In such a big center there are, for instance, several small rooms where different types of activities are held, and a big hall with a stage where people perform, usually, traditional folk songs and dances. There are also a public bath and a rehabilitation room with much equipment where physical therapy as well as simple exercises are given with a help of a specialist. In addition, more than a thousand small-scale club houses for the elderly are now in existence.

Another significant recent movement for the self-defense of the elderly is the birth of the Japanese Federation of Retired Persons' Associations. The organization of this federation was promoted by the General Council of Trade Unions of Japan, the largest, strongest, and most radical labor organization of Japan. The main purpose of this federation is social action for the creation and improvement of public measures for the elderly. This organization is very young, and its influence is not yet very strong. When it is developed, it will be more progressive and more political than the Japanese Federation of Old People's Clubs, which is a federation of community-based, local clubs open to all the aged in the community.

The local old people's clubs and their federations at different levels are playing an important role in providing both a chance for meaningful leisure-time activities and, at the same time, an effective channel of participation in the society. Though the traditional culture of Japanese old people is that old age should be spent quietly, free from worldly cares, this attitude is changing rapidly. And we now have a new term, whose literal translation is "old people's power," which is used by the mass communication in reporting organized actions of old people. Old people's power! This term is symbolic in showing the change of our culture toward aging. Even though the concept of self-defense is rather new to us Japanese, I am sure that more and more old people will be aware of their potential power as citizens. At the same time, the general public too will come to understand that old people should no longer live in hiding but should participate fully in making this world a better place in which to live.

PART III

CHRISTOPHER N. W. SIGANGA

DIRECTOR OF SOCIAL SERVICES AND HOUSING,
CITY COUNCIL OF NAIROBI, KENYA

THERE IS no established age limit in the Kenya society to which the words "aged" and "elderly" may be affixed. In some parts of the country old age starts at fifty or seventy; in others, old age starts as soon as the person involved is considered "overspent." A recent country-wide survey revealed that persons forty years of age were classified as "old," particularly if they were destitute and in need of assistance. There are cases of extreme old age here and there, but on the whole Kenya is a young, developing country whose population is said to consist mainly of young people.

In the past, members of the community who achieved old age were held in great esteem. Their roles in the society were those of counselors, teachers, and custodians of tradition and information. They were often consulted on some community affairs. As a result they occupied an exalted, traditional place in the family and in the community as a whole.

Extended family traditions made certain that essential services required by the elderly were in abundant supply as and when required, although in certain cases aging males always made certain of suitable care and affection during their dying years by a late selection of youthful spouses.

The immediate question is: What are the traditional methods for the defense of the elderly? The problem of the elderly in Kenyan society was mainly a family problem. The elderly were and are an inevitable part of the social setup, geared to the traditional and practical aspects of community life. It is recognized that the elderly have as equal a claim to human dignity as any other member of the society.

Consequently, the established Western methods of providing special institutions or living accommodations for the aging are mainly nonexistent in the social setting of the community. Old people remain within the family circle, hence avoiding the agonizing experience of family separation, loneliness, and the feeling of being unwanted in their latter years.

The services provided for the aging in this setting were, therefore, highly individualized and varied from area to area. Among the pastoral groupings, in addition to concern for food and accommodations, there was the question of providing adequate transportation for the old and disabled members of the community. Constant mobility in search of new pastures for domestic animals inevitably meant that the transportation system had to be fashioned to such degree that it could be available at short notice. But such transport as was available was crude and often uncomfortable, leading to the aged being abandoned some place in the care of young members of the groups until the inevitable arrival of the end.

While services provided for the aged among the more settled groups of the society could be described as adequate, they lacked the ingredients of cohesion, organization, and coordination. There were no old people's clubs to cater to the needs of the elderly and no governmental legislation to protect and advance their special interests.

The extended family system takes care of those unable to find support from their immediate families. This becomes necessary when those involved have no children of their own; or when the children themselves are adults and have responsibilities of their own; or when close relatives, such as cousins, uncles, partners, are all dead. Although the system of extended family care has a significant role to play, it is sometimes attended with strains and stresses. Apart from the possibility of applying the accumulated wealth of the elderly to the wrong purposes, there is also the human element of neglect to which many old people in these circumstances may be subjected.

Kenyan society, like every society in the developing world, is making rapid social changes, changes which throw considerable strain on the traditional methods which once upon a time served the community well. The advent of the cities and large towns has dealt a devastating blow to close-knit family units and to the much coveted extended family units. New economic systems, following on the inevitable changes, have brought in their wake a readjustment in family relationships, thus affecting the existing social setting.

Although there is no accurate census of the number of old people in Kenya, it is estimated that in the urban areas approximately 18 percent of the total population consists of those fifty years of age and above; 22 percent are thirty-five but below fifty, while 60 percent are below thirty-five. The situation in the rural areas is slightly different. Here it is estimated that 37 percent are fifty years of age and above; 23 percent are thirty-five and below fifty, while 40 percent are thirty-five and below.

It is obvious from these data that there is a growing number of old people in the rural areas whose younger relatives may be away in the urban areas in pursuit of paid employment. There is substantial migration by the young and the middle aged, from the rural areas to the urban centers, while the countermovement of retired and old members of the urban centers moving back to the rural areas has been brought to a halt. The aged are thus left to their own devices, for only the very young and possibly those of their own generation are available to provide the required services. A similar situation is beginning to manifest itself in the urban centers, where there is a growing population of retired and aging people whose welfare and well-being must be taken care of outside the family and extended family units.

In a modern society, it is the duty and responsibility of the community as a whole to look after the interests of its members, and it is in this context that the services for the elderly must be viewed. In Kenya organized services to the aging and the aged have been largely left in the hands of voluntary agencies, mainly religious groups who have taken their responsibilities seriously and have provided a service in places which neither government nor local authorities could easily reach. There are old people's homes, particularly in the urban settings, which are established and operated by these voluntary agencies. In these the elderly are provided with food, shelter, and company.

However, one has to overcome the traditional thinking in terms of social interaction vis-à-vis organized community or institutional living before the full benefits of an old people's home can be realized. Rapid social change may bring this about sooner than expected, but the fact remains that under normal circumstances the elderly prefer to spend their last years in close proximity to their immediate family circles rather than surrounded by groups of their own generation.

Generally there are three types of assistance that is normally given both by the voluntary agencies and by governmental bodies:

1. Residential care for aged persons who are too old or too weak to look after themselves
2. Financial assistance for elderly destitute persons who are strong and able to care for themselves
3. Medical care for aged persons who are chronically sick and who need special care.

The first social work service to be provided for the elderly was a result of this voluntary service. This, although still in the initial stages of development, is one which as the problems of the aged manifest themselves will require accelerated development in order to cope with the situation.

In the government and semigovernmental sector, some local authorities have provided services to the aged in their areas of jurisdiction. These services have taken the form of grants-in-aid to voluntary agencies to enable them to provide a specified service or services; or to the local authority itself to provide directly such service as is required. It is often argued that it is less expensive to give services through volunteers than through the staff of an organization. It is, however, not clear when the service provided by a voluntary agency is the service that was intended to be given, and whether the volunteers have the necessary training and experience to handle the situation.

However, the immediate question to be answered is whether the services provided by the local authorities and the voluntary agencies are those that are required, acceptable, and timely. Most elderly people prefer living quiet lives during their last years and have a natural hatred of noise, or company. Some prefer community living. It is, therefore, the duty of the supply agency to strike the correct balance so as to attain maximum utilization of available resources.

In recent years, legislative measures in the defense of the aged have been introduced. The retirement age in the public sector varies from fifty-five to sixty, although in government service a person may be permitted to retire at the age of forty-five provided his retirement is in the public interest. In the private sector the situation is left to the discretion of the employer.

On retirement, there are retirement benefits, including pension schemes and other arrangements designed to help the retiree. The central government operates a contributory National Social Security Fund, which takes care of the contributor's hospital bills as well as those of his family. Local authority employees, apart from contributing to the National Social Security Fund, also contribute to the Local Government Officers' Superanuation Fund, designed to act as security during an officer's retirement. These schemes are aimed at warding off poverty and destitution from retired public officers and are considered sufficient security under present circumstances.

It will be appreciated that in a young and rapidly changing society, as is found in Kenya, the problems of the aged are less pronounced than those found in the older countries of Western Europe. But, since services have to be developed and rendered as and when required, traditional methods of performance will inevitably be inadequate to deal with the changed situation. They would then give way to modern methods.

Defense of the aging and the aged through traditional methods is primarily a family affair. It is based on the premise that the elderly are entitled to the respect and dignity that every other member of the community enjoys. The system does not lend itself to institutionalized care, and the services tend to be individualized rather than organized for group or mass consumption.

In a rapidly changing society, services that are rendered on a family basis rapidly become inadequate. These have to be supplemented if not wholly taken over by the community at large, hence the efforts of government and semigovernmental bodies to provide services for those who require such services.

Services for the aged are still undeveloped in Kenya, hence the reliance on the age-old traditional care and affection, but with the current pension schemes and the various retirement benefits, care of the old and the sick is adequately covered, at least for the time being. There is need for improvement, and perhaps the formation of a national association for the aged would assist in accelerating the pace of assistance that may be required.

# The Use of Volunteers in Development

PART I

## ANGELA CHRISTIAN

CONSULTANT, WOMEN'S PROGRAMS, GHANA

IT MIGHT be useful to remind ourselves what we mean when we say "volunteer" and "development."

Development has been defined as an over-all process of transforming men and societies in such a way that every human being can achieve material and moral well-being. It is a process which calls for the provision of opportunities for a better life, including facilities for education, health, nutrition, housing, employment, an equitable distribution of income, the promotion of justice and cultural well-being, and social acceptance of every individual.

A volunteer is a person who serves of his or her own free will, without expectation of monetary or other personal material gain. In another sense, a volunteer is a person who from compassion and love for his fellow human being seeks through humanitarian acts to bring about social change so that none will suffer physically, morally, or spiritually.

The Second World Food Congress of the United Nations Food and Agriculture Organization (FAO) held at the Hague in 1970 maintained that "if development is essentially the changing of people, it should be a process of the people, and by the people, as well as for the people." In this context, all who participate in self-development programs are volunteers.

In its document entitled *Africa's Strategy for Development in the 1970s,* the United Nations Economic Commission for Africa identifies among other key areas and activities the development of human resources. Recognition of the importance of developing human beings is fortunately gaining ground, and the Economic Commission's own Human Resources Development Program is making an invaluable contribution, and points the way to what is required.

But why is there a need for volunteers? Governments are duty bound to provide social welfare and community development services, and do. That is so, but governments have neither the means nor the personnel to devote to the whole task. Volunteers from among the people must share the responsibility. To ensure, however, that voluntary efforts do not overlap or duplicate government services, it is essential that right from the beginning of any program or project there be coordination by the government body charged with the provision of social services and community development and that the various voluntary agencies and groups in the field collaborate and cooperate with one another.

Greater service can be rendered by volunteers if, before attempting any program, they identify the priorities of the national development plan. Having done so, it is absolutely necessary to establish the felt needs of the community. Without this, there will be resistance on the part of the community, and the program will be doomed to failure. If the community is not sufficiently vocal, or unable to express its felt needs, it can be diplomatically guided.

This is where "conscientization" comes in.

The report of the Consultation on the Participation of Local Volunteers in Rural Development in Africa, held at Tema, Ghana, in 1973, defines "conscientization" as "a process by which groups and communities build up their capacity to analyze their own situation and take action to attain self-defined goals."

Voluntary agencies now recognize that those whom they seek to help prefer them to be partners in development rather than humanitarian donors who dictate. Rural communities need development programs more than urban dwellers, and it is in the rural areas that volunteers can do the most useful work.

Because of the important role that African women play in the social and economic life of the family and community in general, they should be actively involved in both the planning and the implementation of development programs in rural as well as urban areas. In Africa, women's organizations are fruitful sources of volunteers and volunteer leadership. There is a danger, however, that a few dedicated, educated women will undertake more than they can accomplish. Such women tend to serve on too many committees and spend the limited time they can spare from home or professional responsibilities going from one meeting to another, often leaving one meeting before it ends in order to attend another elsewhere. This state of affairs results in prolonged planning and decision-taking on projects envisaged, which are sometimes abandoned through lack of time or sustained interest.

Often the projects launched by volunteers from within these organizations overlap. It would be beneficial if women's organizations would hold joint annual meetings to outline their planned social welfare and community development programs for the year, and allocate areas of operation to avoid overlapping and duplication.

Young people also have a part to play in development. They can, through voluntary youth movements, contribute substantially by direct participation in programs they have helped to plan.

Every volunteer group needs a leader to coordinate its efforts and ensure maximum achievement. A leader must be trained for the work to be undertaken, or at least have the capability for such work. She must have leadership qualities. She must be resourceful, democratic, and decisive in action. The autocratic leader achieves very little in the long run; for when her presence is withdrawn, the group she leads, more often than not, abandons the project she imposed. The laissez-faire leader, on the other hand, does not tap the full potential of the group, nor make the maximum use of its time.

Volunteers no less than their leaders must have the training and aptitude for the work they volunteer to do. First and foremost, they must have the time required. A trained volunteer who is never there when needed is no help at all.

Even when volunteers have the necessary skills, specific

training in the field is desirable, and backing with government technical and financial assistance is essential. Many countries have government-supported trust funds from which monies are disbursed to accredited charitable voluntary organizations. Contributions to the fund are made by individuals, organizations, firms, and industries.

Information is an element of development, and communicated through mass media it can be of great assistance to volunteers. Use of the people's own language makes for quicker, clearer, and better understanding. An idea or information channeled through an interpreter often gets lost in the process. An apparently stupid reaction on the part of illiterate people may be nothing more than lack of comprehension of the language in which a communication is made.

The question as to whether developing countries want or need foreign volunteers has often been asked. The usefulness of local volunteers has also been questioned. It is agreed that both local and foreign volunteers have a place in national development, given the conditions already stated. In addition, it may be said that where possible a local volunteer should belong to the community in which he operates. It is better still if he lives in the community and has an uninterrupted work association with the people.

The Second World Food Congress of FAO recognized that where a foreign volunteer is sufficiently trained, is a "doer" and not an adviser; stays long enough to make an impact on the community in which he works; falls in with the objectives of the national development plan and projects conceived within it by the local authorities; confines himself to his terms of reference; has the right education and attitude to enable him to work in traditional societies, and with his local counterpart, and can adapt generally to conditions in the country in which he serves, he can make a valuable contribution.

If I may echo the words with which Montaigne concluded a lecture to a gathering of illustrious philosophers in the sixteenth century, "All I have done is make a bouquet from flowers already picked, adding nothing but the string to tie them together." Yes, what I have said has been said before, and will undoubtedly be said again, for the conditions which motivated the original discussion are to a large extent still with us.

It is, I am sure, the wish of all of us that with accelerated mobilization of people for development action, and the full development of human resources, we will, if not within the present decade, at least in the foreseeable future secure for all our peoples a better life, conducive to peace in the world.

PART II

## MARY RIPLEY

PRESIDENT, INTERNATIONAL ASSOCIATION FOR VOLUNTARY
EDUCATION, UNITED STATES

VOLUNTEERS ARE the inheritors of a great tradition. Before the caseworker, before the group worker, before the health worker, before the agency executive, there was the volunteer. The volunteer *was* social work. Volunteers were and are the heart, hand, mind, and voice in stirring the social conscience of the community's responsibility for the health and welfare of its citizens. But more than anything volunteers are people, and now more than ever people need people. We cannot computerize society and expect that human needs will be answered. Volunteering and freedom go hand in hand; we cannot have one without the other. There cannot be meaningful volunteerism unless there is freedom within a society. Individuals must be free to choose a course of action, and individuals must be free to associate with others and organize around common goals. However, I would argue that volunteers should not be *used* but should be *involved*.

There are today many, many more opportunities for volunteers to become involved. There is a growing recognition of the value of the volunteer citizen participating at all levels. The status of the volunteer has been elevated. Why is this? Basically, it is due to the greater acceptance and recognition of the volunteer by the professional; the involvement of the volunteer as a member of the team, working in partnership with the professional but never supplanting that professional, only supplementing and extending the role of the professional. With the higher status of the volunteer has come a marked expansion of the opportunities for volunteers. They are moving from the traditional roles of bandage rolling, envelope stuffing, fund raising, and so on, to exciting new opportunities in school tutoring, working in the courts and prisons, helping the mentally ill, staffing family-planning clinics, using their skills in policy-making, public relations, research, and other technical fields.

With the increased involvement of the volunteer have come other changes. First, it has become essential to have adequate and appropriate coordination of the volunteer programs. The majority of hospitals in the United States have paid coordinators of volunteers. Several universities offer courses for volunteer coordinators. There is a national organization that licenses coordinators and directors. Another change has been in the shared decision-making process. We can no longer plan *for* people; we must plan *with* people. The volunteer is involved with the staff in planning the work schedule, the job description, the goals, the priorities, and, most important, the division of responsibility. It is partnership in action. In this way there is an elimination of job conflict and an opportunity for continuing evaluation of effectiveness.

The most dramatic change we have seen in volunteerism in the last decade is in the new sources of volunteers, namely, the young minorities, the elderly, the poor, both men and women. It is now recognized that it is everyone's right and privilege to be a volunteer. Everyone has something to give: his time, his talents, his caring. Traditionally in the United States volunteers came from the middle-class, white, female community. It was assumed that people needed money to volunteer and lots of leisure time. It is recognized in our changing society that the needs for, and delivery of, human services must go far beyond economic values. Agencies and organizations, recognizing the need for volunteers, are setting up what are called "enabling" funds—monies to assist a volunteer with carfare, baby-sitting, lunch money, cost of uniforms, and so on. This, then, makes it possible for all to volunteer.

As we have opened these doors to the elderly dramatic results have happened. There is a program known as Foster Grandparents. Older persons with low incomes are recruited to work in children's institutions and agencies, reading, playing, talking, tutoring the children, and generally bringing grandparents into the lives of children who ordinarily would not have had this wonderful experience. In talking with these foster grandparents we have found that the program is a two-way street. The elderly person who felt that life was over and no longer had any meaning suddenly felt needed and a contributing member of the community while bringing joy to these lonesome little children. Seniors are finding all kinds of jobs open to them. Retired business executives are offering their services and using their skills. This has become an answer to boredom, alcoholism, and even suicide. Other new sources are in industry. Companies are releasing employees to do community service, recognizing not only that this is good public relations but that it is the responsibility of business to take its place in the life of the community.

The young as they search for careers are looking to volunteer work as a career-testing experience. Colleges and universities have coordinators to assist with the job-finding process and to assist agencies to decide where the young volunteer can best fit in. Some universities give credit for volunteer work. All these efforts are opening up new sources of volunteers. But as we recognize the rapid and significant changes around us in the world today with the increased emphasis on material goods, with the changes in family life, with relationships becoming more complex, it is going to be necessary to increase the volunteer involvement to bring people more and more in touch with people. "Much of the depersonalization and social disconnection of the work process of our current technology-based society results in a sense of non-involvement and non-relevance which can best be coped with by opportunities for significant volunteer involvement roles and service." [1]

An international conference offers a unique opportunity to share not only experiences but challenges. Naturally, our major challenges are related to the differences in our own and national experiences. Each country has its own concept of volunteerism and its own type of programs involving volunteers. Of necessity these are based on the needs and the acceptance in the individual country. But we can always come together with the hope of finding solutions.

Whether one lives in a rich land or a poor one, it is serving one's country in a positive manner that one achieves spiritual harmony . . . . any action undertaken should be motivated by a firm belief that our life was given to us that we could live not vegetate. To participate in life not merely exist. To embellish this life not to spoil it. To love those with whom we share it. To help those who are in need of help. This is how I envisage volunteerism.

These words were written in 1970 by a Swiss delegate to an international conference on volunteerism in the United States. Following the conference, this woman returned to her country and set up the entire drug education program for Switzerland with volunteers as implementers. The key is to develop a program around the most important needs of a community or a country. We can help each other by sharing tools and expertise. Because that international conference was such a success, the parent organization that planned the 1970 effort is beginning to plan for another conference to be held in San Francisco in 1976. It will be an opportunity to celebrate the Bicentennial of the United States by highlighting the volunteer movement. People interested in volunteerism will be invited. We hope in this way to build bridges of understanding through volunteerism. There will be ample opportunity to observe volunteer programs, to study methods and procedures, and most of all to share experiences. Perhaps together we can find some of the solutions to our community problems.

One of our basic needs is that of sharing. To this end in the

[1] Ron Lippitt and Eva Schindler-Rainman, *The Volunteer Community*.

United States there is a clearinghouse at the National Center for Voluntary Action where information about programs dealing with volunteers, the cost, the numbers, the goals, and the leadership needed is catalogued. In other words, if a city wishes to set up a program for volunteers in prisons, information can be sought on the hows and wherefores. We do not all need a complicated computerized system but we do need to have tools to assist us in defining methods and assessing resources—an interesting job for a volunteer.

In today's world communication is the key. We are surrounded by gaps that are dividing and threatening our way of life. There are gaps between the black, the white, the brown, the yellow; there are language gaps; gaps between labor and management; between men and women; between government and those who are governed, the establishment and the nonestablishment. If we are to bridge these gaps we must learn the art of communication. With true communication comes understanding. Our challenge is not just to *help* people but to *understand* people. Volunteers can and are the best kind of communicators, they can bridge these gaps. Volunteers can bring the community into the agency and the agency into the community. Volunteer service becomes an antidote for the movement of societies toward materialism and impersonal living.

If, however, volunteers are to fulfill these challenges they must be trained, oriented to the job that is expected of them. This training must be planned for as a specific part of the volunteer program. It does little service to an agency to have persons involved who have little or no knowledge of the purpose of the program, its focus, and the responsibilities of both the staff and the volunteer. Training tools are available through many national and international sources such as the YWCA, Red Cross, and the National Center for Voluntary Action in the United States.

As communities and nations are in the process of developing they will need to look to people power; they will need to tap all those human resources, bringing them together to accomplish unified action. Development can mean many things—testing new programs, finding new resources, building new systems—but ultimately it means involvement. As Nellie Sachs has said, "let's walk together into the future and try again and again to build a new and better way."

# The Family's Participation in Development

## CATHERINE S. CHILMAN

SCHOOL OF SOCIAL WELFARE, UNIVERSITY OF WISCONSIN-
MILWAUKEE, UNITED STATES

IT IS moving to talk about families. It is moving because families have such deep and personal meaning to all of us. Our family bonds tie us to our particular families, to the families of our own countries and of the world. They tie us together because we are partners in the most fundamental of human experiences.

It is difficult to discuss the role of families in development. There are many reasons for this, reasons of both the mind and the heart. As a citizen of the United States, I am compelled to feel shame and grief for my own country, which once had the temerity to see itself as the hope of peoples everywhere. This country proclaimed a dedication to freedom, equality, justice, and opportunity for every man, woman, and child. This country, perhaps the prime example of a super-technological, highly developed society, is experiencing a crisis of character. The question facing the United States, and perhaps much of industrialized Western Europe, is whether this nation—these nations—can survive the spiritual crisis associated with a materialistic mass society dedicated to individual pleasure and fulfillment.

The crisis that many nations of Africa and Asia face is one of *physical* survival, which by contrast makes the Western world seem especially selfish and lacking in a community conscience. The plight of families devastated by starvation and disease makes the plight of unhappy families in my own country look paltry indeed. But I must speak of families of my own country and, to a lesser extent, of other highly modernized ones, because my history, traditions, values, and knowledge are limited to these places.

## THE UNDERDEVELOPED "DEVELOPED" COUNTRIES

The so-called "developed" nations of the Western world are far from adequately developed, if by development one means the building of a society that provides a high quality of life for all its people. The United States shares with a number of other predominantly Protestant nations an ambivalence between familialism and individualism, with the latter value usually predominant. Many of us in the Western world are looking to the South and East for philosophies that are new to us, but rich with ancient wisdom about a more communal, less materialistic way of life.

In my own country, in many other postindustrial nations, problems of poverty and racism are far from resolved. Progress has been made in decreasing these injustices, but much, much more needs to be done.

## SOURCES OF FAMILY VARIATION

It is always difficult to speak about "the family," for there are many kinds of families. Variations in family patterns occur both within and between nations. Within nations, these variations are related to social class, region, ethnicity, religion, and the particular form and experience of each individual family. Between nations, these variations are related to the history, traditions, political, social, and economic patterns and situation of a country.

Views of family patterns in various societies do not tell us much about how families actually feel and behave. Statements about a group's values and customs are apt to be more idealistic than realistic. Thus, the traditional extended family may be far less harmonious and cohesive than often described; the nuclear equalitarian family is apt to be more entangled in the kinship network and less democratic than is generally believed.

Although social science researchers are learning more and

more about different kinds of family life, the depths and complexities of the family experience are apt to elude them. Feelings about family membership are intense, private, and partially hidden from the members themselves.

DECLINING POWER OF THE FAMILY

The power of the family as a system is likely to decline in a mass industrial society; the power of other systems, such as business and industry and the human services, is apt to become greater and more impersonal. Although families in simpler village societies can often demand that social systems adapt to family needs, the opposite condition is likely to prevail in modernized communities. There is a tendency for social systems in these communities to use and abuse families rather than seek to understand and support them.

Ironically, when families show signs of deterioration in response to these stresses, the larger social systems tend to blame parents for their weaknesses. Families are asked to take responsibility for a staggering array of social problems: poverty, children's learning problems, physical and mental illness, delinquency, alcoholism, drug addiction, and the revolt of angry youth. But problems in the larger social systems, vis-à-vis the family, are more likely to be the root cause of deficiencies in family behaviors. Moreover, the behaviors of families are not the only forces that shape developmental outcomes for their members. This is especially true in modernized society where children, youth, and adults are apt to be in daily interaction with so many other influences in school, work, recreation, community activities, and exposure to the mass media.

It is questionable whether the family, as a system, makes much of an impact on the development of a society. There is considerable recent consensus among social scientists, especially those of the United States, that families can do little to shape their own destiny, to say nothing of the destiny of society. Although such a consensus is growing, this does not necessarily mean that it is totally accurate. It may be a reaction, in part, to the failure of an earlier assumption that families were *the* basic building blocks of society, that an enlightened democratic society devoted to peace and world brotherhood could be built by the perfectly reared children of enlightened, democratic, peaceable parents.

The middle-class parents of the United States in my own generation entertained this illusion. Trying to live up to the parental ideal drove us to agonies of guilt and overwork. Some of our children, assimilating the values we strove to impart, led the youth revolt of the late 1960s: they revolted because they found the world so different from the one we, the parents, strove to create through them. We, the United States parents of the 1940s and early 1950s, cannot believe that family relationships and child-rearing patterns play much of a part in a national development. If we did, we would have an even harder time living with ourselves than we do now.

The same might be said for those professionals who committed their careers to family services. For instance, despite extensive efforts by public and private family social agencies in the United States during the 1960s, research showed that those activities had no measurable impact on the reduction of family poverty and related problems.

There is growing evidence to support a more sophisticated understanding that development of families is an outcome of dynamically linked social, political, economic, and psychological forces in the larger society interacting with families and their particular characteristics. Despite the present emphasis on forces outside individuals and families that appear to shape their behavior, this view seems somewhat limited and deterministic. Fate and the social environment are *not* synonymous. Although people respond to political, economic, social, and psychological conditions, these conditions were created by people in the first place. *Individuals* challenged the status quo, *individuals* invented new ways of doing things.

Families have played an incompletely understood role in the development of society's leaders. We know of great families that have provided leaders from generation to generation; we know of great families that, as a group, have acted to bring about more humane conditions in their own societies. We also know of severely destructive people who have come from miserably inadequate families. Conversely, some great leaders have also sprung from miserable families; some destroyers have come from great families. These outcomes probably relate to the mysteries of genetics plus the infinitely complex factors of interaction of the many familial and societal forces that create human behavior and its impact on a society.

DEVELOPING A SOCIETY

The development of a humane society is puzzling; it requires the acquisition and pulling together of many component pieces. The pieces may be generally labeled economic, social, political, and psychological.

*Economic development.* Economic development, of necessity, varies in detail from country to country and from group to group within countries. For the so-called "developing" countries, it involves a massive undertaking in respect to acquiring many kinds of resources. Strong economic foundations are so important to the well-being of a country and its families that other concerns are likely to be ignored while these are being constructed. The resulting problem is an overemphasis on material gain to the detriment of the quality of life.

*Social development.* Social development should be concerned with problems in social stratification, social organization, and social planning within a society as well as with the provision of needed human services. The well-being of families is closely linked to all these activities.

Most, probably all, societies have a stratified social system, but some are more rigidly stratified than others. There is manifest injustice, not to mention inefficiency, in a society ruled by a powerful, hereditary elite that retains most of the wealth and opportunities for itself. Strong pressures for social change must generally come from the members of the under classes who push the elite into less self-protecting attitudes and behaviors. World-wide, we have experienced these pressures for social change; some have erupted into social revolution, some have proceeded through the more orderly processes of social evolution.

One aspect of social development and its young sibling,

community development, involves efforts to make rigid bureaucratic organizations more responsive to *all* people and to recognize the family as a dynamic interaction system rather than a mere collection of individuals. Ideally, social development also includes local, regional, and national planning for the well-being of individuals and families. This planning should be closely linked to economic planning and emphasize consideration of personal and familial factors in such programs as housing, transportation, zoning, and the like.

One would hope that developing countries could learn from the mistakes of the more developed ones and not have to repeat their painful errors of unrestrained, asocial, economic development. The UN recognized these problems long ago and since the early 1960s has strongly encouraged close links in social and economic policies and planning.

A more generally accepted concept of social development centers on the establishment of vocational training, social and health services, recreation and child care programs. By and large, these services are not likely to reach and help effectively those who are most in need unless they are accompanied by allied changes in the social and economic structure of society. There is need for a partnership between basic social and economic change *and* the provision of free or low-cost human services.

*Political development.* Political development is a particularly sensitive subject. The whirlwind of political, economic, and social change has been blowing strongly through the world since at least the fifteenth century. Starting in Western Europe, numerous events lead to restructuring of social, economic, and political power groups, the rise of modern science, and the push for democracy.

The most recent democratic push has had many facets: self-determination by nations and an end to colonial rule; votes and political power for members of minority groups; increased participation by under classes in community decision-making and program development.

Growth of popular demands for equal political power has many effects on families. Increased popular representation in government is likely to lead to policies and programs that benefit the majority rather than the privileged minority of families. However, a related problem is that democratic values generally emphasize the importance of the individual. This emphasis on the individual may lead to *under*representation of family interests in public programs.

Individualistic, democratic, political values can also cause revolutions within families. The patriarchal male who once ruled, or thought he ruled, the women, children, and youth of his household is sorely beset. Rising demands for equal rights in making family decisions, for opportunities to participate in the larger community and for shared sex roles are sending tremors throughout family structures around the world.

It is probable that families are most likely to survive the demands of modernizing or modern conditions and the push for family democracy if they flexibly adapt to the requirements of their times. This adaptation is likely to involve more equality and sharing within the family, increased family interaction with the community, more open communication between family members, a loosening but not destruction of extended kinship ties, a gradual development of new cultural patterns that define the values and norms of family life in the new world.

Destructive revolutions within families seem most likely to occur if there is a rigid insistence on authoritarian traditions that applied well to earlier forms of social and economic life (such as the isolated rural village) but do not apply to conditions of the present and future. It may be that developing countries will evolve less individualistic families than those of Western Europe and the United States. Their histories, situation, and traditions are different in many ways, including customary views of the family. Industrialization does not necessarily mean a total adoption of Western family patterns.

*Psychological development.* Rising popular aspirations for a better quality of life often include the search for a better quality of psychological life in terms of intellect, emotions, and values. These aspirations are most likely to become primary when more basic survival needs have been met. In a sense, the search for self-fulfillment is a luxury accorded to more afflu-ent peoples. In another sense, agonies of the heart, mind, and spirit may be recognized more acutely when more basic physi-cal needs have been satisfied. Psychological distress can also be associated with the breakdown of earlier cultural values that gave structure and assurance to life.

Rising psychological aspirations and anxieties probably find their most vulnerable target in the family. This is true for many reasons. For example, the former functions of families have been partially or completely taken away by the super-technological society.

Psychological nurturance is the main function left for the more prosperous families in such nations. And this kind of nurturance is the most difficult kind. It is much more difficult for husbands to share their thoughts and feelings with their wives than to share their pay checks; it is much more difficult for wives to sustain their husbands' needs for love and under-standing than to nourish them with well-cooked meals. It is more difficult to heal the hurt in children's hearts than to mend their tattered clothes.

As aspirations grow for a psychologically fulfilling family life, high levels of interpersonal skills are demanded in rela-tionships between mates and between parent and child. If these skills are to flourish, family members may need particu-larly skilled help through education for family living, through group, family, and individual counseling.

But skill and sensitivity in human relationships, child-rear-ing competencies, do not grow only out of heightened under-standings. Skills of these kinds are most likely to flourish when basic life conditions free people from corrosive anxieties fed by too little family income, unemployment or under-employment, poor housing, and the like. This provides yet another example of the importance of a close partnership be-tween human services and economic and social development.

It is disturbingly obvious that aspirations for a higher qual-ity of family life in industrialized societies are falling short of their goals. Divorce rates are rising; marriage rates tend to be lower; out-of-wedlock births, higher. Birth rates are low—a welcome trend for most countries because of the problems of overpopulation. People are living longer, and the care of the elderly, especially as chronic illness develops, poses an ever-larger problem.

Statistics of these kinds provide only a small part of the family story. Other trends include the apparent growth of overt homosexuality; premarital and extramarital sex relationships; experimentation with alternate family forms, such as group marriages, communes, and single-parent families; conflicts between the generations and early departure of young people from their homes; a seeming increase of child abuse and neglect by parents.

Some social scientists and writers for the mass media view the modern family as a wasteland of hypocrisy, hatred, and hidden horrors. Although this may be true for some families, though all families probably contain at least a small amount of these ingredients, in-depth studies of family life in the United States suggest that the majority of parents and young people have mostly positive views about their families. It is the fashion among the intelligentsia to see modern society as ridden with terrors. Problems rather than nonproblems make news. Although many of today's families may be failing in whole or in part, they are not about to become obsolete as some would claim.

Agonies of the human spirit, as frequently displayed in individual and family behavior in the highly developed nations, may be the agonies of labor pains associated with the birth of a new society. The widespread decadence observed in many of these countries may signify the decay and disintegration of old cultural patterns that fail to fit a changed and changing world.

Out of this decay, out of these spiritual agonies, may be born new social and psychological guidelines for living. Some of the observed family behaviors, such as communes, cohabitation of couples without the formality of marriage, extramarital love affairs, divorce and remarriage, may be expressions of an idealistic search for a higher quality of human relationships that involve person-to-person intimacy, honesty, commitment, and responsible sharing of the self rather than mere conformity to custom and the law.

This search involves, too, a more enlightened and equalitarian view of human sexuality. Sometimes this search appears to degenerate into a hedonistic hunt for the mechanically perfect orgasm; more often it involves added understandings of human relationships and new ways of fulfilling partnerships.

The women's liberation movement also represents an exploration for more humane ways of family and personal living. Although some of this exploration involves hostile confrontations, these are probably necessary to force changes in former patterns. This liberation movement can free both males and females to live more effectively in an industrialized society that no longer requires heroic acts of physical exertion from males or endless child-bearing and domestic dedication from females. There is an enhanced opportunity for males and females to share their lives with each other in work and play both outside and within the home. As they share more of their experiences the way is paved for more open and complete communication between them: one key to satisfying marriages.

As the concept of liberation and equality for *all* peoples spreads, it becomes necessary to reexamine traditional assumptions about *the* "right way" for families to live and raise their children. As social, economic, and political conditions bring about changes in all aspects of life we cannot be sure what *are* the best patterns for family living.

It seems advisable, then, to help individuals and families explore life styles that are both satisfying to them and satisfactory to society. This does not imply that just *any* kind of life style is acceptable. The push for freedom must have its limits. Freedom without constraints can breed anarchy, unrestrained violence, and self-centered impulsivity. These trends are observable in many nations, especially, perhaps, in the United States.

At the beginning I ventured that the United States and, seemingly, many of the highly developed societies, are suffering a crisis in character. Such qualities as self-discipline, self-sacrifice, responsibility toward others, and commitment to human welfare seem to be going out of style. As I see it, society cannot continue to function if it fails to value the well-being of the group along with the well-being of the individual, if it fails to establish limits on human behavior as well as cherishing human freedom.

These values cogently apply to the family. For viable family life depends at least as much on altruism as it does on personal fulfillment, as much on defined limits as on self-expression. Perhaps the family is the most crucial group in all society for the development of social character; without this development, the family may fall apart, and its fall will reverberate throughout society. Through these qualities, family life provides an endless circle of giving and receiving, grieving for and rejoicing with others, comforting and being comforted, learning and teaching, forgetting the self but not being forgotten, loving and being loved, doing the impossible in times of family crisis and finding that the impossible can be done, rejoicing in the miracle of new life and mourning the departure of old.

My own family life covers nearly sixty years and stretches nearly around the globe. Times and places have changed radically over the years and yet, in heart and mind, my family and its many generations, living and dead, are with me and give me continuing faith about the enduring strength and vitality of human life, enduring commitment to families everywhere. Except we give our lives to others as well as ourselves we shall be lost.

NEW AND OLD ROLES FOR SOCIAL WORKERS

Perhaps most social workers have equally deep feelings about their own families and derive from this a dedication to family services. This dedication is important but should also be buttressed with knowledge and skills. Like all social institutions, including the family, the profession of social work has been undergoing disruptive yet hopeful change. Possible roles for social workers have expanded as the profession seeks to meet more effectively the challenge of changing conditions. These roles include the more familiar ones of social treatment (casework and group work) along with newer ones of supervision and training of paraprofessionals, launching and administration of complex human service systems, social planning and development, formation and implementation of social policy, and research and evaluation. These roles are difficult; they require that we learn and do more. But they are in a vital cause: the well-being of individuals and families everywhere.

PART II

# AYESHA NABI

ASSOCIATE PROFESSOR, INSTITUTE OF SOCIAL WELFARE AND
RESEARCH, UNIVERSITY OF DACCA, BANGLADESH

THE FAMILY has been intensively and extensively studied by scholars in various disciplines, such as anthropology, sociology, social psychology, economics, social work, and so on. But the study of the family in the processes of planned development efforts is a comparatively new trend. The practical implications of such study raise many questions bearing upon the future roles of the family, significant to development practitioners as well as to social scientists. The recent interest in developmental study has turned our focus to the family in its role as a recipient and also as a contributory unit in the developmental service programs. This subject assumes particular significance in the context of the current social structure and the needs of development in the Asian countries.

The concept of development in current usage puts emphasis on the following major elements:
1. Development as a process
2. Economic growth as an important target
3. Creation and provision of essential social services like health, education, housing, and so forth
4. Redistribution of resources on an equitable basis

5. Increase of individual and collective ability of all citizens to participate democratically in the development process.

The traditional definition of "development" leans heavily toward economic growth and puts more emphasis on the tangible criteria of development. This sometimes has overshadowed the intangible (referred to as "subjective" and beyond physical measurement) social aspects which can no doubt accelerate the process of development. On the other hand, the term "social development" can be used in a broader sense to include economic development, social justice, and provisions to raise the standard of living. Thus, it should put emphasis on the development of the totality of society in its economic, political, and sociocultural ramifications; and in this, the part played by the family in the over-all developmental organizations of the society cannot be minimized.

The present-day challenge to social development is not only one of mobilizing economic resources, but also of mobilizing and motivating people to participate in the total spectrum of social development programs so that all the economic, sociocultural, and political institutions can be made more responsive toward development and will also integrate individuals, groups, and communities into the larger whole of a national society.

One of the basic potential contributions that a family makes to development lies in its basic and primary function, that is, its role of socializing the members. Basically, it acts as an educative agency while it inculcates positive attitudes among its members, especially the children. Provision of security, identification, love, care, and emotions as well as acceptance of authority and discipline are essentially provided through families. The emotional climate in the family is to the child what water and sunshine are to the plant. We cannot expect our children to blossom into responsible adulthood without a positive role of the family.

If the greatest need of the hour is our concern for national development both socioculturally and economically, then the family gains all the more importance as a strategic social unit to play a purposeful and meaningful role in development.

The basic preparation of an individual to play an effective role in the development process is gathered in the family. The family, therefore, has to have sufficient strength to prepare its members to participate in the process. But those families which do not have such strengths have first to be consumers of development services such as education, housing, health, hygiene, nutrition, social security, social welfare, and so on. And this should be regarded as an "investment in human resources" so that families can first build up strengths for future contributions to the national development.

LEVELS OF PARTICIPATION

Families can participate at the various levels of development to different degrees, and at international, societal, regional, and community levels. Direct participation of families on the international level, however, may not be always feasible in the general sense of participation, though individual contributions to progress like those of the Curie family in the field of science and of Will and Ariel Durant in the lessons of history cannot be discounted.

Participation on the other three levels may be possible in direct and indirect, tangible and intangible ways. On the regional and societal levels the participation may be rather intangible, but still may be considered significant and important. This may be achieved in an indirect form which attends to the task of imparting preliminary lessons on societal values and concern for social issues and social problems. On these levels, societies may perform the ground work in preparing families for greater participation on the community level by arousing interest in common concerns, in awareness of socioeconomic problems of a society, in the changes that take place in the society, in the cause and effects of varied social problems and issues. Different mass media—newspapers, booklets, brochures, television, radio, film strips, movies, and so on—may be fully explored, utilized, and mobilized for achieving these goals. Besides these, holding regional and national seminars, workshops, conferences, discussions, and so on might be very effective.

The family, therefore, has a substantial contribution to make to development in securing intangible gains. This, however, does not mean that the family as a social institution has not been achieving tangible gains. The difference in the present context would be the emphasis of new concepts, such as arousing social interests, stimulating family education, and encouraging attitudes of sacrifice, sympathy, tolerance, sharing, social values, social problems, and utilization of discussion, seminars, and other media.

But under existing conditions we would wish our families to play a more direct role in development and we may think that role would be played more fruitfully at the community level. A community is nothing but an intergroup organization, and the family constitutes the integral part of such a community. Families as such can participate and contribute more effectively at the community level in some of the following important areas of development:

1. *Family planning.* Family planning is not only important for economic growth, it is equally important for social development as well. The family can directly and indirectly participate in an effective program to check population growth in a community. In Asian countries where children are considered as assets and security in old age, where infant mortality continues to be about twice as high as that in the Western countries, the family-planning concept does not receive much incentive. Thus bringing down the birth rate to a level consonant with the country's developmental goal cannot be attained by formulation of legislative policies or enactments only.

Family planning has been part of national development policies and programs in most of the Asian countries. But effectiveness of their successful operation is altogether a separate issue. In communities where families are convinced of the gravity of this problem they can easily influence both directly and indirectly a change in people's behavior. They can modify attitudes, values, and beliefs, and so on, so that a small-sized family can become the accepted social norm of the country.

By participating in the development of a sound family-planning policy and program, families can make major contributions to social development. Most of the national governments of the Asian countries have emphasized family planning as part of the population policy, for they realize its inevitable positive impact on family welfare, which ultimately leads to the socioeconomic development of a country. Social workers, like other behavioral scientists, may become more effective in bringing about the desired change in the motivation of family planning.

2. *Health.* The broad areas of health, hygiene, and sanitation, the drainage systems of a community, and so forth, become a direct concern of the families in a country. Healthy families mean a healthy community, and healthy communities mean healthy societies.

Health consciousness, attitudes toward medical treatment, health education, drainage, water supply, and health services are of primary importance to health. These are essential elements for development of healthy manpower for national progress. Such needs of families have prodded the national governments to expand the network of health measures for families in the communities. Families thereby can face the new challenges, consequences of changes in the societal structure, family life patterns, and the effects of rapid urbanization and industrialization, drawing upon the services provided by the social workers who have been incorporated into the medical team.

3. *Nutrition.* The objective of good nutrition is to benefit all individuals and families for a healthy, happy, and productive life so that the longevity of human beings is fully and substantially utilized. If this objective can be realized the families would be positively contributing to the development of the country. The problem of malnutrition, which is quite acute in the Asian countries, makes the family lethargic, creates inertia, and hampers the attainment of developmental goals. Malnutrition caused by poverty brings along with it poor health, illiteracy, unhealthy environment, vice, and criminal tendencies, any one of which is sufficient to limit families' capacities for achieving a productive and satsifying life. Nutrition itself af-

fects one's ability to be productive to the family and to society as well.

If the families of a community can develop proper food habits and are able to determine proper and desirable attitudes in regard to dietary values, methods of cooking and eating habits, the life spans of the familes are expected to be lengthened. As a result, the families at the community level may participate more constructively in its development.

4. *Education and literacy.* In the field of education and literacy, especially in the movement to eradicate illiteracy at the community level or to initiate mass education, the family can play a positive role. Education in the family starts with the birth of a child. It is the family which rears the children from the beginning with expanding "we" attitudes. The "we" attitude, belonging first to the family and gradually shifting to the community, creates an incentive in the family to be productive and concerned about the community welfare. This positive attitude leads to a fuller and a more enjoyable community life. Within this educational process families as teams bring natural flow and direction.

The socialization process within the family is part of the total educational process which connotes the process of preparation for life, just as a child growing up undergoes a change of roles when he attains adulthood in the family. Family education plays a key role among the children and youth of the family, and in the long run determines the way of life in the society.

Once the total educational process in a community system can incorporate the feelings of community belongingness among its families' developmental programs for the sake of national progress, there are bound to be positive responses. When educational policy and planning become integral parts of the socioeconomic development planning, the families get incentives to participate in the processes.

5. *Women's emancipation.* Until the seventeenth century, women received very little formal education, and as a result the society looked down on womenfolk as an inferior segment of the population which was supposed to play the role of

homemakers primarily. By the nineteenth century, with the spread and expansion of female education, jobs for women outside the home, economic independence and new avenues for women in the labor market, division of labor at home, reduction of family size and of household units, and labor-saving devices at home, new horizons opened up for women. This relative emancipation of women and their liberation from traditional outlooks have brought a radical change in the status, role, and responsibilities of women. At present, housekeeping is not the exclusive job in a woman's life.

We are not going to probe the advantages or disadvantages of such changes and the dilemmas thereby created in the woman's life. We are rather accepting that such change is inevitable today or tomorrow for the sake of the socioeconomic development of a country. We may only say that the whole philosophy of the family life, pattern, and life style has undergone major changes, at the basis of which at present are, love, equal status, companionship, mutual understanding, cooperation, and shared authority.

If any country is to make progress it simply cannot afford to keep almost half of the population (womenfolk) idle, economically unemployed, and socially unaware of their contribution to the national progress. Yet this is the case in most of the Asian countries. While we talk of women's emancipation, women still live in a man-dominant society; man still decides for woman; and discrimination against women exists in many occupations, and in pay, allowances, privileges, and so on.

Families have to be motivated so that women are convinced of the necessity of increasing women's education, technical training, and social awareness in order to enable them to initiate community action in this direction. This would strengthen family solidarity on the basis of equal understanding.

6. *Supplementing the family income.* Men are even now considered to be the major breadwinners in any society, and women generally assume the responsibility of looking after the family expenditures. But with increased prices of essential goods everywhere, more and more women are coming forward to take up economically gainful jobs outside the home to supplement

the family income. In spite of its side effects on the family, this at least helps the family to attain a better life, and the joint pooling of resources helps the family budget to obtain the necessities of life.

Women in Bangladesh, whether they earn or not, value family solidarity as the key focus in their life. More than 80 percent of Bangladesh consists of rural areas, where women share the agricultural activities with the menfolk equally without any dispute. Whether in villages or in urban areas, women are trying to make money either as wage earners or by putting labor into activities which will ultimately increase the family income and thereby help raise the standard of living and bring material comforts and happiness to their families. A family's participation in monetarily gainful work not only helps to raise the economic level of the family but also helps the community to maintain a steady momentum in economic development. Even in Russia, where private enterprise is prohibited, an exception is made in the case of a family enterprise to augment the family income.

In addition to participation at the community level, there are various ways and forms through which families can participate in and contribute to, the development process itself. Some of these are:

1. *Social action programs.* Communities where conflicts are resolved through positive group processes are contributory elements in the developmental process itself. Problems do always exist; but the process of tackling these problems, the task of enhancing better community life or planning community programs and determining the areas of services and the problems for community action, needs effective family participation. To obtain the goal of social action, properly utilizing human and material resources, mobilizing youthful energies, and initiating proper communication media are some of the relevant areas where families can be fruitfully engaged in bringing the desired change through appropriate and timely social action on a community and national scale.

2. *Participation in national development goals and tasks.* So far in development, the popular emphasis has been on achieving

material prosperity, a higher ratio of the gross national product, or greater physical targets, and participation has been limited to receiving direct benefits and consuming services. Instead of that, if the families of a given society are informed and made conscious of national goals, their hopes and aspirations are well-projected in these goals, and scope is left for their participation in the decision-making or development phases, citizens will become convinced that social improvements can be achieved by them and through them.

3. *A point of entry to community involvement.* The developmental process entails successive stages of thought and action for bringing desirable changes in the society. Such results cannot always be measured in terms of quantity. The means or methods by which change takes place need to be considered. Tangible results are no doubt sought, but a more decisive test of the success should be in terms of whether a society fosters the popular democratic principles, values, social thinking, and creativity and can control the changing forces instead of merely adjusting to them. In the successive phases of development processes, the family as a group may be considered as a point of entry into the process of participation and involvement in the greater developmental task.

4. *Social reform.* Families have always been powerful units of society. Through initiation, motivation, and strong ties families may bring social reform and even formulate social policy and social enactment. This was evident when through social action, families, especially the womenfolk, urged the government of Pakistan to pass the Family Law Ordinance of 1961, according to which a husband was legally prohibited from having more than one wife at a time without some compelling reason; and this was subsequently adopted in Bangladesh. Thus we observe that if once families are convinced of the usefulness of a developmental program, they can participate and help to enlarge the concept so as to embrace a whole community and thus attain that objective.

This has been a theoretical analysis and conceptualization of the possibilities of the family's participation in development. Social workers in their long history of practice with individuals and families have established their familiarity with family problems and have recognized the family's potentials in the context of varying social situations. Now it is a new challenge for social workers to help increase the family's strength to cope not only with the individual's stress and strain in the present complexities of human life, but also with the demands of social development as a vital need for the task of national development. While carrying these responsibilities social workers have to face the hard realities of the day. It is now crucial for, and demanding on, them to realize the need to innovate, probe, and work out policies and programs with new dimensions and strategies in working with families, so that the families as social units can be effective participants in the developmental goals and tasks of a country.

# Development: a Case History

## MARTA CAMPOS TAUIL

SOCIAL WORKER, BRAZIL

THE RESEARCH reported herein was conducted in a Brazilian town, Porto Nacional, situated in the northern part of the state of Goiás, in the Amazon region. The municipality, on the east side of the Tocantins River, is 340 km. north of the state capital. The climate is tropical.

The economy of the state as well as of the municipal territory is based upon cattle raising and rice growing. The state's per capita income in 1971 was just over half that for the whole of Brazil.

The demographic density is 1.68 inhabitants per square kilometer, and the population growth rate is 4.37 percent for the state as compared to 2.9 percent for the country. The municipal area is 13,682 sq. km., with a population of 27,278 when this work started in 1968. Of these, 7,200 lived in the urban area, where currently the total population is approximately 12,000.

The town was founded 100 years ago as a cattle, commerce, and supply post for the region, benefiting from fluvial transportation. Its early development was derived from gold searching. After the construction of the Belém-Brasília highway (60 km. from the city on the other side of the river), the economy of the region was modified, and the town's leadership is moving to other centers closer to the highway. Nevertheless, due to local facilities such as schools, airport, a banking establishment, government agencies, justice administration, and health services, it maintains so far an important position in the region, mainly for the communities situated along the east side of the river.

The economy of the region is not dynamic enough to create

employment opportunities adequate for the population growth. Industrial activity is practically nonexistent. Therefore, stagnation is being prevented by external investment mainly from government sources.

This image—an old town with a past of more importance and development—is reflected in the population's conservatism and traditionalism and its lack of faith in future development.

All these factors are important in analyzing the work of improving health conditions that was attempted with emphasis on community participation.

*Work team.* The interdisciplinary team—doctors: one surgeon-sanitarist, one surgeon, one pediatrist, two internists, three social workers, one public health nurse, and one high school teacher—moved to the region from São Paulo in January, 1968. This team included the minimum necessary personnel willing to work in the conditions offered by the region. Pitifully, the team could not include other kinds of professionals, such as a nutritionist and an expert in health education, because they were not available.

Another important aspect is that although the team underwent modifications in its composition during the six years of the work this did not change the development of the work significantly. It is also necessary to note that the group met other professionals living in the town—an agronomist, a veterinarian, schoolteachers, and, specifically in the health sector, a sanitary doctor, a private doctor, and one dentist, as well as auxiliary personnel such as nurses, hospital laboratory technicians, and so on. All these people participated in the work.

*Health situation and work programming.* The group, with the exception of the high school teacher, was hired by the state health agency. The salaries for the whole group amounted to approximately $6,500 monthly, permitting all the personnel to live locally with no other source of income.

The state health agency was already active in the region, maintaining a sanitary post which was founded ten years ago. The recently built fifty-bed Unity Hospital had a good layout and a good surgical and obstetrical center. It started with 1.2

employees per bed. In addition, there was a small maternity and infancy center offering medical attention and an orientation to child and prenatal hygiene and one federal agency for the eradication of malaria.

In all the large region surrounding Porto Nacional there were only six other doctors in private practice, and two of them worked on a part-time basis. There was no public health nurse in the region.

The existence of some health resources in the town had two important consequences for our work. First, when the community was approached, to secure its participation, the population was already familiar with the usual procedures in the health field, notably those relative to preventive action. Unity Hospital, to which the team attached itself, was already well-known and accepted by the community, mainly by the poorer people.

Secondly, although it had been formulated unsystematically, there was already in existence a diagnosis of the region's health situation:

1. Caloric-proteic undernutrition in general, and particularly proteic (kwashiorker) in the child population in both urban and rural zones (This was the most serious problem. The infancy death rate was exceedingly high during the period referred to here.)
2. A high prevalence of intestinal protoparasitosis, reaching almost 100% among school children
3. Malaria, affecting 15 percent of the population
4. Trachoma, mainly among children
5. Pulmonary tuberculosis, with 104 new cases in 1970
6. Endemic integumentary leishmaniasis, foliaceous pemphigus, infectious hepatitis, Hansen's disease, tetanus, measles.

Based on this situation the following priorities were given to the various programs:

1. Child medical-sanitary care
2. Pregnancy medical-sanitary care
3. Control of contagious diseases
4. Basic environmental sanitation
5. Medical-sanitary adult care.

From the point of view of the methodology of community development work we can say that the group did not develop a survey of local health conditions that allowed the population to gain insight into their needs, but did not impose its views. The surveys that were carried out every three years by the sanitation service and the registration that had been done over the past ten years by the local health service allowed the action to be based in real community problems.

It is important to mention that the group tried to develop this project not only through direct action but also through stimulation of the active participation of the people. Coordination of health resources, the search for new sources, and cooperation for social and economic development were considered important factors in the improvement of health conditions.

COMMUNITY PARTICIPATION

Community participation was very effective in the following activities:

1. Verminosis eradication program
2. Municipal health committees
3. Medical-sanitary surveys
4. Nutritional recovery and educational center
5. Housing improvement program.

*Verminosis eradication program.* Two phases can be recognized here. In the initial one, involvement of the whole population was tried. A second phase was carried out under the supervision of the Basic Sanitation Service with the participation of those benefited by the program. The verminosis program was chosen because it was deeply felt by the population to be an important health problem.

It was also useful for the group to get a better understanding of the community and conversely. The town was divided into sections. Community groups were organized to visit the homes to evaluate the problem of inadequate disposal of sewerage and to make the campaign known and stimulate dwellers to find a solution.

Local leaders met several times. Schools were mobilized for the presentation of puppet shows, and educational posters contests were organized in connection with the problem being tackled.

The work took on the characteristics of a campaign with a real impact on the community, of which a considerable part was mobilized. The majority of the social strata participated. Actual results were relatively good; during the time the campaign was undertaken, from May to October, 253 cesspools were built as compared to five a month previously.

It is important to mention that no financial help was available for the population in this work. The population only received technical information, and this emphasizes the good results obtained, considering the low social-economic level of the people.

Later, an attempt was made to solve the financial problem. A kind of partnership was organized among dwellers for the purchase of concrete covers, the most expensive item in the cesspool construction. This type of association only worked for a few months and was discontinued. After that, resources were gathered from outside the community to finance the concrete cover for those willing to build a cesspool. This cover is only delivered when part of the work is done and the necessary materials to finish the construction are available.

The permanent work of the Basic Sanitation Service has been in action in this way since the end of 1971. In 1973 it was extended to rural areas. In the urban area the program acts in the poorest sections of the town. Sanitary education, technical information, and people motivation are carried out by systematic home interviews. There are complementary meetings with groups of people, and audio-visual aids are utilized.

In the rural area, motivation was attained through meetings organized by sanitation workers. They gave technical instruction on building the concrete covers. These were built in a collective work project to avoid breakage due to transportation hazards.

Initially, the project anticipated the donation of a large quantity of construction materials. Due to the good reception of the program, the number of cesspools that were built was almost triple that expected.

*Municipal health committees.* Due to the lack of medical assistance in the region, the team set up a monthly medical service in two towns where there were no doctors. Local health committees were organized in these towns to improve the results of the medical trips. These committees selected the most acute cases to be examined by the doctors. They also arranged for lectures on health and sanitation problems during the visiting days. Sanitary surveys were also carried out by these committees as well as supervised preventive health action. The financial resources came from one part of the population. Notwithstanding the fact that the work was discontinued because in one of the towns the air line interrupted its flights and in the other a doctor established a private practice, this kind of relationship between technicians and community proved to be highly productive.

At Porto Nacional a health committee was organized, but its characteristics differed from the ones described above. Here it was a voluntary work group acting as an auxiliary group in close connection with the local health services and with the municipal administration.

The committee started from an actual problem: the lack of hospital beds. This hospital was the only one in a 700-km. radius, causing many people to stay in town under very poor conditions. Initially, the committee aimed to build a lodging place for convalescents. Gradually, the committee realized that other problems had to be solved, like garbage collection and a water supply system, both nonexistent in the town. Also, better sanitary standards for housing, odontological assistance, rat eradication, control of pig raising, better conditions in the trade of food stuffs, and so on, were needed.

The practical results of the committee's action were: reform of the market place, with routine supervision; a municipal law enforcing periodical medical examinations of people engaged in food selling; and the organization of garbage collection by the municipal administration.

It is important to note, too, that the work of this committee had indirect beneficial results in educational, agricultural, and cattle-raising activities. Even among the members of the committee a better sense of social responsibility developed in connection with the general problems of the community. This was also noted among people who did not take part in the committee.

The main obstacles to the committee action were:

1. The difficulty in accomplishing its first aim (lodging convalescents) because of the lack of financial resources
2. The difficulty in transmitting to the community some of their objectives and standards
3. The difficulty in replacing some influential people who left town.

The permanent results obtained by the committee demonstrate the importance of community development work being considered as a part of any action in the field of public health.

*Medical-sanitary surveys.* The medical-sanitary surveys, including a specific one in connection with child nutrition, were carried out with the participation of high school students to collect field data. The surveys were conducted in 1968, 1970, and 1971. Families were interviewed by high school girls who were trained for this kind of work. It is important to note that these surveyors became very conscious of the health problems in the whole community.

*Educational and nutritional recovery center.* In this center the main objective is education in the field of malnutrition. The mother's participation is therefore absolutely necessary during the period in which the child goes to the center. While the children are at the center, daily in the morning and staying until afternoon, they receive balanced meals, medical care, and psychological stimulation through games. Mothers help in the housekeeping once a week and at the same time become familiar with hygiene and child nutrition. They also attend educational meetings every fortnight. (As a policy and to guarantee the continuity of the nutrition policy after he leaves the center, a child is only admitted when his mother can participate in the work in the center.)

The center is partially (about 25 percent) supported by members of the community of higher economic level.

*Housing improvement program.* Housing and sanitary conditions of the poorest people are obviously highly unfavorable. Moreover, the people are worried about not having adequate shelter, especially in the rainy season. Having this in mind, and since there was a section of the town where a great number of lots owners had built very low-level dwellings, a program of housing improvement was designed and is being carried out. It consists of supplying these owners with construction materials which are used by groups of residents who work together in rotation.

The criterion for forming a group involves ownership of the lot, the need for help, and availability of manpower. The group meets weekly to evaluate and plan their work, which is done on weekends. During these meetings the next improvement work is decided according to criteria discussed by the group. Whenever possible, local materials are used, like wood and sand from the neighborhoods, in order to cut costs. Diocese and municipal administration cooperated by providing transportation of these materials.

In spite of the slow rate of the work it has been constant and efficient. No group member has given up after his own needs were satisfied. The sanitation workers cooperated in preparing layouts and planning the houses in such a way as to get the best conditions of air circulation and sun (there is no architect in the town).

## OBTAINING, IMPLEMENTING, AND COORDINATING HEALTH RESOURCES

In this region, the nonexistence of traditional health agencies and the magnitude of the problems make obvious the necessity to integrate the several services. The coordination of existing health agencies, as well as trying to attract new ones, was a team purpose. Therefore, during this six-year period, several social security agencies, a federal welfare agency, a federal manpower training agency, rural credit entities, and the Federal University of Goiás were mobilized. The experience made it possible to prevent duplication of effort in all fields and to use resources that had been underutilized.

As a general conclusion it can be said how important is the action of a group determined to improve the general conditions of a community, making it conscious of its needs and learning ways and means to solve its own problems.

# Participation and Development in Different Political Settings

## PART I

## BERNARD J. COUGHLIN

SAINT LOUIS UNIVERSITY, UNITED STATES

I HOLD that social development is a form of social change, and as such implies a shift in societal resources. Therefore, it is resisted by those who stand most to lose and encouraged by those who stand most to gain by a relocation of resources. It is a form of planned change of some major social institutions, not change in individual, small-group, or organizational behaviors, although these also are affected by social development.[1]

Moreover, I propose that an adequate conception of development encompasses not only economic change, but social, cultural, and political change as well. Although economic growth is perhaps most frequently the immediate target of development, economic factors should not be considered and planned apart from the total societal fabric nor from the total person who ultimately is the object of development. To conceive of development in economic terms alone tends to breed only greed. Marshall poignantly laments this as the end result of too many development programs. "The rich are covetous, desiring more than they need; and their covetousness is rapidly spreading to poorer people. A greedy world can only be a divided world, ethically sordid, heading toward barbarism." [2]

It is critical, therefore, to distinguish ends and means. The

[1] Denis Goulet, *The Cruel Choice: a New Concept in the Theory of Development* (New York: Atheneum, 1971), p. 104.

[2] Alfred Marshall, "Principles of Economics," in George W. Wilson, ed., *Classics of Economic Theory* (Bloomington, Ind.: Indiana University Press, 1964), p. 632.

end is human development and the good society, as understood by the society in question; every other goal, with reference to these, is a means. Development programs have stressed such things as roads and highways, water supplies, agricultural production, and industrial growth; but unless these are seen as means to the end of personal and societal development as defined within the culture of the people themselves, the attainment of these intermediate goals may not be development at all, in the ultimate analysis, but nondevelopment. Defining development thus thrusts us into a discussion of the function of values. What is the good life? An abundance of automobiles and television sets? Power plants, refrigerators, and air conditioners? Full employment and a high gross national product (GNP)? Social development cannot avoid making fundamental value judgments about the goals of social life.

A second observation is that economic advance, technological progress, modernization, and social development are not interchangeable concepts, even though they may be closely related. Technology offers the tools for modernization and economic growth. It is measured in quantitative units, such as the rate and yield of data from a computer or of automobiles from an assembly line; economic development is similarly measured by the GNP in terms of some monetary unit. Social development is not subject to quantitative measures since it is a function, at least in part, of the values and, so, of the thoughts, beliefs, styles, and tastes of the society. Observe the rich and enduring cultural developments of countries like China, India, and Egypt alongside their present economic and technological underdevelopment. A society may be technologically and economically far advanced but culturally backward; or it may be culturally developed but economically and technologically underdeveloped.

A third observation is that democracy and socialism are not mutually exclusive. Indeed, in many places they have become so intertwined as to be fused in the writings of some theorists, and in the policies of some nations. Democracies are daily incorporating into their programs and practices much of the theory and policies of socialism. England, along with Canada

and many other nations, adopted many of the central principles and practices of socialism without at the same time relin-
quishing a basically democratic political system. Israel, the
Scandinavian countries, India, Great Britain, and many other
nations are socialist countries that are also functioning democracies. They see no inconsistency in this. The same is true in
the United States. It is true that in the 1930s alarmists shouted
"Socialists!" to the likes of Franklin D. Roosevelt and Harry
Hopkins; and in the 1972 elections there were those who
shouted "Communist!" to Senator George McGovern. History
in America shows that today's so-called "socialists" and "com-
munists" are tomorrow's conservatives. The conservatives of
the 1930s have long supported social insurance, minimum
wage laws, the progressive income tax, public housing, unemployment insurance, and workmen's compensation—all from
the pages of socialism—without batting an eye, and without
thinking they have abandoned democratic government. No
one of Robert Theobald's followers, who advocates the
guaranteed minimum income, would see this spin-off from socialism as incompatible with democratic government. They see
it as democracy at its best. I leave it to my colleagues to discuss
the opposite phenomenon; that is, the extent to which socialist
nations are incorporating into their political and economic systems, principles and practices that historically and ideologi-
cally are democratic.

From my point of view, a fourth equally important observation is that capitalism and democracy are not synonymous.
Capitalism refers to an economic system based on the market
concepts of supply and demand and stresses the importance
of private property, free enterprise, and the profit motive. Its
herald was Adam Smith, whose classical economic theory
championed a political theory of laissez faire on the ground
that the market mechanism, if allowed to work, would result
in a just society. Democracy is a political system of government
of the people and by the people, generally through some form
of elected representation. In the nineteenth century both economic capitalism and political democracy held that the government governs best which governs least. Thus, a laissez-faire

philosophy of government that was to the liking of political revolutionaries and postrevolutionaries because they feared tyrannical governments was also to the liking of capitalists because it allowed them to accumulate economic profits.

Therefore, in the late nineteenth and early twentieth centuries, democracy and capitalism, though distinct, developed together. The shibboleths of personal freedom and private property, free enterprise and laissez faire were powerful weapons that the wealthy wielded to their personal gain. The nineteenth-century history of Western democracies is an account of the exploits of wealthy industrialists and entrepreneurs, so-called "capitalists," and how they bent the political system to their economic advantage. This unholy alliance bred social and economic injustices to which widespread reaction began early in the twentieth century and has gained momentum ever since. In recent history Western democracies have taken a steady walk away from laissez-faireism toward democratic socialism. Western democracies have shown a remarkable flexibility in adjusting to outside influences and to demands of the economic system. Whether they will continue to do so, is for the future. The hard questions for the democracies are not basically economic but political, social, and moral. As Heilbroner wrote:

The questions which face us in the future are not the purely economic ones of whether corporations will naturally grow larger or whether we will suffer from unemployment, but the moral ones of whether we will *let* corporations grow unchecked and whether we will *allow* unemployment to develop unchecked.[3]

I have made these observations as expressing my view of the nature of social development in itself, wherever practiced, without specific reference to the United States or any particular country. There are probably certain features of development that are determined by the history, structure, and values of a nation. And so I shall now limit my remarks to the United States and propose three features of development in that country.

[3] Robert L. Heilbroner, *The Worldly Philosophers: the Lives, Times and Ideas of the Great Economic Thinkers* (rev. ed.; New York: Simon and Schuster, 1961), p. 283.

First, development and participation in the United States grow out of and reflect a democratic tradition. There are many threads in that tradition. Its leaders are selected in free elections. Public authority is dispersed and exercised by three major branches of government: legislative, executive, and judicial. Each branch is subject to a written constitution that embodies the society's basic political values and guarantees to each citizen certain fundamental rights. The Constitution is the law of the land to which all citizens, officials of government included, are subject. It is a government of laws, not men, and those entrusted by the people with the powers of the state may not with impunity violate the law or the rights of citizens. Among those rights are, for example, freedom of religious worship, freedom of speech, including a free press, freedom to assemble, to organize, and to express one's views on public issues.

The separation of the three powers of government operates as a system of checks and balances of one branch against another, as a guarantee against tyranny in government. The legislative branch makes laws but neither executes them nor judges their constitutionality; the executive branch has no power to make laws, and its actions are subject to judicial review; the judiciary has power neither to legislate nor to execute laws, and its judicial interpretations are subject, in turn, to the Constitution. Government is thus responsive to the popular will. Public opinion, therefore, is a mighty force, and as a result interest groups play major roles in the United States. Social development, accordingly, moves on the wheels of interest groups that vigorously voice their views and promote their causes, seeking to direct public opinion and determine the course of public policy.

Secondly, the United States places a high value on citizen participation in decision-making. Life in the United States has changed considerably since those early days in New England when the entire local community met in the town hall to decide issues like the construction of roads and schools, the hiring of teachers, the salaries of local police, and the method of taxation to finance all these things. This was the "town hall democracy" that attracted the attention of that famed nine-teenth-century French social analyst who compared participation in America to that in classical Athens, and then added: "At the present day the principle of the sovereignity of the people has acquired in the United States all the practical development that the imagination can conceive." [4]

Most of those towns are now sprawling cities, and that kind of direct participation in government is no longer possible. But the principle of what we colloquially call "grass-roots" participation in government is deep in our culture and is popularly dramatized by the real power and autonomy exercised by the thousands of city and county and state governments throughout the land. Today it is recognized and established, even more than in those early days, that every citizen has the right to participate in this kind of political activity and decision-making. It is a citizenship right, and so not based on social or economic class. It is a political right, legally guaranteed, and jealously safeguarded by liberal and conservative alike.

I am not saying, however, that all participate equally. For the exercise of political rights hinges on other things, such as one's social and economic power. There are socioeconomic classes, and those on top seek to remain on top. Thus, there is unequal participation by groups whom the law equally protects. Democracy, perhaps like all politics, is a kind of game that groups play. The game has its rules, and people are expected to abide by them. The stakes are more power, privilege, and prestige. People with similar interests unite to strengthen their hand and expand their power. It is the game of interest-group politics in which the contestants compete for the public confidence, but on an unequal footing.

Many issues, therefore, pit the powerful and the privileged against the underprivileged. In the unequal contests, however, the underprivileged are not without their sources of power, as history shows. The American landscape is spangled with social movements of the disadvantaged struggling for their place in

[4] Alexis de Tocqueville, *Democracy in America* (New York: Vintage Books, 1957), I, 59.

the sun. At the turn of the century, the Populists challenged the business and industrial tycoons and legislation that favored business interests, and finally won the day. In the 1930s, with encouragement from a "New Deal" government,[5] laboring men organized and swept the land. To ignore the labor vote today is political disaster. In the 1950s and 1960s many interest groups coalesced to form the civil rights movement. As a result of that, a series of steady and significant changes is occurring in social and political life. In this "grass-roots people" movement, the poor marched alongside the rich, children alongside adults, housewives alongside university professors, whites alongside blacks, and vast changes have been made. Although racial equality has been the most hotly fought, there are other significant civil rights issues currently on the fire—the rights of children, the rights of women, the rights of offenders, the rights of the mentally ill, and the rights of the poor.

Citizen participation is perhaps nowhere more characteristically illustrated than in the Community Action Program (CAP), one of the weapons of the war on poverty aimed at increasing the power of the poor. CAP held that there should be "maximum feasible participation" of the poor in selecting, designing, and staffing programs to eliminate poverty in the United States. This piece of federal legislation required the participation of the poor at local levels of government where decisions regarding poverty programs were made. The economic and political power groups in the community should not decide programs for the poor without the poor themselves having a voice in those decisions, and that voice should be as loud as is feasible—this is the thrust of CAP. In the opinion of some, maximum feasible participation is unquestionably an important principle of development in America, and its enunciation in federal legislation has had, in my judgment, considerable influence in American life.

A third characteristic stands in opposition to, but not in con-

---

[5] This campaign slogan is illustrative of the political game played in democracies. Under Franklin D. Roosevelt, the Democratic Party promised to deal a better hand to the underprivileged so they could more effectively compete.

tradiction with, the second. Notwithstanding the ideal of maximum feasible participation, the reality of decision-making in the United States allows a wide road for elitism. Students of decision-making line up behind two theories of the distribution of power in American society. Pluralism holds that power is widely distributed and decision-making broadly shared, many interest groups participating, with the outcome in any given public issue depending on the issue in question. Elitism holds that power is in the hands of a few, regardless of the issue in question, and that the decision-makers form groups that interlock into what Mills called "the power elite." Pluralism, of course, more comfortably fits the American democratic ideal; we like to think that decision-making power is broadly shared. But Schattschneider's gibe is probably true: "The flaw in the pluralist heaven is that the heavenly chorus sings with a strong upper-class accent." [6] The reality of decision-making in American society is probably somewhere midway between the elitist's and the pluralist's positions.

That there is a gap between the ideal and the real is no surprise. Democracies must continually uphold basic democratic values such as broad citizen participation in order to keep alive the citizen ideal toward which it educates. When the citizen ideal is lost, social goals cease, and the society, void of purpose and definition, degenerates. That ideal in this case is conditioned and modified by the social phenomenon that widespread active participation in development is rarely, if ever, achieved over any extended period. On the contrary, insistence on mass participation can be dysfunctional. Studies of development programs reveal that in many instances failure results from uncompromising insistence on mass populace support. Goulet reminds us:

Communitarian movements have repeatedly foundered because they have not come to terms with the real motives which impel men to sacrifice. Only the naïve will suppose that large numbers of men can long sustain a commitment to such values as solidarity, community, austerity, and the common good." [7]

[6] E. E. Schattschneider, *The Semisovereign People: a Realist's View of Democracy in America* (New York: Holt, Rinehart, and Winston, 1960), p. 35.

[7] Goulet, *op. cit.,* p. 145.

Where leaders have assumed that elitism is inherently bad and insisted on mass participation, development has tended to break down and a functional elitism to develop spontaneously. What seems important is not so much the number of participants as the quality and purpose of the participation. To impose an elite from the outside is not only counterproductive to the goals of development, but ethically questionable. But to foster the identification and rise of "natural" elites from within the populace at large is altogether consistent with the goals and methods of development.

Observers throughout the world have testified that most groups contain in their midst individuals with the capacity to grasp the problems affecting their community and to lead their peers in group response to that challenge. These "natural" elites are often distinct from formal, hierarchial leaders—chieftains or their sons, elders, or members of respected classes. "Natural" elites are individuals who can perceive, with an understanding of the forces at work and a sense of synthesis, the deep *meaning* of changes proposed.[8]

A democratic model of development employs strategies for change that suitably foster the emergence of such leaders.

Development in the United States, as we have seen, is effected through interest groups and the roles they play in decision-making; second, the political system fosters broad participation in the development process. But because in the United States the development outcome is ultimately determined by the power that interest groups can muster for their cause, the participants are not always equal. Development, therefore, frequently finds the powerless struggling to take from the powerful some of their privilege and prestige. And strong ideological and legal support for political equality is the major leverage that the underprivileged use in seeking a reallocation and redistribution of resources. It is, of course, a perennial struggle that all societies face regardless of their political patrimony.

[8] *Ibid.*, p. 149.

PART II

# MIECZYSLAW KARCZEWSKI

DIRECTOR, MINISTRY OF HEALTH AND SOCIAL WELFARE,
POLAND

POLAND'S SOCIAL welfare system is both very simple and highly complicated in its conception. Poland's economic, social, and political system differs considerably from those of the majority of countries represented at this conference.

Those taking part in this conference come from different countries in different parts of the world, from developed countries as well as from the developing nations. There is a great diversity of systems represented here. As a result, where social welfare is concerned, the experience of the participants is, by the nature of things, heterogeneous, varied, and in some cases even fundamentally different. This is so because experience arises out of, and is a function of, the conditions within which social welfare activities are conducted within each country. Experience is derived from institutional principles as well as from economic, political, and social conditions. The possibilities, the forms, and the methods of social work also result from these factors.

As the representative of a socialist country, a country with a planned economy, I feel it important—not so much in order to facilitate understanding of our social welfare system in its entirety, but to give some idea of our conception and organization of social welfare—to present a general outline of the structure of our administrative and planning system.

This planning system is the element which most differentiates our social welfare system. A good many people have already visited our country, and a good many more will be doing so in 1974 as Poland celebrates the thirtieth anniversary of its liberation at the end of the Second World War and of its independence. These people will have an opportunity to observe the results of our work and the success of our socialist system; at the same time, they will have an opportunity to familiarize themselves with, among other things, our planning system.

First and foremost, planning embraces every sector of the national economy. Decisions concerning the distribution of national income between individual and collective consumption and capital accumulation are centralized.

In Poland, the organization of social welfare work is the task of the State, which plays a vital role in this field, with the collaboration of trade unions and benevolent organizations. At the central level, organization and administration are rather similar. At all levels, we have divisions of the Ministry of Health and Social Welfare with social welfare sections.

The Polish social welfare system may be defined as a system which attempts to analyze fully existing social needs and which is characterized by a constant increase in efforts aimed at the maximal satisfaction of these needs by means of the most rational utilization of available resources possible in a given period.

In my country, the type of social aid essentially consisting of charitable activities funded by philanthropic individuals or associations and various other bodies is now but a memory of a bygone age. Thanks to the progress brought about by the construction of socialism, the basic tasks and objectives of social welfare work have evolved and continue to change in line with the radical transformation of the social base, of the kind and quality of needs and of forms of activity. Nowadays, the chief clients of social welfare are the aged, the retired, and, in particular, old people rendered incapable of living alone without outside help because of old age and loneliness. This development is reflected in the constitution of the People's Republic of Poland. Perhaps it is worth pointing out here that although Poland was the youngest nation in Europe, demographically speaking, immediately after the last war, she has tended to become a demographically aged population since 1968.

Four social welfare systems are currently employed in carrying out the tasks under discussion:

1. Help in the form of services

This is the most widespread and fully developed system.

2. Help in the form of cash benefits

Over 80 percent of the population is insured, and health insurance covers the entire population.

3. Help in the form of benefits in kind

This system is due to disappear, with the exception of the low-cost meals service.

4. The network of welfare homes.

Of the highest quality, many of our institutions are among the most modern geriatric centers in existence.

The social welfare planning system in Poland is absolutely inseparable from social planning in general and thus, in turn, cannot be dissociated from the planning of the country's overall development. By their very nature, national plans serve society's progress and development in the sense that they tend, in socialist countries such as my own, toward the satisfaction of the material and cultural needs of the population. Plans determine priority objectives by stages and as a function of a given period of time, having regard for prevailing conditions. The explicit premise of this planning system is that national income growth must be optimalized and that individual and collective needs should be satisfied. Now that we have resolved the education problem (free education from primary school to university), the health problem (all treatment, including hospitalization, is free), and now that we can look back on thirty years of full employment, we are at last in a position to devote our full energies to the problems of social welfare. Broadly speaking, the planning process covers:

1. The assessment of needs
2. The determination of objectives to be achieved in the year or period under consideration
3. The definition of priority policy areas
4. The distribution of manpower and resources
5. Evaluation of the plan's impact.

In Poland, social planning includes both manpower and resources of the State as well as those of trade unions and social organizations. Thus, they all participate in the elaboration, discussion, and choice of orientation. At the bottom lies obviously the analysis of needs, an analysis which is undertaken by social workers each year in my country. This analysis serves to establish assessments of local needs and resources. The assessment of needs should balance with available resources to satisfy the requirements.

Financing of the social program is provided for in the State budget. It is included in that section of national income set aside for collective consumption, along with the allocation of funds to trade unions and social organizations.

In view of the fact that even when funds from all these resources—State, trade unions, and social organizations—are brought together they are still insufficient to satisfy all the needs, it is clearly essential to determine priority objectives when drawing up local and national plans. As a result of this, the social administration's activities are fully in harmony with those of the trade unions and social organizations (benevolent). Tasks, and the means whereby they are to be carried out, are identified on the basis of the foregoing assessment of needs.

Consequently, the choice of means and the allocation of resources for the attainment of objectives thus strictly defined can only take place upon completion of the planning stage. In what follows, therefore, I shall assume we have assessed our needs, that we have quantified them, that we know their pattern of national distribution, their degree of urgency, and so forth.

At this stage, the most important step is to define priority tasks. For this, we need to know what the appropriate criteria are going to be. But selecting these is neither easy nor simple. So many factors have to be taken into account that it seems impossible even to enumerate them all.

As I mentioned, Poland has for some years belonged in the category of demographically aged countries. The aged section of the community is growing much faster than the population as a whole. It is precisely the needs of this group that are going to determine the tasks and the extent of social welfare.

Of all the many problems with which social welfare is concerned, those concerning the aged were recognized some years ago as taking priority over all the others, and all activities in social welfare are subordinated to this group of problems.

The next step is to determine priorities. We must now decide which groups of aged people need help ahead of which others, which forms of assistance ought to be favored, which amenities and installations are to be developed straight away, and which objectives can be put off until tomorrow or relegated to an even more distant future. So, before programming the means required for the fulfillment of the tasks and objectives set, we must draw up a hierarchy of needs.

Thanks to the assiduity of its social workers, Poland possesses relatively complete and up-to-date information concerning needs. For social welfare purposes, the country has been divided into more than 48,000 social constituencies manned by over 66,000 social workers, each having a thorough knowledge of his area of competence.

Once needs have been assessed and ranked in order of importance, discussion at all levels, starting with individual localities, now turns to the question of the amount and quality of means required for the satisfaction of these needs and to possible sources of financing. Representatives of the administration—representatives of the People's Councils, of social organizations concerned, and of the trade unions—also take part in these discussions. Social welfare activities are strictly coordinated in conformity with directives from the Ministry of Health and Social Welfare, and each of the organizations involved specializes in a specific field and in specific forms of assistance. Thus, for example, the Polish Red Cross organizes assistance to sick people in their own homes; the Polish Committee for Social Welfare organizes domestic help for invalids living alone, and so on.

In order to carry out these and any other tasks, each organization receives a State subsidy which is intended to make up the difference between its own resources and the cost of the services or benefits it dispenses. The directives issued in this respect by the Ministry of Health and Social Welfare are derived from a law authorizing the minister to coordinate all social welfare undertakings and activities.

Each year, the planning process deals with the year ahead, while each annual plan constitutes a step forward in the implementation of longer term (generally five-year) plans elaborated beforehand. The detailed list of identified needs of available resources, and of allocations of supplementary means required, along with supporting arguments and analytical documentation, is then submitted to the social welfare department at the next level, the district level. After adding up these requirements and analyzing stated needs and resources at the district level, and after consultation with the district plan commission, the district passes the dossier on the services to the *voivodie,* where the operation is then repeated at the corresponding level. All the *voivodies* then submit the fruit of their labors to the social welfare and planning departments of the Ministry of Health and Social Welfare.

At this stage, the dossiers are subjected to thoroughgoing analysis from the viewpoint of their conformity to State directives and social policy orientations. After correction (where needed), the over-all plan is then laid before the National Planning Commission, where the needs thus determined are matched against available resources. Once the means the State can afford to make available have been determined, we move on to a detailed analysis of additional possibilities and resources outside the budget, enabling us to come as close as possible to the full accomplishment of the tasks arising out of recognized needs.

Where planning is concerned, the simplest problem, relatively speaking, is that of social welfare institutions, the vast majority of which form part of the State apparatus. The totality of their expenditure is therefore covered by the State. In so far as the staffing and expenditures of these institutions are covered by a series of norms easily expressed in monetary form, the determination of means is a purely technical operation.

With respect to social institutions not dependent upon the

State, the problem is slightly different. Each institution receives a State subsidy intended to cover all expenditures exceeding its own income: retirement pensions, family allowances, and so on.

Thus, in so far as there are social institutions and in so far as we are able to organize and manage these institutions, they all have sufficient means—thanks to State subsidies—to cover all planned expenditures. Here, the vital question is not so much one of financial resources as one of qualified personnel; as many countries know, this resource is in very short supply.

The contribution of the press, radio, and television (of which we make heavy use in Poland) in this field is relatively economical and entails no extra cost on the part of social welfare bodies. This expenditure is generally covered by the publishing houses and other mass media.

The last phase of planning with which I am chiefly concerned here has to do with the analytical assessment of methods employed in programming means, of the volume of means thus determined and allocated to different objectives, and, finally, of the way in which they have been employed and the results obtained. If carried out correctly, this analysis and assessment should lead to an improvement in the programming of means for the following year, ensuring a more rational deployment of resources, avoiding the repetition of mistakes (if any), and thus leading to more satisfactory results. In fact, the success of all subsequent activities in this field depends upon this first, vitally important stage in the planning process.

The system I have described is the system currently prevailing in Poland, But I am sufficiently familiar with social welfare activities in other socialist countries to say that there are a great many similarities, especially where planning is concerned, and that the planning process in these countries is equally methodical.

If I have dwelled almost exclusively on our social welfare planning system, this is because, in my view, it is most characteristic. The rest of social welfare work is very similar, and sometimes even identical, from one country to another throughout Europe.

PART III

# LUNDONDO MUMEKA

ASSISTANT SECRETARY, MINISTRY OF RURAL
DEVELOPMENT, ZAMBIA

ALL OVER the world there is considerable concern at the rate of development deterioration. The World Food Conference to be held in Rome, in November, 1974, is symptomatic of this concern. Both national and international communities and institutions have exhibited this concern through their desire and willingness to explore and adopt new methods for effecting programs which will not only induce development, but will induce the kind of development which will become self-servicing.

DIFFERENT POLITICAL SETTINGS

Understanding the theme of my subject requires an appreciation of the origin of economic systems of the developing world, and that appreciation requires a mental journey back to the days of the colonial era. The colonial economic system was characterized by capitalism. Under capitalism, mobilization of labor as a factor of production was engineered through the market-steering system. Under this system the working relationships were purely secondary and contractual. In the capitalist societies of this model the state mobilized people through party systems only as voters. The people's economic, social, and spiritual needs were left to the devices of capitalists and friendly societies. In the colonial world capitalism was introduced by the colonizers, but this was capitalism with a difference. The state became the mobilizing agent for economic growth. It was the colonial administration which mobilized the indigenous people to work for white settlers who took up land in the fertile highlands for commercial farming. As a steering system for economic growth, the British Government spent vast sums of money in order to induce Englishmen to settle in Kenya. The picture was similar in Zambia and Malawi. In Kenya, the colonial government exercised wide compulsions to coerce Africans to work for white employers. These harsh laws and economic policies turned Kenya, Malawi, and Zambia into settler countries.

It is interesting to state in passing that colonial laws as facilitative laws differed from one colony to another. While the British Government spent several million pounds to attract white settlers to Kenya, Malawi, and Zambia, colonial laws turned the Gold Coast (now Ghana) into nonsettler territory. Practically the only whites were officials. In the Gold Coast, by and large, whites were forbidden to purchase land. Unlike Kenya, there was no forced labor. In these and many other ways the governments and economic policies of Kenya and the Gold Coast were as different as night from day. In the light of these circumstances the highlands of Kenya were par excellence the locus of British colonialism in sub-Saharan Africa. During the long night of colonial control political and economic participation by Africans was effectively nil.

Malawi, Rhodesia, and Zambia were no exception to this colonial device. The state systematically intervened in the economy with a series of overt measures to organize it in a way conformable to settler interests. First it was land, then labor, then the corporate organization of the economy. The progression was toward ever-increasing direct intervention.

As a result, Africans living in what were legally known as Native Reserves reached employment sectors on the highland farms and in the copper and gold mines not by market steering but by state intervention resting ultimately on coercion. While the state positively intervened in the economy of the East and Central African colonies, it took no social, economic, or spiritual responsibility for African workers. Instead, the state encouraged separate development for different races and ethnic groups. In the colonial economy the African worker was simply a cog in the wheel whose motivation to work sprang from fear; therefore he could not be called a participant. European managers and African workers did not act as social units. It can be said that the colonial government encouraged the use of naked power which did not take into account the basic human needs of African workers. These, in turn, became alienated from the economic system.

The third model may facilitate our appreciation of the reasons that the developing world is moving away from a pure capitalistic economy in the search for the kind of economy and development which will provide the necessary stimuli for the workers' participation. This model is the socialist model. Since 1945 the central political issue has been to what extent industry and trade, or at least their larger units, should remain in the hands of private enterprise or should be taken over by organs of the state. It was in Britain that the Labor Party made a bald experiment thought to involve a significant process of socialization. The *modus operandi* in the socialist economy is to vest the undertaking in a corporation specially created by statute, subject to some measure of state control by the relevant Minister, but not itself being a branch or department of government. Perhaps it is pertinent at this juncture to mention that this device of establishing an organization which is both public authority and an independent corporation is not a unique English discovery; on the contrary, it has been adopted for similar ends by countries as divergent in their ideas as the Soviet Union and the United States, and it is being used extensively in developing countries.

Socialism as an economic system seems to be favored by independent states of developing countries because it enables the state to act on behalf of the masses for the creation of political and economic conditions which recognize the need to develop the whole man and whole woman and to assist him or her to develop his or her mental faculties to the full so as to make it possible to participate actively in the political, social, and economic development of the country. In this model the state intervenes in order to correct development disequilibrium.

It is for this reason, *inter alia,* that political systems in the developing world have become means to such important ends as mobilization of the masses for self-help projects, eradication of illiteracy, conservation of natural resources, construction works, and establishment of development-oriented institutions which have become positive vehicles for the masses' meaningful participation in the social and economic development of their communities. Through this system of political and social engineering a good number of governments in the developing world have managed to establish a positive alliance between people and technologies. Through these institutional infrastructures people identify themselves with development plans and programs. In this way, the relations between ruling political parties and governments have been fostered to promote jointly human progress. Because of such national ideologies as "Harambee," Ujamaa, and humanism, the new states of Kenya, Tanzania, and Zambia have brought about humanization of development plans and programs. As a result of the establishment of one-party systems in Kenya, Malawi, Tanzania, and Zambia "development" has become a household word in these countries, and the quest for meaningful social and economic development has become the preoccupation of the rank and file.

PARTICIPATION AND DEVELOPMENT

This general survey of the role of political systems in development shows that the stand taken by one-party systems of the East and Central African states on questions of economic reforms epitomizes the concept of production as a means of enhancing the human dignity. However, my experience in planning rural development programs has shown that it is easy for plans to be based on wrong assumptions, resulting in displacement of goals. This type of planning engenders frustration among recipients of development. Experience has taught me that in order for development to be meaningful to the recipients, participatory devices must be embodied in the plan so as to enable the recipients to become active participants in the planning and implementation of development programs. As a planner I have learned with regret that although planning teams essentially put together comprehensive packages of economically and socially viable technologies which are likely to redound to the benefit of the people and the country, the tendency is for these plans to fail rather than succeed. Like shooting stars, these plans burn briefly in the glare of publicity, then are gone and forgotten. This tendency is a function of errors of omission rather than commission on the part of planners. And almost invariably omitted are techniques and strategies for total involvement of the people whose development is sought.

In my view this is crucial because technologies themselves are useless unless they become stimuli for enlisting support and participation. In other words, planners must learn to plan for planning. This is not a deliberate calypso of words, but an indication of the amount of thought which should precede our plans. The planning approach I am advocating discourages the application of mechanistic principles. It requires that planners be drawn from various disciplines so as to constitute a team of planners which will be in a position to see various facets of the desired development holistically, that is, as being interrelated. If conditions generated by lack of development are to be ameliorated, governments and planners must not only be capable of selling development plans to the people, but must also enable people to identify with development plans and programs. In order for people to identify with plans and programs they must be enabled to participate in the process of plan formulation and program implementation. By "participation" I mean mental and emotional involvement rather than mere muscular activity. A person's self is involved rather than just his skill. The peasant's or factory worker's involvement in his work must be a product of his mind and emotions. The degree and quality of participation must be such that it will motivate people in target areas to contribute to the program. They are given an opportunity to release their own resources of initiative and creativity toward the objectives of the plan.

From these assertions it is apparent that among planners and plan-implementing staff there must be men and women who are trained in social engineering. To be specific, social workers must form an integral part of every planning team. If programs are to be of impact design, we have to accept as a hard fact that planning is no longer the monopoly of economists as the world has been made to believe. If the objective of development programs is to improve the quality of life in target areas, we must accept as a fact that the success or failure of a given program cannot be determined on the basis of quantifiable results. Lest I am misunderstood, I should add that the effect of an economic crisis, for example, could be either to strengthen or to weaken the social cohesion. Planners must take into account value systems and roles of people in target areas if the quantifiable effects of plans and programs are to be as desired. In my view, social workers are more qualified than others to make a real contribution in this vital area of planning. Social workers will enable planners who represent the "hard" production-oriented sciences to appreciate that goals should have economic as well as social implications in order to secure a more orderly and self-lubricating development.

Development is a movement toward new and constantly rising goals. It is the process by which people change their goals of the past, devise new and appropriate programs to achieve new goals, and adjust their way of life and a variety of personal and group aspects in order to implement these programs. Development is never fully accomplished and is therefore always in process. As preliminary and then intermediate goals are attained, still others are identified. The purpose of the development process is to satisfy these ever-rising expectations. Basically, development is a reciprocal relationship between growth and development. Neither process is likely to continue for long or go very far without the other. Therefore, qualitative transformations must occur concurrently with quantitative increases. Hence, development must be seen to mean change and growth. The process of development is one of infinite variety. The change may be from agriculture to industry or from a rural to an urban way of life. The change may involve a repudiation of some or many traditional values with concomitant effects on various facets of personal or community life. Religious values and their influence on social and political life may change. Political systems may also change. It will then be appreciated that planning and plan implementation should involve every aspect of the government system. This is important, for the planning process should be seen as comprising the following:

1. Identifying development goals or purposes for which development is undertaken.
2. Determining the resources actually or potentially available for achieving specific goals
3. Formulating the policies necessary to achieve these goals
4. Implementing these policies through the process of systematically coordinated government and political machinery.

Given the above principles, the success or failure of a national development plan will depend upon the political climate under which it is born and nurtured.

Considering the multidimensional and complex nature of the problems inherent in the question of participation and development in different political settings, this discussion is far from exhaustive. Nevertheless, I hope it has touched upon the central issues of participation and development with which most countries must deal if they are to attain development that is permanent and self-sustaining. Development issues have tended to be colored largely by inherited colonial methods and even objectives. Development plans proclaim the need for skill development and employment creation but are, for the most part, notoriously devoid of any manpower plan or employment strategy. Even the exceptions that prove the rule tend narrowly to concern themselves with the manpower requirements of significantly small, formal sectors, neglecting the vast, low-productive, but economically dominant rural and other informal sectors. It is a result of realizing the political, economic, and social dangers inherent in these tendencies that Africa's leaders of vision have called for production by the masses in contrast to mass production through democratization of institutions and processes of development.

# Man and Development

## PART I

## A. ABDALLAH

DEPUTY GOVERNOR, CENTRAL BANK OF KENYA

ALL NATIONS of the Third World as well as many industrialized countries have development plans of one kind or another. In fact, economic management or planning has become a universal cult practiced by governments of all ideological colors and persuasions. The reason for this is that all governments seem to accept some role in guiding the economy to certain goals. If they have no other motive for doing so, they at least want to be sure that estimated tax revenues will be there for collection and that sufficient foreign exchange will be generated to enable them to repay foreign debts.

A government without a plan is like a person driving a bus full of people but knowing neither where he is going nor how to return to where he started. The parallel is even closer today with the world gripped with a serious energy crisis and ever-rising prices. This inflationary situation was substantially reinforced by last year's steep increase in crude oil prices. As a result of the escalating prices the international economic and monetary system has been thrown into disarray.

Nearly all oil-importing countries are faced with serious balance-of-payments problems. But while wealthy industrialized countries are able to weather the economic storm with possibly only small discomforts to their people, the countries of the Third World are confronted with problems of survival. The economies of even the luckiest of these countries will register little growth in the immediate future, while the majority are certain to experience economic stagnation at best with recession the fate of the others. This means not only that the standard of living of the poor half of mankind will stay at the present level, but that of many people will actually decline.

God knows how low and intolerable the present living standards really are! In most parts of the Third World the majority of the people are already at the very bottom of the economic ladder, leaving no further depth to which they can fall. The only way for them to absorb further economic squeezes is through their bodies, most of which will experience increasing malnutrition, greater emaciation, and for some, even starvation.

"Development" in any meaningful sense of the word is out of the question for most of the Third World nations unless international aid is extended on a massive scale. It is far from clear at this stage whether the international community will provide the aid in sufficient quantity and in time to avert mass misery of unprecedented proportions. The omens do not look terribly good, though it is reasonably certain that there will be sufficient international cooperation to prevent mass deaths from disease or starvation.

Bearing these possibilities in mind I suggest that people concerned with social welfare might usefully discuss after "man and development," "man and survival." It is no exaggeration to say that a good many developing countries face at the moment no less a challenge than how to survive as nations. This somewhat alarmist statement is based on a belief that something fundamental and irreversible actually occurred in 1973. The oil producers seem suddenly to have discovered as a group that the prices they were receiving for their product were terribly low compared to the utility value of petroleum and the real demand for it. This realization made them decide in December of 1973 at one go to more than treble their asking prices for crude oil.

This phenomenal increase in price and the immediacy of its application sent shock waves throughout the world. Suddenly the consuming countries found their oil-import bills quadrupled and that the only way to lessen the cost was to reduce consumption. Producers of other raw materials and commodities will never forget this startling lesson: as soon as one reaches the position of a monopoly supplier, one can virtually dictate the price at which his product is dealt.

The leverage now possessed by the oil producers has definitely affected the balance of economic power in the world. The rich, industrialized countries have suddenly found themselves virtually dependent for their essential energy requirements on production policies of people over whom they have no control. They obviously do not find this either a comfortable position or one which they should accept passively.

The present international economic situation is both bewildering and unstable. The hitherto economically dominant countries of the world find their current account positions reversed, with the necessity of permitting substantial outflows of foreign reserves because of oil imports. The oil producers, who will be receiving huge payments from the poor countries as well as the rich ones, have still not grasped the full extent of their new position. They possess enormous economic power which everyone hopes they will use responsibly and constructively.

But if this makes the continued affluence of the industrialized countries at its present levels somewhat uncertain, the same factors make the economic future of the oil-consuming Third World look dismal and grim. These countries have no room for economic maneuvering, and if the inflation that is now raging in the industrialized countries gives rise to recession, developing countries stand to receive less income from their commodity exports when their import costs will be edging upward. Already, commodity prices have begun to decline while prices of manufactured goods are rising steadily, and the indications are that this will continue.

What is the strategy for survival in such an unfavorable economic setting? Clearly, governments of the developing countries will need to embark on painful adjustment measures involving drastic revisions of their budgets and the cutting down on all nonproductive expenditures. Such exercises in most countries (developed and developing alike) tend to begin with social services which are generally regarded as nonessential. If people concerned with social welfare consider this a mistaken way of looking at social services, then it is up to them to make a case why the social welfare expenditures should be retained if not increased.

Developing countries will also have to cut down on their imports with a view to allowing only those goods that are absolutely essential to national survival. A great deal of national reorientation and improvisation will be required, particularly among the least developed countries in this group. All of them may find it necessary to urge their people to go back to the land and to concentrate on self-sufficiency in food production, using local resources. Such imported items as chemical fertilizers and insecticides may have to be forgotten because the foreign exchange may not be there to pay for them.

The elites of the developing world will also have to go without new cars because their countries may be forced to choose between importing buses and lorries on the one hand and private cars on the other hand. There may be increasing resort to traditional herbs and medicines because certain imported drugs and medical preparations may be in short supply. Some staple commodities as well as imported consumer goods may disappear from the shops.

The revolution of rising expectations that was talked about so much in the 1960s may be replaced by disillusionment, frustration, and political instability. Persistent balance-of-payments deficits will set in train recessionary forces that tend to drag everybody downward, thereby causing powerful social and economic units to try to improve their position unmindful of the public good. Economic struggles are usually won by those who are already economically strong.

In a world of dwindling economic opportunities, full of strife and self-seeking, the handicapped, the aged, the sick, and the lazy will cry out to Heaven for help. They will beg for manna that will never fall. That is the time when those who can give hope where there is despair, teach self-reliance where there is fatalism and apathy, and offer guidance where knowledge and leadership are lacking will be in greatest demand. Will you be there?

PART II

# GIUSEPPE PETRILLI

PRESIDENT, ITALIAN COUNCIL FOR THE EUROPEAN
MOVEMENT; PRESIDENT, INSTITUTE FOR INDUSTRIAL
RECONSTRUCTION, ITALY

EVEN IF the notion of the historical development of man which
dominates contemporary thought is of comparatively recent
origin, broadly coinciding with that of evolution, the linear
conception of time is characteristic in general of the entire
Judaeo-Christian tradition, going right back to its earliest
beginnings—Genesis. As opposed to cyclical representations of
reality, the creation figures as the starting point of a progression founded upon a deliberate act of the will of God, a progression that unfolds in stages and whose culminating point is
the advent of man. The mission with which the latter has been
invested by the Almighty, namely, to cover the earth and to
dominate it, is, in a manner of speaking, the prolongation in
time of God's act of creation and, so to speak, the metaphysical pivot of history. The Messianic expectation of the Kingdom of God, to which Christianity is heir, as well as the tendency toward the eschatological fulfillment of God's promises
to his people ever since his covenant with Abraham would be
inconceivable if we ignored this linear conception of time
which lies at the roots of our sense of history and onto which
the fundamental notions of contemporary civilization, from
evolution to revolution, have been grafted.

But this tension toward the future which characterizes the
Judaeo-Christian tradition cannot be reduced to its historical
expression alone. History and prophecy, civic commitment
and religious annunciation, appear as inseparable, though dis-

tinct, perspectives in the eyes of those called to work in the world to hasten the advent of a kingdom which, in the words of the Evangelist, is not of this world. Seen in this light, any historical event may be considered as both an episode in the process of temporal evolution and as a chance for salvation. Even if Christians have on occasion tended to regard historical success as a manifestation of divine blessing, much in the way the Old Testament so frequently presents the longevity of the patriarchs as a sign of God's favor, radical fidelity to the Judaeo-Christian tradition undoubtedly prohibits us from seeing this as the supreme goal of our existence. We are consequently forbidden to sacrifice to the idols of progress seen as an end in itself while forgetting the instrumental nature of all historical progress. As a result, conversely, we cannot attribute an absolute value to any given civilization while forgetting that salvation was promised to man, and not to institutions as such. This transcendence of man over institutions and even over the law was confirmed by Christ when, criticizing the excesses of the Judaic mentality, he reminded us that "the Sabbath was made for man, not man for the Sabbath." We would be justified in concluding that, on the one hand, the Judaeo-Christian tradition excludes all indifference with regard to history and hence with respect to the historical development of man and that, on the other hand, it also excludes any kind of blind confidence in the automatism of historical forces and the illusion that it is possible to achieve the consummate human order, guaranteed proof against sin or, if one prefers, against involution, before the end of time.

Seen from this angle, all historical situations are, by their nature, ambivalent: consciousness of this state of affairs is the true prerequisite to a "prophetic understanding" of history enabling one to discern the "signs of the times," that is, the visible manifestations of a divine intention. This intention is not—and I repeat this once again—to be seen in terms of a necessary evolution, fulfilling itself mechanistically or deterministically like natural laws and before which man has merely to submit, but as the possibility of a human development truly in accord with man's nature as created by God and yet whose accomplishment depends upon the choices man makes in exercising his freedom. This is what was meant by a contemporary Italian philosopher of Christian inspiration when he said: "Man's first task, his first duty, at the same time as being his most profound desire, is to realize his humanity and, from a religious point of view, this realization is none other than the fulfillment of the will of God." Through his study of the signs of the times and his scrutiny of history, then, man is in reality seeking himself and his calling.

These general considerations bring us to the problem which lies at the heart of our discussion, namely, our judgment of industrial civilization seen as a contemporary phase of human development. As we are all in a position to observe, this civilization is characterized by the growing invasion of the natural environment by man, which has radically altered our living conditions. I am referring to such well-known phenomena as urbanization and the gradual freeing of man from difficulties arising out of the insufficient availability of natural resources, from physical fatigue, and even from temporal limitations upon his existence. This evolution is accompanied by the acquisition of a planetary frame of reference and by a kind of "gradual desacralization" of the natural world. Modern man, in effect, lives less and less off nature and increasingly by the fruit of his own labor.

I should like to say straight away that there is nothing negative about this desacralization of the natural environment, in my view, in so far as we consider this in the light of the Judaeo-Christian tradition. I would even go on to say that it is only by growing out of naturalist and hence fundamentally "magical" religion that we can hope to attain a higher and more intimate notion of the sacred. The humanization of the world thus corresponds to its veritable sacralization, if one accepts the principle that there is no other way to accomplish God's will than by realizing man according to His creative idea. If it is true that human development is to be conceived as progress toward the infinite, constantly outgrowing its own product, namely, all specific historical structures, then the demythologizing or demystification which progress entails not only does not lead to an impoverishment of man's horizons—as certain Romantics held—but, on the contrary, creates the conditions for his growth, by calling on man to participate actively in God's creative plan. By claiming a liberating signification for industrial civilization one is by no means guilty of blind optimism, seen from this viewpoint, but rather one is drawing attention to the historic occasion that this civilization is capable of offering to man's free will, provided, of course, man is ready to seize it.

However, we all very well know that in reality the possibilities of genuine human growth offered by industrial civilization have more or less been wasted by the total subordination of human activities to the objectives of production conceived as an end in itself. This subordination has led to an ever-sharper opposition between the increasing rationality of existing technical means, on the one hand, and what one might term the declining rationality of the objectives of development. This opposition justifies, moreover, the protests—increasingly widespread among our contemporaries—aimed at a model of development that is constantly giving rise to increasing contradictions. The all-too-frequent blind confidence in technology has led to a very dangerous tendency to delegate to technicians the solution of problems which can only really be solved by reference to values and hence to alternative choices. In political terms, this kind of mentality obviously runs the risk of inducing society as a whole to resign itself to the power of technocrats, whose power is necessarily authoritarian in inspiration.

In the final analysis, the debate concerning the negative consequences of industrialization from the point of view of the deterioration of ecological conditions, which has been going on for some years more or less everywhere and particularly in the most developed countries, is aimed at the model of civilization that has grown up in these countries along with the scale of values which determines, however indirectly, the political and economic choices characterizing their current development. The debate on ecology has increasingly led public opinion to express itself on a subject which, for too long, had been accepted as an objective factor, namely the general orientation of the process of development. We should bear in mind, at all events, that the possibility of correctly posing a problem of this nature, in an operational perspective and not merely as a statement of principle void of all practical consequence, is a function of the means placed at our disposal by scientific and technical progress. And yet it was precisely Western civilization, with its Judaeo-Christian tradition, which played a pioneering role in triggering off the process of industrialization through scientific and technical research. And it is this same tradition that is today in a position to indicate for the whole of humanity the threshhold yet to be attained: this involves a kind of maturing of our consciousness, enabling us to cover the distance that has opened up between the extraordinary expansion of the technical means available to man and his true freedom, that is, his ability to make independent choices.

This problematic conception of development enables us, moreover, to grasp its real universality in the contemporary world. The opposing situations of overdevelopment and underdevelopment existing in various parts of our planet are in fact no more than contradictions arising out of the model of development we have known till now, and the problems posed by these situations cannot be solved validly, in my opinion, if we ignore the fact that they are historically simultaneous. Conversely, all too frequently we find that, inside industrialized countries, the problem of the quality of life is treated as a kind of luxury, a problem which only arises beyond a certain level of development and corresponding in some way to a price that has to be paid for the level of well-being attained. In developing countries, on the other hand, one comes across a line of argument opposing industrial civilization, seen as something exclusive to a small number of islands of well-being, to the agrarian civilization which characterizes the vast majority of countries still dominated by a primary economy. Nowhere, in reality, do we find radical solutions to the problems of development, on account of the interdependence between the different aspects of a single process of development which has now attained planetary dimensions. While it is true that contemporary men of science are increasingly aware of the moral implications of scientific thought, the same problem can be said to be posed from a geographical point of view, imposing on us a universalist conception of human development. Industrial civilization rediscovers thereby the ecumenical inspiration it draws from its Judaeo-Christian roots.

It would, therefore, evidently be absurd to continue to juxtapose supportive measures in favor of backward areas alongside ecological reclamation measures on behalf of areas characterized by heavy industrial concentration, without combining the two within an organic synthesis. As we can see, even in industrialized countries the problem is a global one, incapable of resolution in the absence of a modification of the model of development designed to encourage a more balanced localization of new investment and of reversing the current tendency of labor to drift toward the most highly evolved regions. It is not by accident, moreover, that we are currently witnessing efforts to consider the cultural component of development (know-how) no longer as an objective factor, but as something to be adapted to the needs of different countries as they perceive them at various stages in their evolution. It would be illusory to suppose that the contradictions of industrial society must necessarily come to a head at the terminal point in the development process; in other words, in the most advanced countries, for this would assume that progress is always linear and that the last in the queue must necessarily go through all the stages already experienced by the older industrialized nations. Following this line of reasoning, it is of great importance that we recover a more positive estimate of the value of the traditional cultures characterizing different countries; these traditions should rather be treated as factors of individualization, often liable to assume unpredictable forms.

Finally, we should recognize that despite the pluralism which characterizes it in other respects, Western civilization was long marked, and especially from a religious viewpoint, by an intransigent and exclusive defense of its dominant ethic, which is a far cry from the symbiosis between different religious beliefs to be observed, for example, in Indian civilization. In this, the Christian tradition, which had started out by contesting over-Judaic interpretations of the old Covenant in the name of the universality of the "promise," undeniably ended up in its turn by long taking refuge within the fortress of institutions and customs forming part of the West's age-old heritage. While it is true that by triggering the process of industrialization the Western world has created the conditions for a genuine unification of the world, we must not forget that this unification has frequently been accompanied, from a cultural viewpoint, by the forcible introduction of values and models of institutional organization that were alien to local traditions.

In this respect, I am inclined to think that the criticisms nations belonging to other spiritual families have frequently made with regard to the West during recent years should be heard by peoples belonging to the Judaeo-Christian tradition, and especially by Europeans, as a call to conversion. For while it is true that our linear conception of time in itself supposes, by its very nature, that progress is achieved through the interplay of dialectical contradictions, with their imbalances and their ruptures, we may take it that these criticisms are also made in the name of the values of our own tradition—values to which we have not always been as faithful as we might. They demand that we rediscover our awareness of the universality of our message, and that we employ the means placed at our disposal by contemporary technology in order to enable humanity as a whole, and not merely a privileged minority, to attain the full historic realization of its possibilities and its destiny. I believe that, underlying their criticisms, the other spiritual families are saying to the West today what the lady of the old Eastern legend said to the prince who had outraged her while drunk: "I shall call you when you are no longer drunk."

# Participation—an Ideology

PART I

## A. T. ARIYARATNE

ADMINISTRATIVE DIRECTOR AND ORGANIZING SECRETARY,
LANKA JATIKA SARVÓDAYA SHRAMADANA SANGAMAYA,
SRI LANKA

DURING THE last decade or so the expression "participation"— or, to be more exact, "people's participation in development"—has slowly crept its way into the official documents of planners and bureaucrats, both at national and international levels. Being a village-level worker, struggling with village people to make their voices heard, their human dignity reestablished, and their just rights realized, my experience has conditioned my mind to cast doubts on the seriousness of these expressions. If we are not cautious enough, we can deceive ourselves into a situation of mistaking manipulation of the people by a bureaucratic establishment as a genuine attempt to bring about people's participation. Therefore, a clear ideological base for the concept of participation must be established, at least by those who genuinely desire to attain a more egalitarian society in our countries.

In most countries of the world, the present generation has inherited a legacy of certain oppressive instruments in economic, administrative, and political spheres. These are so interlinked, and sometimes so complex and subtle, that they keep vast masses of people enslaved without ever making them conscious that they are the victims of one form of exploitation or other by a privileged elite. This situation becomes more dangerous when the oppressors themselves are "good-hearted" men who genuinely feel for their people but who have not realized that in actual fact they are manipulators and not liberators of their brother human beings.

Any definition of participation or an approach to bring about people's participation must take into account this complex situation in our societies irrespective of the fact that they are the so-called "developed" or "developing" nations. A terminology understandable only to the elite is never a substitute for real-life situations where the human being feels he is the master of his own personality awakening, leading to a joy in living within the broad framework of a society where he does not infringe on the freedom and liberties of his fellow men.

People's participation can be a reality only if situations are created where both the privileged and the underprivileged are given an opportunity to awaken their inner selves in accordance with certain commonly accepted principles. This should result in changing the relationships of both. In the Sri Lanka Sarvodaya Shramadana movement (a movement where the members share their time, thought, and energy to awaken all in society) to which I have dedicated myself, we try to awaken our personalities based on four traditional principles:

1. Respect for life (*metta*)
2. Compassionate action to remove the causes that lead to suffering (*karuna*)
3. Learning to get joy out of living through service (*muditha*)
4. Bringing about a psychological stability leading to equanimity (*upekka*).

The first principle helps us to look at all our fellow human beings as belonging to one human family. This leads us to transcend man-made barriers of caste, race, color, religion, and national prejudices. We learn to look at man as man.

The second principle is an action based on the first—the thought. We organize *shramadana* (gift of labor) camps where everybody joins together to live and work together to alleviate the suffering of one another. Programs are decided upon by the participants themselves and are implemented without creating two classes—those who plan and those who implement.

People from all strata of society work together in our camps knee deep in mud, transplanting or weeding paddy fields, cutting dusty tracks to villages that need access roads, building houses for families who have no proper accommodations, and clearing jungle lands to open up collective farms for unemployed youth. They meet thrice a day at a meeting called the "family get-together" at which all participants, as equals, join in making decisions on the project at hand. This practice results in a spiritual, psychological, social, and cultural integration of a people who were divided among themselves earlier. They all get the joy of living when they work together for the common benefit. A continuous program of this nature results in great self-confidence for the human being, culminating in a balanced personality.

These four principles of human awakening are further strengthened by four other concepts of group behavior, namely, sharing, pleasant language, constructive activity, and equality.

There cannot be genuine participation without sharing with one another wealth and power as much as physical and mental energy. In this context, political and economic decentralization becomes an important prerequisite for people's participation. Removal of political and economic inequalities demands structural changes in our societies. In my country this is being realized today by a democratically elected government through legislative enforcement. Injustices and inequalities in land ownership, tenancy rights, inequitable housing, hoarding of essential commodities, and corrupt practices are removed by law. It is a revolution taking place by using only the legislative arm.

Structural changes alone will not do unless a change in the value system also takes place. This is where the voluntary organizations can play an important role. New methods and techniques have to be introduced into the communities without disturbing those traditional elements which are yet progressive and adaptable to a new way of participatory living.

An excellent beginning can be made at the grass roots. Still, the vast majority of the people of our world, as much as 85 percent, live in about two million villages, they say. The future of the world, in all aspects, lies in the village. The village community needs the liberty and freedom to express itself. A vast untapped human and material potential is there in the rural areas.

In Sri Lanka the Sarvodaya movement launched a 1,000 villages development scheme. We are already working in 500 selected villages. An integrated program of development involving the laying of a psychological and physical infrastructure—a social reorganization in which all men, women, and children in the village are involved in development action—is being carried out. Leadership training, training in skills in agriculture, crafts, and village technology, debt redemption and capital formation through a revolving fund, cooperative marketing and purchasing are some of the activities. Self-reliance, self-discipline, and self-development are the strongest features of this program. The entire exercise is centered on the human being—on his total development, spiritual, moral, social, and economic—who participates with others as equals in a dynamic social situation.

Total participation is most effective in small units. In our experience, 150 to 200 families make an optimum unit to bring about strong participation. The tendency in the world, with the advancement of science and technology, has been for bigger and bigger social, political, and economic units to emerge, which results in alienation of man from man. The human being degenerated in the national context to a mere statistical digit. The progress of a nation was not measured by the quality of life its citizens possessed, but by the amount of goods and services they could have at their disposal. Thinking in terms of growth and per capita income, the large society lost sight of the total human being and development of the individual human being and the small groups. In other words, the benefits of science and technology went to the already affluent, and the poor became poorer while the rich became richer. But is it not a fact that this same science and technology could be used for efficient coordination among smaller units on a national and global scale? Cannot man realize the dream of a universal social order where each nation becomes a commonwealth of village republics?

It is only when the small unit is vested with the maximum decision-making power that people's participation becomes real, that man controls the instruments of government, the economy, and social organizations rather than these structures controlling man; in valueless, dead, self-perpetuating systems, controllers themselves, not of their choice, become inhuman oppressors of their own people.

One final point. In our craze for increased material wealth, produced through large-scale organizations, we have not only polluted our biosphere and atmosphere we have also poisoned our psychosphere. By "psychosphere" I mean that envelope of mental energy that is the result of the aimless and uncontrolled thought energy that we release every moment. Just as material form is the result of certain phenomena like hardness, cohesiveness, heat, and expandability, mental formations are the result of certain root causes which are mind-based. In our part of the world what we call "spiritual awakening" is the depth of our understanding of our own mind.

In the Buddhist doctrine that I follow, this type of self-realization results in one's understanding of certain principles. First is the principle of change; whether it is mind or matter it changes every moment. Secondly, if one holds with desire to such changing phenomena it invariably brings about sorrow and unhappiness. Thirdly, if there is no permanence to enjoy, ego is only an illusion. This right understanding brings the human being into a situation where his mind and heart are filled with compassion toward all beings. Such spiritual identification is the ideal situation in which man will accept man as his brother, and participation will naturally follow. In other words, while we are dabbling with political, economic, and social problems, let us not lose sight of the importance of a spiritual reawakening of man. In this age of science where there is so much potential for good let us try to rebuild this world as a harmonious combination of scientific and spiritual development.

PART II

# MILOS STEVANOV

UNIVERSITY OF NOVI SAD, YUGOSLAVIA

IDEOLOGY IS, first and foremost, a coordinate system of values and aims created by a human group in order to direct its conscious action in the present and in the future. This system of values is, in reality, the projection into the future of the profound and constant aspirations which men feel and formulate, founded on a philosophical viewpoint which they adopt concerning the world, man and his position in the world, society, and all emanations of humanity. This projection into the future of man's highest intellectual and psychic potential is a sort of normativization of the knowledge acquired by the human group at a given point in time and represents the passage from experience to development, from what has been to what ought to be. This is why ideology constitutes the dominant philosophy and the norm, practice, and theory, the explanation of man's situation in the world, but also at the same time the determination of his role in development.

The elaboration of ideology is a long, constant process, involving all the members of the group. But the social elite and certain persons undeniably contribute far more than the rest of the group. In the past, and depending on the period, this task was fulfilled by prophets, priests, poets, artists, scientists, philosophers, politicians. Yet, while setting up ideology as a sacred, disinterested, and superior creation, its creators, by the very nature of things, and by the definition of ideology itself, could not help but mingle their interests and the interests of the more or less broad groups to which they belonged. To recognize this or to ignore it had little effect on reality. Thus, each ideology is steeped in the class interests of its creators and its avatars. This is inevitable, given the definition of ideology as the coordinated system of values and aims of a human group.

Looking at the history of humanity we observe a multitude of ideologies and, for each period, we can distinguish those which, whether singly or severally, were dominant. We can also observe their conflicts or their coexistence, their evolution, and sometimes even their disappearance. But, as long as an ideology continues to exist, it is always operative, for it binds together the vital forces of the group, committing them in each action the group may undertake.

In this sense, it becomes utterly reasonable to reflect on the role of ideologies in the general development of humanity and of each social segment. Simplifying somewhat, we can say there are two dominant ideologies in the world today, capable of affecting the course of human development: the ideology of the Western world, capitalist, calling itself the "free world," and the ideology of the Eastern world, socialist, calling itself "progressive" and "revolutionary."

These two dominant ideologies are well enough known to make any attempt to present them a waste of time: nothing new would be added thereby. It would be more useful to show how a concrete ideology, in a state of constant formulation, can influence the conscious action within a concrete society, Yugoslav society, which drew inspiration from Marxist, workers', revolutionary ideology in carrying out its revolution and in order to build an original path which we call "self-management" socialism and which others sometimes refer to as "human" socialism.

By taking development as our starting point, and by thinking about the consequences which development has had and could have on social measures as a whole, the reference to self-management socialist ideology may provide us with some interesting directions and provoke some very fertile reflection.

According to this ideology and, we can already say, on the basis of the practice arising out of this ideology, self-management differs radically from participation, so much so that we cannot call self-management a kind of extension of participation; it is an entirely new quality, a new method of social organization that aspires to touch upon every aspect of life and to change each one radically.

Participation is merely one palliative among others. It respects all the existing social structures, concerned solely to open up tiny side roads in order to enable men involved in a given activity to "express their opinions, to exercise a certain control, to protest and, above all, to organize independently— this right being granted to individuals and to groups." [1] What this amounts to is that nothing changes: on the one hand, we have the governors, the possessors, the privileged, the educated, the leaders, "untouchables" of every stripe; while on the other hand are the governed, the penniless, workers, the multitude, the masses, the people, simple operatives, those at the bottom of the social pyramid. Nothing is changed, the only difference being that the former now permit the latter to express *an opinion* concerning the social complex in which they are involved; they later are to be allowed to intend to control this social complex affecting their lives, to protest, to relieve themselves psychologically by speaking their minds, though with no guarantee that they will be able to change anything whatsoever.

Nothing is altered: the organization of production, the utilization of resources, the distribution of national income, the representation of the masses by elected representatives, decision-making and power centers, the crushing burden of the State and the legal system, the multinational companies, wars and other evils. Nothing is transformed and everything remains as it was, except that people now have the right to speak and to give their opinion.

Participation, therefore, is a social policy and a social welfare measure designed to open one more safety valve, aimed at eliminating certain relativities, improving things slightly, quieting the consciences of some while pulling the wool over the eyes of others; in the meantime, the *status quo* is preserved.

[1] Final Report of the European, Middle Eastern, and Mediterranean Basin Region.

Self-management, on the other hand, demands that everything change in accordance with the model derived from its ideology.

Man is the most important social value of all, and he must be placed at the center of all preoccupations, of all development. This also means that man takes precedence over things, and that things should be at the service of man. Man must free himself from the blind laws of economic and social life which have separated him from nature and alienated him, which have enslaved him and reduced him to the role of mere instrument. And when we speak of man we mean every man, the lowest on the social ladder, the man in the crowd. Thus, development cannot be identified with economic development that leaves man out of account; economic development must occur in such a way that it serves man, permitting his fulfillment and his well-being.

Social policy, with its utterly human goals, should guide every type of development, including economic development. In this sense, social welfare will not merely be the curative and the preventive form of the fight against the incidences of development, but it will find expression in a social policy that will form an integral part of every conscious activity of the society as a whole; its goals shall preside over all development.

With man as its starting point, and taking into account the need for development, self-management socialism determines man's position in society in accordance with two criteria: work and solidarity (the latter being largely assimilable to the former in the form of future work, or youth, and past work, or the aged, and the handicapped being the only ones to be covered by solidarity as such). All existing wealth belongs to all, being social, while all members of society have both the right and the duty to work. Their social position and their well-being depend upon the results of their labor: from each according to his abilities, to each according to his labor. We soon realized, however, that labor and rewards based on results do not automatically lead to the liberation of man, for a certain bureaucratization and institutionalization have led to a further kind of exploitation of the worker, and thus to a new form of alienation.

It is for this reason that we have sought, by means of self-management, to eliminate all intermediaries between the world of work and the distribution of its fruits. We have sought forms of direct democracy permitting those most concerned to decide for themselves on everything that affects them and, above all, on their working conditions and the distribution of the results of their work. Let them decide for themselves, without intermediaries, without interference by the State and its representatives, without any other kind of representative, hence directly and of their own accord. At the present time, every type of human activity capable of being termed *work* is so organized that the workers belonging to each basic work unit, such as a factory shop floor, decide, in their assemblies, on the most important matters affecting them. Without exaggeration we may say that they possess sovereign power when making decisions concerning themselves. The entire edifice of bodies, including the State and its subdivisions such as the commune, is derived from these workers' assemblies and from the territorial assemblies formed along the same lines by means of a rather complicated electoral system.

We believe that we have found in this a form of organization which enables a populous modern society made up of a great number of individuals to exercise direct democracy; that is, permitting all those concerned to participate, giving the opportunity not only of expressing an opinion but also of deciding for themselves and of deciding upon all matters of vital interest to themselves, as directly as possible and, in the last resort, sovereignly.

Man considered as the supreme value, the means of production and all the wealth of the country nationalized, work considered as the determining element in the social position of each person (to which should be added, as mentioned above, solidarity), direct democracy as instrument—these are just some of the essential elements of self-management which give rise to reflection concerning what is called participation elsewhere.

This manner of organizing society upsets the normal course of things encountered in so-called "liberal" democratic societies and in the peoples' democracies where, one way or another, the masses elect their governors and leave them to make the decisions, through the intermediary of the State and its panoply of instruments of constraint, in all matters concerning them.

Thus, self-management is essentially an attack on the State and its organization, and especially on the traditional principles of its organization, such as centralism, hierarchy, the bureaucracy, and all its consequences for the economy, for education, for health services, and so forth. Self-management introduces a profound change wherein man, the worker, with his primordial, inalienable, and sovereign rights occupies the place of honor.

Within such a social organization, it is easy to place so-called "social" and "social welfare" questions at the center of primary decision-making. For workers are directly affected by these questions, and, since it is they who create national income and who dispose of it, it is perfectly natural they should take a close interest in all aspects of social welfare, and especially in those which enhance their social security and their well-being. Thus, child care, maternity services, and, generally speaking, the social position of women, the family and everything concerning the family, the aged—all these aspects of social welfare have become the direct concern of the producers themselves, that is, of all the avatars of self-management. The principle of solidarity, which is founded on self-management, has taken on even wider importance, covering all the other aspects of social welfare such as care for, and reeducation of, the handicapped.

We may say that self-management is of interest to and is capable of mobilizing and actively committing all workers to the development of society; we may add that its organizations have bound up social questions with that of general development as a result of the eminently humanist orientation of the ideology underlying self-management.

The few ideas concerning self-management just outlined, dealing mainly with the development of social welfare, show that the best possible choices man can make where his fate and his history in the world are at stake must take as their central object man—man as worker, man in his greatest numbers, man as creator of social goods. In order to activate his creative possibilities to the fullest, it is necessary to liberate him from the secular constraints of class oppression; he will then be able to regulate the course of events by placing his own, human, and noble interests above the blind laws of exploitation and submission.

Yugoslav self-management is an original road to social change, arising out of the specific conditions of Yugoslav society as a whole. This experiment is currently being conducted in every sector of our society. It is the direct creation of an ideology which itself is in a state of constant formulation. This year, even, we have promulgated a new constitution representing the latest formulation of our self-management practice as well as the expression of our ideology.

Yugoslav society is an open society, independent of blocs and aspiring to the highest degree of independence and tolerance. Internationally speaking, its first principle is coexistence, by which we mean active, committed, and above all peaceful coexistence. This implies another important principle, that of noninterference in the affairs of other countries: each must be master of its destiny. It is for these reasons that we have no wish to impose either our ideology or our way of life and self-management organization on anyone else. But we do believe our experiment is of interest to all, and especially to the developing nations, enabling them to reexamine their options and to rethink their orientations. Even those who do not intend to revise their fundamental choices may take a closer look at our experiment.

We think a meeting such as this throws up the following points for reflection:

1. Can man, with his available intellectual and psychic powers, direct his destiny, his life, his history; or is he doomed to submit to the blind and oppressive forces of a development in which things take precedence over man?

2. When we claim that man is the supreme value in society, which man are we talking about? Should we not be talking

about man-as-worker, man as the creator of social wealth, man in his greatest numbers in each society?

3. This man-as-worker is also capable of using his powers outside his strictly professional role as worker. He is capable of governing himself, of managing his labor relations as well as disposing of the income he creates and deciding upon its use, not merely for the satisfaction of his individual needs, but also for the satisfaction of the most varied social needs.

4. In order to do so, he is capable of creating a social organization which enables him to exercise his influence directly and to decide for himself on vital matters concerning him. He is also capable of delegating his representatives in order to decide on other questions of general interest while remaining subject to his permanent and effective control.

5. Consequently, we need to revise not merely our notions or our principles, but also such institutions as the State, with all that implies. Thus, "destatification," "debureaucratization," and decentralization are orientations opening up the way to participation, self-management, and direct democracy.

6. The engagement of all the active members of society in running that society and in making decisions concerning vital matters affecting them opens the way to the disalienation of man, to the liberation of his true nature, and the suppression of all forms of exploitation and oppression.

7. Thus organized, humanity will be better able to master the forces conditioning its development. Those social aims most intimately linked with man and his well-being will thereby form an integral part of all development. Social welfare will lose its curative character and will become an inherent part of life itself.

I am certain these few reflections will encourage all people of good will to develop their own ideologies and to contribute to the development of social welfare in their societies.

# Maldistribution of Wealth—an Obstacle to Full Participation in Development

## PART I

## WADOOD A. JILANI

DEPUTY CHIEF, MANPOWER DIVISION, GOVERNMENT OF
PAKISTAN

DEVELOPMENT, AS we understand it, is the process of glorifying the socialization and culturization of man by providing opportunities and facilities for him to grow and to develop himself, his environment, his habitation, and his community, individually and collectively, to have a decent living. This is the version I have assimilated after going through the voluminous books on economics, social welfare, political science, and sociology. Can this development be gauged by counting the automobiles in a country or by counting the palaces and skyscrapers? No, not at all. Development means harnessing the natural resources of a country for the ultimate gain and benefit of man. Economic and national development requires the common man to play his part effectively in raising the national income, production, and savings so that he may participate as an active agent of development. Maldistribution of wealth always takes place when the common man is denied, socially and politically, an opportunity to participate in the process of development.

In Pakistan, during the last two decades, four five-year plans were put under way. The object of this activity of economic planning has been and should have been the welfare of the common man. And if the man, or rather we should say the common man, is to play an effective role in the development of the country, he has to be involved in the process of planning. The expertise, no doubt, will be needed to determine the methodology to attain the objectives and the targets to be achieved for the welfare of the common man, through planned and processed prescriptions for national development, but unless the common man is enabled to participate in this process, no spectacular and tangible results can be expected.

However, although the common man was not allowed to participate fully in the process of development in the past, by denying him the opportunity of exercising his will through established political institutions, development did definitely take place but at the cost of the maldistribution of wealth. The rich became richer and the poor became poorer. The wealth of the country circulated among the few.

The first prerequisite for the participation of the common man is his ability to read and write and thus to understand his social environment so that he can play his part effectively as a patriotic citizen and join hands with government and nongovernment, national and international agencies in nation-building programs. With 15 percent to 20 percent literacy in many of the countries, including mine, how can we expect the common man to have a chance to participate in development? That is a question to ponder.

Maldistribution of wealth, no doubt, debars the majority of the people from participating fully in development, since they are not taken into confidence as to why development is necessary and what will be its impact on their socioeconomic conditions. They are just watching the activities of the haves to multiply their wealth in the name of development since they are in the category of have-nots. But this cannot be called fair play or justice. This state of affairs cannot be allowed to go unchecked for long. The time comes when things have to be set right.

In the first budget of the present government in Pakistan, the rich and the well-to-do who had been enjoying unreasonable concessions were called upon to bear a greater share of taxation. The income tax on the higher incomes was raised. The tax holiday was abolished. Rates of state duty and wealth tax were enhanced. The rich were taxed, and the poor were afforded relief.

Maldistribution of wealth directly or indirectly affects agricultural and industrial production since the tillers of the soil and labor do not get their due share and feel disgusted and disgruntled and do not get any satisfaction out of hard labor. Policies had to be framed and pursued to avert this situation. Previously, prices of agricultural commodities were kept low with the objective of transferring money to the industrial sector. The new policy restored the proper balance between the agricultural and industrial sectors.

Poverty stands in the way of development. If development should, therefore, aim at reducing, or rather eliminating, poverty and not widening the gaps of economic development between man and man, and the poor segment of the society gets its share of wealth, the common man's participation in development would be better and so would his performance in the process of production. By allowing 100 percent tax exemption to the segment of the society whose income does not exceed Rs.12,000/- a year the burden of taxation has been shifted to the higher-level group. More facilities like free education up to matriculation, free school books up to the primary level, merit scholarships, free health and medical services will have an impact on reducing the stigma of maldistribution of wealth.

Industrialization and urbanization have made the people much more self-centered and, to a great extent, selfish too. Society as a social unit has ceased to exist. Sharing joys and sorrows with one's neighbors and the community is no longer feasible. To bridge this gap voluntary social work and, in its wake, professional social work came into existence. Provision of social welfare services by the federal and provincial government agencies of social welfare and by the voluntary social work agencies and social workers is another proof of the joint efforts to remove maldistribution of wealth.

The intention of the government to remove maldistribution of wealth is embodied in the following articles of the Constitution of Pakistan:

37. The State shall:
    a) promote, with special care, the educational and economic interests of backward classes or areas;
    b) remove illiteracy and provide free and compulsory secondary education within the minimum possible period;
    c) make technical and professional education generally available and higher education equally accessible to all on the basis of merit;
    d) ensure inexpensive and expeditious justice;
    e) make provision for securing just and humane conditions of work, ensuring that children and women are not employed in vocations unsuited to their age or sex, and for maternity benefits for women in employment;
    f) enable the people of different areas, through education, training, agricultural and industrial development and other methods, to participate fully in all forms of national activities, including employment in the service of Pakistan.

INCOME DISTRIBUTION

All the socioeconomic reforms introduced by the people's government are aimed at narrowing the differentials in minimum and maximum incomes and to taxing the rich and providing relief to the poor. Government policy in this connection is reflected in the following provisions of the Constitution of Pakistan:

38. The State shall:
    a) secure the well-being of the people, irrespective of sex, caste, creed or race, by raising their standard of living, by preventing the concentration of wealth and means of production and distribution in the hands of a few to the detriment of general interest and by ensuring equitable adjustment of rights between employers and employees, and landlords and tenants;
    b) provide for all citizens within the available resources of the country, facilities for work and adequate livelihood with reasonable rest and leisure;
    c) provide for all persons employed in the service of Pakistan or otherwise, social security by compulsory social insurance or other means;
    d) provide basic necessities of life, such as food, clothing, housing, education and medical relief, for all such citizens, irrespective of sex, caste, creed or race, as are per-

manently or temporarily unable to earn their livelihood on account of infirmity, sickness or unemployment;

e) reduce disparity in the income and earnings of individuals, including persons of the various classes in the service of Pakistan.

To avert the maldistribution of wealth which was considered by the people's government of Pakistan as an obstacle to full participation in development, some major reforms were introduced.

NEW EDUCATION POLICY

In the new education policy (1972–80) which was introduced by the Prime Minister of Pakistan on March 15, 1972, and is under implementation by the government, one of the objectives is:

Building up and nurturing the total personality of the individual, dynamic, creative and capable of facing the truth as it emerges from the objective study of reality; an individual able to comprehend fully the nature of technical and social change and having deep concern for the improvement of society.

Another objective is:

Mobilizing the youth for leadership roles through participation in programs of social service and environmental improvement, and by inculcating in them the dignity of labour.

Under this policy, education has been made free and universal up to Class X for all children throughout the country. In the first phase, education up to Class VIII has been made free for boys and girls in both government and privately managed schools. In the second phase, starting October 1, 1974, free education has been extended to Classes IX and X in all schools.

At present only 8 percent of the youth of secondary and intermediate age attend secondary schools and intermediate colleges in Pakistan. Elsewhere the figures are: the United States, 100 percent; Japan, 86 percent; United Kingdom, 72 percent; Soviet Union, 67 percent; United Arab Republic, 30 percent; Turkey, 24 percent; Iran, 21 percent; and India, 15 percent.

The present rate of increase in enrollment at the secondary

and intermediate levels is about 10 percent per annum. It is estimated that by 1980 the enrollment will more than double, rising from 400,000 to 850,000 in Class IX and X and from 160,000 to 360,000 in Classes XI and XII. The proposed program provides for an increase in total enrollment in Class IX and X from 560,000 to an estimated 1,200,000. This will cover 15 percent of the age group by 1980. It is possible that with the introduction of free education up to Class X, the rate of enrollment growth may become still higher.

*Nationalization of education.* According to the education policy, privately managed schools have been nationalized since October 1, 1972, and the colleges from September, 1972.

*Schools and Centers.* The targets to be achieved by 1980 are:

|  | Schools and Centers to be Established |
|---|---|
| Factory schools | 500 |
| Farm schools in association with the Agroville scheme | 3,500 |
| Special women education centers | 5,000 |
| Out-of-school youth centers | 300 |

*New boards of intermediate and secondary education.* To provide more convenience to candidates coming from far-flung areas, five new boards are to be established at Saidu, Rawalpindi, Gujranwala, Bahawalpur, and Khairpur.

*New universities.* Three new universities are being established at Saidu, Multan, and Sukkur. The Agricultural College at Tandojam and the N.E.D. Engineering College, Jamshoro, are to be raised to university level. A constituent medical college is to be added to the University of Baluchistan, and facilities for science and rural home economics are to be added to the Agricultural University, Lyallpur.

PEOPLE'S WORKS PROGRAM

By way of introducing the People's Works Program, I am prompted to quote the following paragraph from the philosophy and concept of the same program:

Despite the psychological advantage of the sense of belonging together and having a common destiny that independence brought, we failed to build truly and well the foundation of our national life. This was in a large measure due to a failure to recognize contemporary reality, that while the capacity for national survival is measured in terms of vast physical, material, economic, technical and human resources, even the merest national existence demands an organic unity, a social cohesion in the community in addition to a minimum of the requisite resources; that given these minimum resources the social cohesion cannot exist unless the people fully participate in their development and have an equitable share in the rewards of such development.

The principal aim of the program is to improve the quality of life of the general mass of people by improving the rural economy and living conditions in villages, towns and cities and developing local leadership. Its specific objectives include:

1. To combat unemployment and underemployment by significantly enlarging opportunities for gainful work
2. To undertake, within the framework of the country's over-all development plan, such productive projects as will build up the economy through the provision of basic capacities and amenities (The projects undertaken will be split into comparatively small units and will materialize quickly.)
3. To mobilize local resources and to motivate the people for a massive productive effort so that the process of development gets institutionalized and is associated with a large segment of the population
4. To provide opportunities for constructive leadership and draw upon local initiative to the maximum extent
5. To generate confidence and self-reliance among the masses through proper training and skill formation so that they become worth-while productive assets for the country.

INTEGRATED RURAL DEVELOPMENT PROGRAM

In the words of the Prime Minister of Pakistan, Zulfiqar Ali Bhutto:

The Integrated Rural Development Program is our last hope to improve the economic position of our vast majority of small farmers and thus improve the quality of life in villages, afford employment opportunities, reduce the gap between the urban and rural areas so that the people living in the villages may participate with their colleagues in the cities with pride in political, social and economic life of the country.

Since about 85 percent of the population of Pakistan are predominantly agricultural, earning their livelihood directly or indirectly from farming, the impact of the Integrated Rural Development Program on the youth can very well be imagined. This program, as a matter of fact, is, in other words, a rural community development program.

According to the authorized version, the concept of the program is: to select a production area comprising fifty to sixty villages mostly with small and medium-size farmers with a view to improving their socioeconomic status by an intensive rural development program with an initial thrust to increase productivity by providing technical guidance, supervised credit, supply of inputs, machinery on hire, storage and marketing facilities, and so forth, based on a sound physical infrastructure, by intensification and commercialization of agriculture through a social cooperative system under a total approach.

LABOR AND INDUSTRIAL RELATIONS

Since the present government came into power, it has shown a major concern for initiating steps to promote the interests of workers. It introduced labor reforms in February, 1972, appropriately called "a new deal for labor." These were elaborated and enlarged in August, 1973, after detailed discussion in the Pakistan Tripartite Labor Conference, 1972. Another such conference was held in November, 1973, to discuss the results achieved in the implementation of labor reforms and to lay out new proposals for further improvements. The labor reforms seek to guarantee to the workers their fundamental rights of freedom of association and collective bargaining and provide for greater security of service, participation in management, and a number of financial benefits, including a share in profits, compulsory payment of bonuses, higher rates of compensation for injuries, group insurance, old age pensions, free education of one child, and housing and medical facilities. The labor laws have also been made applicable to the provincially administered tribal areas.

The new labor policy charted a new course for creating a dynamic socioeconomic structure that the people's government has taken the lead to establish. This is enshrined in viable and effective labor-management relations designed to achieve industrial peace and maximize production. It was based on three interrelated principles of having a strong and representative trade union movement, effective participation in management, and assurance of employment security. These reforms cover all matters of interest to the workers and have brought significant gains. There is no end to the benefits that can be provided to the workers, but under the present situation, higher production, greater savings, and more investments need to precede further benefits.

Under the Companies Profit (Workers' Participation) Act, 1968, the workers' share in company profits, which was earlier raised to 4 percent from 2½ percent, was further raised to 5 percent, and the workers were enabled to cash their shares or leave them in the fund for further investment at their discretion. The scope of the law was extended by Companies Profits Workers' Participation (Amendment) Act, 1973, to industrial undertakings employing fifty or more workers.

The quantum of various benefits under the West Pakistan Employees' Social Security Ordinance, 1965, has been enhanced. The death grant for funeral expenses of a "secured" person has been raised from Rs.50/- to Rs.500/-. Sickness benefits to "secured" workers have been made payable for 121 days as against 91 days previously. In tuberculosis cases, this period has been increased to 181 days. The waiting period for receiving the sickness benefit has been reduced from three to two days.

The social security scheme, which was previously confined to Karachi, Hyderabad, and Lyallpur, covering only the textile workers now covers 4.50 lakh workers of industrial and commercial establishments in about forty cities and towns of Punjab, Sind and North West Frontier Province (NWFP). The three social security institutions of Punjab, Sind, and NWFP have set up about 140 medical care units of their own besides having contractual arrangements with government and private hospitals and clinics. The Sind Social Security Institution has already built a 200-bed hospital in Landhi and a 50-bed hospital in Kotri which are expected to be commissioned soon.

Some other major reforms which have resulted in removing the maldistribution of wealth in Pakistan introduced by the government of Pakistan are nationalization of major industries, nationalization of the banking system, nationalization of the life insurance business, and exchange reforms. These reforms, as a matter of fact, revolutionized the whole economic system of Pakistan by making available to the national government the money for improving the lot of the common man and bridging the gap between the rich and the poor. The money which formerly was circulated among a few people and the fruits of all development that used to remain within a limited circle have now been channeled to the masses of the country.

Other countries of the world, and particularly the developing countries, including mine, have still to do a lot in removing the maldistribution of wealth which definitely is an obstacle to full participation in development.

PART II

## ELISABETH THIAM

DIRECTOR OF THE CABINET, MINISTRY OF LABOR
AND SOCIAL AFFAIRS, IVORY COAST

ONE CAN look at the problem of development in many ways. The way one approaches this question clearly has something to do with the results sought and the specialty of the person who is doing the looking. I shall discuss this subject in my capacity as a social worker.

In order to be effective, development should be seen as a global notion, general both in its range and its objectives. It should cover every aspect of life and mobilize all strata of the population. As one of the most complex of all phenomena, there is no lack of examples where development has failed disastrously because economic and social leaders in particular have not taken sufficient pains to ensure that the development process embraces all the different aspects involved.

The best-qualified authorities unanimously agree that, in the first development decade, and especially in the case of retarded countries, the accent has been placed on the maximization of economic growth without paying sufficient attention to the social consequences of this growth. As a result, social indicators have revealed some very worrying phenomena that tend to lower the value of man and deepening despair. Most prominent among these social indicators are:

1. The increasing backwardness of the traditional agricultural sector
2. The pauperization of village populations
3. The acceleration of the rural exodus and urban unemployment
4. The disorderly growth of the major urban centers, with the proliferation of shanty towns, and so forth.

By tackling the problem of the direct impact of the distribution of wealth on participation in development we are in fact bringing together the two key components of development: material factors, such as financial resources, raw materials, natural resources, and acquired wealth; and intangible factors, essentially consisting of human resources. In one sense, human resources may be included among natural resources; in other words, among spontaneous resources, since their plentiful availability influences the amount of the material factors of development.

THE INFLUENCE OF THE DISTRIBUTION OF NATURAL AND
ACQUIRED WEALTH ON DEVELOPMENT

Any development undertaking presupposes the prior existence of a number of factors we shall term *primary,* or *original:*
  1. A more or less organized human group founded upon a common will to existence.

At the present stage of the political process, the State is the symbol of these groupings.
  2. Physical factors: the territory or geographical delimitation which marks the limits of the zone of influence for action
  3. The known or suspected natural potential of this territory (mines, minerals, and so forth)
  4. Men (seen as a natural resource) living in this territory, whether or not they are prepared for the activities of the community.

To begin with, let us consider those primary or original factors that possess greater or lesser potential and are apt to contribute to the development undertaking. The natural distribution of fertile and poor land, of easily accessible zones and those that are less so, already plays a major role in development. This is merely an observation concerning phenomena on which humans, at our present stage of understanding, have not yet been able to exert any influence.

Most important for us is to see what influence the distribution of acquired wealth has on development. How do we handle problems affecting humanity as a whole? More precisely, who decides what are the fairest solutions to these problems?

I think all will agree that world affairs are influenced by a form of discrimination founded on the possession of acquired wealth, expressed in terms of economic indicators such as the gross national product (or net national product), per capita income, and so forth. These economic indicators continue to dominate at the highest level of the international political structure (the Security Council of the UN) where the leadership of States is a function of their economic and technological power.

The discrimination based on acquired wealth can also be seen in the conduct of the economic affairs of the world, where the financial and commodity markets—these last constituting the principal source of income for the slow-developing nations—are completely dominated by the wealthy nations. Consequently, we are obliged to observe the accentuation of the impoverishment of the raw-material-producing countries; this impoverishment is attributable to the increasing imbalance in the terms of world trade (something of a euphemism, I might add).

At the national level, and referring solely to the example of the developing countries, one notes the existence of oligarchs who have mainly established themselves as a result of their undeniable dynamism at the most difficult moments in the period in which State structures were being established. On becoming national leaders, these personalities assume responsibility for the conduct of the affairs of state, both because of their heroic and successful struggles against the colonial powers and because of their mastery over sociopolitical phenomena. On account of their more ample living conditions (from direct and indirect income), these leaders are more or less omnipresent, and they effectively participate in the direction of national life. They determine the orientation of national activities, they participate in the implementation of policy, and they supervise the execution of programs.

Opposed to this minority, we find various strata of the population which may be classified in two groups:

1. Those with formal, permanent incomes, fixed by the politico-administrative authorities, with a hierarchic scale taking professional qualifications into account.
2. Those with informal incomes—the great mass of peasant farmers, agricultural laborers, and operatives in the secondary and tertiary sectors.

This broad mass, forming 70 percent to 80 percent of the potentially active population in African countries, was, until recently, a mere "object" of development rather than a "subject" because its participation in national life was, if not negligible, at best insignificant—except, that is, where this participation was imposed, as in the case of institutions automatically retaining a portion of income (notably agricultural) in order to redistribute it among rural areas to obtain a better balanced regional development. This is what has happened in the Ivory Coast, for example, through the action of the Caisse de Stabilisation des Productions Agricoles.

The main reason for the effective exclusion of this part of the population lies in the total lack of education, in partial education, or in education ill-adapted to the real needs of social and economic development, combined with the precariousness of material living conditions, due to inadequate income and the consequent obsessive search for the means to ensure immediate survival. In these conditions, it becomes quite illusory to think in terms of associating this great mass of people in discussions concerning the best way of involving them in local, regional, national, and, a fortiori, world development tasks. In fact, participants in the process of development are selected in terms either of intellectual ability or economic capacity due to the accumulation of material (essentially monetary) goods.

In the developing countries we must count chiefly on an improved distribution of accumulated wealth as the fundamental factor in increasing the participation of populations in development tasks. In this particular context one is also forced to admit that money incomes, especially salaries, currently constitute the surest guarantee of even some semblance of a decent material and spiritual life, one that could liberate the individual, both physically and intellectually, thus fitting him to participate fully and consciously in activities in the national interest.

THE IMPORTANCE OF HUMAN CAPITAL IN DEVELOPMENT

In this last quarter of the century we are observing a growing emphasis on human capital as a key factor in development.

Development presupposes the association of two prime factors: material and intangible. The latter are generally referred to as "human resources." Furthermore, underdevelopment is generally characterized by a lack both of capital goods (a question of financial resources) and of suitably qualified or technically trained human capital capable of playing an effective role in the life of the country.

One rather more comforting observation, however, concerns the priority which developing states place upon the accumulation of human capital. Put more simply, this means the training and education of the population by all known means. In the Ivory Coast, the President, M. Félix Houphouet Boigny, has expressed this major concern by defining education and professional and technical training as "the priority of priorities." The proportion of the annual budget devoted to education has grown constantly, now accounting for about one third of the operating budget. In other words, investment in human beings is looked upon as a major factor in development.

The most obvious consequences of this training program are:

1. The quest for a certain level of education or for a greater open-mindedness
2. The prospect of ensuring formal and permanent incomes to entire populations, capable of freeing them from immediate worries about their daily needs in the first place and, consequently, rendering them more available for participation in the development process.

For, the basis of any valid commitment and of any effective initiative in the community must be the ability to understand the need for mobilization of the nation's energies. Yet, without a minimum income there can be no participation in national life. Without some familiarity with agricultural techniques or without some access to more or less advanced intellectual training, there can be no hope of attaining these minimal incomes.

In the developing countries, one way of redistributing incomes, and hence acquired wealth, lies in the social security system, which remains a widely underestimated factor for development. I need hardly emphasize the potential importance of improved use of the social security system, but its underlying principles are going to have to be rethought in order to suit them better to the real needs waiting to be satisfied in our regions. The most urgent among these is the need for a socio-health infrastructure and for family allowances for families falling below a certain poverty threshhold.

Even if we have to admit that money still takes precedence over the heart and reason in the present world, we must also recognize the efforts being made at all levels to improve the status of the latter two in order to make them into enlightened and indispensable interlocutors for the former.

# The Contribution of the
# Physically and Mentally
# Handicapped to Development

PART I

## YOSHIAKI NEMOTO

SECRETARY, NATIONAL COUNCIL ON SOCIAL WELFARE, JAPAN

IN DISCUSSING especially the theoretical and philosophical aspects of this subject, I shall draw from actual experiences which handicapped people in Japan, their relatives, welfare workers, educators, and medical doctors have had during the past ten years and more. These people have made great progress, not only in improving the administration of welfare programs for the handicapped, but also in developing concepts and theory. Moreover, this theory and its practical application have affected a wide sector of programs outside what might be considered strictly the area of social welfare.

In Japan, the handicapped have been subjected to a long and bitter tradition of discrimination and segregation. Historically speaking, during the period between 1600 and 1868, known in Japan as the Tokugawa Era, feudal rulers established a rigid social hierarchy. This hierarchy included, in descending order, the warriors at the top, then the farmers, the artisans, the merchants, and the outcaste Eta-Hinin classes at the bottom. Eighty percent of the population were farmers. The governing rulers were supported almost entirely by agriculture, and they squeezed the farmers of their lifeblood through heavy taxation on the rice they produced. The farmers were thus obliged to live miserable lives with but slight consolation except that there were so-called "special" people, such as the outcastes and the handicapped, who were of even lower social status. As one of these lower classes, the handicapped were used by the rulers for controlling other levels of society. By manipulating various class groups in this way, the Tokugawa rulers were able to maintain a surprisingly stable society, but not without the sacrifice of human rights and dignity.

In 1868, with the Meiji imperial restoration, Japan emerged from the feudal era and ended her long period of political isolation. The new imperial regime, in contrast, pursued an aggressive policy of overseas contact, using as its slogan, "A Rich Country through Military Power." The handicapped fared even more poorly under this policy than they had under the Tokugawas. They were considered unable to contribute to either military might or the wealth of the nation. The mentally handicapped were considered to be of weak will and so potential murderers, arsonists, prostitutes, delinquents, and vagrants. For this reason the handicapped and their families were considered antinational and a burden on society. They had to hide from the cold eyes of a society bent in mad fashion on conquering the world.

In 1945 the Second World War ended in defeat for Japan. One year later, a new constitution was enacted. This constitution differed at many points from its forerunner. Especially unique was Article 9, calling for the abandonment of any kind of war. Also of special note was the declaration that the sovereignty of the nation rests with the people. With fresh liberal innovations, this new constitution pointed Japan's way into the future. Of special importance for the field of social welfare was Article 25, which made it clear that all the citizens of our country were to enjoy the right to a minimum standard of daily life and health and that the nation at all levels of its social structure must promote social welfare, social security, and public health.

In spite of the ideals of our new constitution, the actual living conditions of what we might call the "socially weak people"—including, in addition to the handicapped, such groups as the elderly, children, and the poor—were still very marginal and involved many difficult problems. From the latter half of the 1950s and into the 1960s Japan's government energetically promoted a policy of high economic growth. Today, Japan's gross national product has risen to the extent that our country is one of the world's top three economic powers. However, this economic growth has itself created many new problems, such as pollution, increased traffic accidents, an overheated urbanization and an accompanying depopulation of rural areas.

The emergence of these problems changed our whole concept of social welfare. Formerly, we thought of welfare as services for special groups. Now we see all the citizens of the land as being recipients of welfare services and programs. Further, it should be emphasized that the bitter experiences of our past have stimulated the people to regard social welfare not as the gift of a magnanimous governing body, but as their lawful "right" in the truest sense of the word. We are coming to realize that true rights cannot be achieved through ready-made programs handed down from above. Rights can only be achieved and enjoyed when the people themselves are involved in the process of formulating the services and programs.

Having been to a certain degree liberated by these developments, the handicapped people and their families, realizing their right to a normal life, surmounted their limiting circumstances and organized associations among those of their own number who faced similar problems. In 1953 one group of parents who had mentally handicapped children attending special classes in a public school organized a small association based on their common burden and sorrow. They appealed to all parents of mentally handicapped children in Japan to overcome their sorrow and urged them to pioneer in developing a future for their children. This association was welcomed enthusiastically by the people concerned and was called the Association for the Educational Nurture of the Mentally Handicapped or, more familiarly, the Parents' Helping Hand

Society. After some twenty years of experience and practice, this organization has recently announced a new set of program objectives:

1. Autonomy of daily life for the lightly handicapped
2. Adequate protective care for those with severe handicaps
3. Guaranteed care after the parents' death
4. A program of prevention and early discovery
5. An immediate program of countermeasures to existing problems.

At present there are about fifty organizations of this kind, each specializing in one particular form of handicap. Most of these organizations are members of our National Council of Social Welfare. The activity of these organizations is largely directed toward government social welfare policy-making and has involved both parents and teachers as well as others concerned with the handicapped. From this effort has resulted the enactment in 1970 of the fundamental law for the protection of mentally and physically handicapped persons. In accordance with the provisions of this law, the Central Association to Protect Handicapped People has been established under the direction of the Office of the Prime Minister.

In another related development, The National Study Association for Problems of the Handicapped was established in 1969. Its purposes include: guarding the rights of handicapped people; securing means for proper development of the handicapped; promoting movements for autonomy and democratization of the handicapped and for the integration of theory and practice regarding the handicapped. And so, after a long history of neglect, the nation has come at last to promote actively the welfare of the handicapped. Furthermore, this has resulted directly from the efforts of these handicapped people and their families.

We should note that during the 1960s, as a part of the establishment of various associations, including those of the handicapped, there emerged several resistance movements initiated by service recipients themselves. One example is that of Shigeru Asahi, a public assistance recipient in Okayama Prefecture, who in 1963 brought suit against the government in the highest court of the land, claiming that his welfare payments were inadequate. He contended that "to live" is not "to live in an animal way" but to live in "a healthy and civilized way," as provided for by Article 25 of the Constitution. This case is the first instance of a court procedure against the government by a public assistance recipient. A similar example was a movement begun around 1960 by mothers who wanted free oral polio vaccine for their babies. It is encouraging to report that the number of examples of service recipient participation in movements to improve policy and expand services is on the increase. Many more examples might be cited.

In my opinion the most profound contribution to the understanding of the handicapped and social welfare comes out of the practical experience of institutions for severely handicapped children. This contribution has come to be referred to as the theory of guaranteed development opportunity and is aimed at realizing the total development of the child. The late Dr. Kazuo Itoga, a director of one such institution, in commenting on a philosophy for work with the handicapped has said: "It is not a matter of society being a light in the life of the handicapped child but rather that the handicapped child should be a light for society." To put it another way, for our welfare policy to reflect pity for the miserable situation of the handicapped is very counterproductive. Even the severely handicapped child has his own personal life and the need for self-realization. The handicapped child is born to live his or her own life as only he or she can live it. It is the children themselves who represent the potential, the rough, raw material which somehow must be polished so that each individual personality will become a glistening gem. To release this potentiality is a unique, creative, and productive activity. The effort of those related to the field of social welfare should be to build a society where all recognize the potential of every handicapped person to be a capable producer for society and not simply a blotter to absorb society's energy.

We must concede that there has been a long history of discrimination, involving race, sex, social class, and economic inequality as well as the handicapped. These complex issues have been left to our generation to solve. The encouraging thing is that today the common people, those who actually experience the handicaps, those who are actually discriminated against, have the opportunity to challenge these issues. If this new spirit of challenge is encouraged and allowed to develop, I feel sure that our generation and the generations to follow will find solutions to every kind of discrimination.

Certainly it is not in the field of services for the handicapped alone, but in every area of service—in education, in medical care, and in labor relations—that this new spirit of challenge is so desperately needed. No longer can we simply plan services for those in need from a position of power, wealth, and prestige, a position we might refer to as the "capitalist ethic." Rather, these plans must be developed through the participation of the recipients of the services themselves, a position which we might rather hope is a true "welfare ethic."

I feel that in Japan we are reaching the dawn of a new age in regard to this kind of understanding. Further, I am proud to be able to point to the activities and participation of a group of handicapped and their families. It means a great deal to be able to report the important influence they are bringing to understanding the problem of welfare in my country. It is to people like these that we owe our thanks. It is their efforts that lead us into the future.

PART II

# VOAHANGY RAKOTONDRAINIBE,

MEDICAL DIRECTOR, INSTITUTE FOR MOTOR
REEDUCATION, MADAGASCAR

IN MOST countries, whatever their ideologies, there is one essential objective: that all should participate in the wealth of the community, and that is to be achieved in the first place by providing each person with work that permits himself and his family to live and confers on him the sense of his own dignity. Full employment has become a fundamental principle of economic policy in virtually every country. If we are to maintain economic growth in a constantly changing world, we must employ our resources to the fullest; all potential workers, including the physically handicapped, must therefore more than ever play their part in the productive process to the utmost of their capacities. By "handicapped" we mean not only those individuals who are physically afflicted or physiologically deficient, but also persons suffering from mental deficiencies.

Each nation, then, must evolve its own constructive policy permitting all citizens to receive from the community the aid required to enable them to lead a humanly dignified and socially effective life. The important thing, in the final analysis, is to make the best possible use of each individual's potential. We must integrate the greatest possible number of workers with their known capacities into the economic circuit, bearing in mind the need to obtain the greatest possible efficiency for the economy. For this, the handicapped must in no way be excluded from the process.

In addition, the right to work, like the right to life, should be equal for all. Every human being aspires to live like his fellow men. And each salary, whether paid to a handicapped or an able-bodied person, contributes via taxes and social insurance payments to financing the collectivity and social insurance schemes.

Present-day society contains an ever-growing number of handicapped persons because it is constantly creating new factors of inadaptation. These are caused by:

1. The rising number of traffic accidents and accidents at work
2. The various assaults (both physical and psychic) upon people due to the pace of modern life
3. The effectiveness of modern medicine, which saves an increasing number of human lives while at the same time increasing the number of survivors suffering from permanently diminished capacities due to cancer, tuberculo-

sis, traumatisms, cardiac illness, nervous and mental illnesses.

But, to tell the truth, who among us is not handicapped in one way or another? It is merely a question of degree of capacity.

Society's attitudes toward the handicapped have changed considerably over the ages. In the earliest times, the handicapped person was quite simply rejected; eugenics was already being practiced in Sparta. The following stage in society's attitudes was comparable to its attitude toward leprosy. Out of charity, society assumed responsibility for the handicapped while at the same time operating a segregation that was no less profound for not being visible, for its first impact was psychological. The first duty of the handicapped, as well of the person looking after him, was to understand that, being infirm, he must resign himself to finding the least bad position for himself in the world of the infirm. For a long time, only very limited employment opportunities were offered to the blind. People were concerned in the first place with providing them with work in what one might call "soft" jobs or minor crafts calling for only rudimentary training. Of course, the returns from this kind of work were correspondingly mediocre and precarious.

In the so-called "developed" countries, where the problem of professional and social rehabilitation of the handicapped has been most studied, if not actually resolved, it took the acute need for labor felt in the course of the First and the Second World War before they got around to mobilizing fully all the labor available, including those members of the labor force apparently least suitable. So it was economic need that gave rise to the notion of social rehabilitation for the handicapped. After the Second World War, the factors brought together in the course of the war were organized into a body of doctrine and, in most modern nations, were employed in order to obtain the total social rehabilitation of the handicapped.

Today, with the pace of technological progress, we are seeing the emergence of an ever-wider range of crafts and jobs requiring very little physical strength. There are already a good many jobs for which physical adaptability is not a major condition. Even in the industrial sector, the more we rely upon mechanical progress, the more we employ automatic and electronically controlled processes, the less the physical state of persons working in factories counts. As a consequence, handicapped persons no longer pose, or pose fewer, insoluble problems.

Experience in many countries shows that the judicious employment of handicapped workers combined with normal profitability is no longer chimerical. The principle of equal opportunity in work has been applied in the United States, where it is held that each person is professionally suited to one or more professions. Consequently, there is no effective difference between handicapped and able-bodied workers.

The first question we have to answer when dealing with the problem of handicapped people working (whether for the first time or returning to work) concerns the number of people to be reintegrated into the normal economic cycle. So far as I know, there has never been any official census of the total number of handicapped persons in Africa. But the European Technical Conference on Rehabilitation, organized in 1959 by the World Health Organization, fixed, on the basis of rough estimates, the proportion of African populations that was handicapped and yet capable of benefiting from rehabilitation and hence capable of participating in the national economy at between one percent and 5 percent. Whether for a developed or for a developing country, this represents a far from negligible percentage of available resources.

But in order to achieve a normal and profitable employment of the handicapped it will be necessary to adapt the physical, intellectual, and moral condition of those concerned as closely as possible to the demands of professional work; at the same time, it will be necessary to work out a job policy and perhaps even modify working conditions so that the handicapped can give of their best. The first part of this program involves professional rehabilitation designed to ensure that the handicapped person suffers from no professional inadequacy. For this, in an economy where rising production goes hand in hand with technological progress and specialization, the handicapped person must increasingly strive to compensate his infirmity by means of ever higher professional qualifications; for overqualification is the key to his problem —qualification tends to eliminate the physical handicap. On the one hand, they work in unison (one makes use of the difficulties in order to develop one's strong points), and on the other hand, qualifications enable one to overcome the handicap. But once the desired level of qualification has been attained, the problem is then to maintain and, if possible, improve it still further in order to keep abreast of new techniques. With this in mind, the more solid the basis for this professional qualification, the more the handicapped worker will be in a position to play an important role in production. But precisely one of the problems encountered in rehabilitation work is the lack of basic culture, both among adults and the young, many of whom suffer from a heavy scholastic handicap due to their illness, and the maximum possible effort must be made to remove this particular handicap.

But in all cases, the social and professional rehabilitation of the handicapped presupposes a uniform process that must be set in motion as early as possible, that is, at the outset of the active phase of care, which should comprise functional retraining, professional guidance, professional retraining or adaptation, and, finally, finding a job.

The important thing, then, is to provide the handicapped with professional training or retraining, enabling them to find and keep jobs under the same conditions as able-bodied workers. In this respect, it is essential to develop professional retraining and readaptation centers. The broadest possible coordination between the various departments of the ministries involved in each country (health, labor, civil service, education, social insurance) is vital to efficiency.

In professional retraining centers, training should be preceded by a precise report on the disabilities of the handicapped person, which amounts to an assessment of the remaining aptitudes on the basis of which a valid professional life can be reconstructed. The conclusions of this report should be matched against the realities of the labor market and its current needs before any decisions concerning professional guidance are made; this should help avoid any subsequent underemployment. One must be realistic; therefore, the more the teaching in retraining centers is adapted to what is known about the labor market, the better the chances handicapped workers will have of being reintegrated into the economic circuit.

In addition to taking account of the realities of the labor market, job-finding for the handicapped should also take certain other factors into account.

1. A lot remains to be done to convince the handicapped person that his condition need not prevent him from doing as well as others. He is a worker like the others. The notion of philanthropy must be eliminated: there are workers and there are employers.

The handicapped person must, moreover, cease to behave as an assisted person and seek profitability above all. Sometimes handicapped people manifest a stubborn egocentricity or else a certain aggressivity largely due to the very real difficulty they have in convincing people of their true worth, a difficulty that is reinforced by the fact that they naturally feel a degree of bitterness or envy. Handicapped people must understand that all conscious beings, whether normally or abnormally constituted physically, have a useful role to play wherever they may be.

2. It is necessary, also, to allay the apprehensions of the employer and workmates of handicapped people. The examples set by a good many firms in France, England, and elsewhere have done much to eliminate prejudices in the last few years. The risk of accidents at work or in travel are, if anything, lessened, since the handicapped person often has a more acute sense of potential danger; in general, he is no more responsible for, or a victim of, accidents than other workers. As for job profitability, this is certain, provided certain vital conditions, such as the proper suitability of tasks and their material, intellectual, and psychological appropriateness, are fulfilled.

Job-finding for the mentally deficient merits special mention here, as it involves somewhat different problems from those of job-finding for the physically handicapped. More than anyone else, the mentally deficient person is especially sensitive to insecurity; if he is not reassured of his worth, if he is not encouraged, if he feels distrusted, he will never acquire anything lasting. Retraining centers for the mentally deficient should be adapted to the particular requirements of these subjects. In general, the mentally deficient person is the more effective in his work the more narrowly he is specialized in its execution, the more clearly defined his responsibilities, and the more clearly his orders are expressed. In addition, his tasks must be made comprehensible to him, and his activities should be more in harmony with his level of maturity than with his aspirations. Each time one recycles the mentally deficient one comes up against specific problems, for the mentally deficient is obliged to overcome a dual handicap: his own, consisting of his inhibitions and his depersonalization, and those, which are more important, which society places in front of him. All too often, a stay in a mental hospital is regarded as a stigma. All therapeutic efforts are in vain if, on leaving the hospital, the patient cannot find an understanding environment but merely prejudice and taboos, still alive in a society which seeks to turn each into the reflection of all. In any case, the social rehabilitation which is the ultimate goal of all psychiatric treatment and the sign of cure cannot be the work of an isolated doctor. It implies the participation and the support of the entire population, and notably of employers.

As a practical conclusion I offer a few suggestions concerning at least those countries where the problem of social reintegration of handicapped persons has yet to be resolved (or sometimes even envisaged). In order to bring about participation in economic development of a not insignificant part of the population, it might be a good idea to set up an interministerial committee made up of representatives of the ministries of health, labor, civil service, education, and so forth. This committee could be responsible for the training, the retraining, and the social rehabilitation of all handicapped persons.

The tasks of this committee would be:

1. To ensure the identification and rehabilitation of the handicapped
2. To ensure the best possible medical treatment for those concerned
3. To encourage reeducation, professional retraining, and hence to encourage the creation and running of specialized centers
4. To organize the employment of handicapped persons in appropriate jobs, taking labor market conditions into account
5. To create, through the press, radio, television, and all other information media, a favorable climate for the rehabilitation of the handicapped
6. To supervise the hiring of handicapped workers, which implies that a law obliging employers to employ a certain percentage of handicapped workers will have to be passed.

By "employers" I mean not only all firms whose staffing system will permit this, whether they be industrial, commercial or agricultural enterprises, but also public establishments. While this is undoubtedly a coercive measure, it should not be applied in such a way that the employer feels obliged to take on handicapped people; it should rather be of such a nature as to persuade him that a handicapped person, after adequate retraining, is just as capable of working as an able-bodied person, provided he has been properly guided and that the job-finding has been selective. Experience in a number of countries that have established a policy of rehabilitation shows that, if these two rules are respected, the problem of reintegration of the handicapped need not be insoluble and that the latter, despite their difficulties, remain and must remain fully active human beings.

## PART III

# JEAN VANIER

L'ARCHE, FRANCE

THOSE WHO live close to wounded people become rather accustomed to hearing talks about how so-called "normal" people should help their unfortunate brothers and sisters. We rarely ask what handicapped people can bring to others. The very thought rarely comes to mind; it seems so remote and far-fetched.

And yet I feel deeply that handicapped people have an important part to play in the development of the world, in helping it to find its equilibrium. They can ensure that development is not just a development of mind and matter, but a development of the total human person, who is certainly intelligence and creativity, activity and productivity, but who is also a heart, capable of love, a seeker of peace, hope, light, and trust, striving to assume the reality of suffering and of death.

I have had the grace and joy to live with mentally handicapped adults over the last ten years. With friends, we have been able to create some forty-five small homes for men and women who were either roaming the streets, locked up in asylums, or just living idly—though frequently in a state of aggression 'or depression—with families who did not know how to cope with them. These homes of l'Arche are in France, Canada, the United States, England, Scotland, Belgium, and Denmark, as well as in Calcutta and Bangalore in India; our first home in West Africa is just beginning in the Ivory Coast. Each of these homes welcomes and finds work for eight to ten handicapped men and women and for their helpers or assistants. They try to be communities of reconciliation where everyone can grow in activity, creativity, love, and hope. Some of the handicapped people leave us and find total autonomy; others, who are more severely handicapped, will stay with us always.

It is this experience of daily living, working, and sharing with my handicapped brothers and sisters that has made me so sensitive to the question of their contribution to the development of our world. A man or woman can only find peace of heart and grow in motivation and creativity if he or she finds a meaning to life. If they are there only to be helped and can bring nothing to others, then they are condemned to a life of simply receiving, of being the last, the most inferior. This will necessarily bring them to depression and a lack of confidence in themselves. This, in turn, will push them into anguish and make them aggressive toward themselves and others. For them to find real meaning in life, they must find people who sense their utility, their capacity for growth, and their place in the community and in the world.

The tragedy of humanity is not primarily the lack of development of peoples, or even poverty. It is the oppression, the despisal, and the rejection of those who are weak and in want. It is the horrible and disastrous inequality of wealth and opportunity and lack of sharing. The tragedy of man is his hardness of heart, which makes individuals and nations endowed with the riches of this world despise and consider as inferior those who are poor and handicapped. They not only refuse to help them, they tend also to reject and exploit them.

The tragedy of mankind is the collective national or religious prejudices and pride which close nations and peoples upon themselves, making them think and act as if they were the elected ones and the others enemies to be rejected and hurt, whose development and expansion should be checked. Our world today, with its terrible divisions and hatred, with its continual sounds of war, with its vast budgets being poured into armaments instead of into works for love and justice, is the result of these prejudices and fears.

The tragedy of our world today is that man is still afraid of man. Far from seeing other individuals and peoples as collaborators in the mystery of universal human growth, we see them as enemies of our own growth and development.

It is of course terribly important that misery and starvation be erased from our earth. It is of course terribly important that everyone has access to social and medical benefits. But it is even more important that the hearts of all men open up to universal love and to the understanding of others, to gentle service to mankind and especially to its weaker members. For if we do not work together to create a world of fraternity and of peace, we will sink in wars, economic crises, and national disasters.

There is a continual struggle in all our countries between traditional religious and moral values, lived through family ties, and economic and industrial development. Highly industrialized countries offer a certain financial prosperity, but so frequently this prosperity has been achieved at the cost of the values of community. Competition and the desire for wealth, individual leisure, and liberty have tended to crush compassion and understanding. So it is that we find old people lingering in homes for the aged, handicapped people in large institutions, and a mass of marginal and suffering people unable to work because of alcoholism, drugs, and social ills. We find thousands of children abandoned and given over to social agencies, a frightening rise in delinquency, and prisons which offer only punishment instead of reeducation and so cause the high rise in recidivism. We find mental disease rampant, because in our search for efficiency we have lost our acceptance of "the other" and prefer to label people "mad" than to understand them. We condemn more and more people to live like strangers, in terrible loneliness, in our large urban conglomerations. The growing population of our cities, our disastrous housing and inhuman working conditions, bring a real disequilibrium of the human heart in its quest for love, peace, and truth.

In the small villages of Africa and India, and in rural areas of North America and Europe, there are still sturdy people living simply off the land and artisans bound closely to the matter with which they work. There is deep love and commitment among families. There is a spirit of gentleness and openness, sharing and welcome for the stranger, which has often been lost in the big cities. Certainly this is a generalization, for there are also tribal warfares and social injustices and individual anguishes. But we must not forget the values of fraternity and community held by simple people, which are so often crushed with the coming of economic development. We can see the gradual breakdown of these values as the desire for material possessions is stimulated, as the attractions of big-city leisure activities become stronger, and the older generation and its ways are rejected.

Of course, it is essential that people should develop and find the benefits of greater wealth and security. It is even more essential that this development takes place in a human context which safeguards and strengthens the forces of sharing, participation, and responsibility. Where economic development coincides with the breakdown of cultural and ethnic ties, where villages are destroyed, where children are displaced, and men obliged to leave their homes for far-off lands, the situation is extremely serious: it can gradually cause the destruction of what makes a human being a person.

In each of us there is a mixture of weakness and strength. Each of us is born in weakness, unable to fend for ourselves, to find nourishment, to clothe ourselves, or to walk. The growth to autonomy is long and slow, and demands many years of loving education. The period of strength and capacity during adolescence and manhood, the period during which we are able to act efficaciously and to defend ourselves, to struggle against the forces of nature and environment, is in fact short. After it, we all enter a period of weakness, when our bodies become tired and sick, when we are hurt by the trials and sufferings inherent in human life. And all of us are then called to the last and final poverty of death.

The child in his weakness has all the potential of activity which must grow in him. The strongest of men is inherently weak because he has a mortal body and also because he is called to love and is vulnerable to the sufferings of love and of infidelity in friendship; he is weak because he is capable of depression and sadness, drowning in the vicissitudes of life.

The society which encourages only the strong and the intelligent tends to forget that man is essentially weak. We are all potentially handicapped and we are all called to suffer and to die. So often the search for riches, or hyperactivity in work, is a flight from these essential realities which we must all face one day. What is the meaning of our life, and of suffering, and of death? Are we called simply to be active and to gather wealth, or does man find peace of heart, interior liberty, and happiness in the growth of love? Is it not in service to others, sharing, and mutual understanding—which is not mere sentimentality—that we find this inner peace and human fulfillment?

If people do not refind this energy of love and acceptance of their own intrinsic poverty, if they do not discover that joy comes more in giving than in taking, we are heading for more conflict. If we do not grow in a desire to give our lives rather than to exploit and take the lives of others, then we are all doomed to destruction.

In all societies there are vast numbers of weaker brothers and sisters: those who are aged or depressed; those who have been struck by sickness while young and cannot take on a working life. Are these people just misfits who must be gradually eliminated? Are they just people we must try to reeducate so that they can become active members of society? Or have they a special place and role in the development of our society? This is the question we must ask ourselves.

My experience of living with the wounded, the weak, is that they have very precious values which must be conserved for the full development of society. Their experience of rejection, their experience of suffering, which is a taste of death, has brought them closer to certain realities which others who have not suffered flee and pretend do not exist.

Handicapped people have all the rights of other men: the right to life, to medical and social help, and to work. They are able, when this is recognized, to develop in so many ways. With the right educational and work techniques, many can find their place in the world of work and become totally integrated in that world. I have seen men who at the age of six were judged incapable of any growth working in a factory at the age of twenty and living quite autonomously. Others who were condemned to asylums, to beggary, or to total inactivity are now finding fulfillment as artisans and enjoying life in their community. With care, loving attention, and the right kind of technical help, many can find their place in society.

Handicapped people, and particularly those who are less "able," are frequently endowed with qualities of heart which serve to remind so-called "normal" people that their own hearts are closed. Their simplicity frequently serves to reveal our own duplicity, untruthfulness, and hypocrisy. Their acceptance of their own situation and their humility frequently reveal our pride and our refusal to accept others as they are.

I had occasion once to appear on television with Helen and some others. Helen has cerebral palsy. She cannot talk, she cannot walk, she cannot eat by herself. She is condemned to a wheelchair for the rest of her life. Her only means of communication is through a typewriter, on which she laboriously expresses her thoughts with two fingers. But Helen has the most beautiful smile. She gives herself through her smile. At one moment in the program, someone asked her if she was happy. She broke out into a big smile and typed: "I wouldn't change my life for anything in the world." Her smile got even bigger, and as the program closed the camera picked up the last word she was writing: "Alleluia!"

Helen, who has nothing except her joy and her love, revealed to me and to so many who possess the goods of this earth that fulfillment does not come from material riches but from some inner strength and liberty. Through her acceptance of herself and her condition she showed how poor we are, in all our petty quarrels, pride, and desires.

At a week's meeting with some two hundred people, there was a handicapped man called Glen. He could not use his legs and he lay on the floor. During the last day, there was a period when each person could express what he felt about the week's activity. Glen propped himself up and just said, "I have only one thing to tell you: I love you all so much." His simple words broke down the barriers of convention and of fear in many of us. He was not afraid to talk of love.

So often, "normal" people have interior barriers that prevent them from relating with others in a simple way. All of us have deep needs to love and to be loved. All of us are in the conflict of our fear of death and of our own poverty. We so quickly pretend we are more clever, more intelligent, and more powerful than we actually are. So often we flee reality by throwing ourselves into activity, culture, the struggle for power and prestige. We lose contact with our deep inner selves. Handicapped people do not always have these barriers. In their poverty, they are more simple and loving, and thus they reveal to us the poverty of our riches.

The weaker members of society are total human persons, children of God. They are not misfits or objects of charity. Their weaknesses and special needs demand deep attention, real concern, and continuing support. If we listen to their call and to their needs, they will flourish and grow. If we do not, they will sink into depression, sadness, inward revolt, and a form of spiritual suicide. And we who carry responsibilities will have closed our beings to love and to a strength which comes from God and which is hidden in the smallest and the weakest.

Those who take time to listen to them, who have the inner peace and patience to respond to their silent call, will hear crying in them the great cry of all humanity for love and for peace. A great Dutch psychiatrist has written of the schizophrenic that he is not insane, not made of wood, but "the loudspeaker from whom the sufferings of our time ring perhaps most clearly." [1] The same can be said for all weak and handicapped people who cannot fend for themselves.

If we listen to them, then we, the so-called "normal" people, will be healed of our unconscious egoisms, our hardness of heart, our search for power and for dissipating leisure. We will discover that love, communion, presence, community, and deep interior liberty and peace are realities to be found·and

[1] Jan Foudraine, *Not Made of Wood* (London: Quartet Books, 1974).

lived. We will discover that these can become the inspiration for all men. We will realize more fully that men are not machines or objects to be used, exploited, tyrannized, and manipulated by law and by organizations, but that each one is beautiful and precious, that each one in his uniqueness is like a flower which should find its place in the garden of humanity for the fulfillment and beauty of all mankind.

If each one of us who holds a responsible place in society pays attention to the heartbeats of the smallest, the weakest, and the companionless, then gradually we will make of our countries not lands of competition which favor the strong and powerful, but lands of justice, peace, and fraternity where all men unite and cooperate for the good of every man.

Then nations will no longer rival each other in their search for power, prestige, and wealth, but will work together. They will turn from fear and from group prejudices and from the creation of large and horribly expensive armies. They will use their intelligence, strength, wealth, and natural resources for the growth of all men throughout the world, and especially for the smallest, the weakest, and the companionless. Mankind will then, through the heart of the poor and those crucified in their flesh, refind the road to unity and universal love, where all can be themselves without fear, growing together in love and in the peace of God, our beloved Father.

# Formulation of Population Policy

## Y. F. HUI

DIRECTOR, HONG KONG COUNCIL OF SOCIAL SERVICE

CONCERN FOR population has grown markedly throughout the world in recent years, and with it concern for population policy. The concern is not everywhere the same; that is, it is not everywhere expressed with the same knowledge or intensity, nor even attached to the same object. Nevertheless, it is there. I hope no country will take an exception in this respect. Although some countries may not have a population policy as yet, I am sure the concern is present.

By "population policy" I refer to governmental actions designed to alter population events or that actually alter them. This definition refers to actions by government, whether statements of position, laws, decrees, or administrative programs.

When the Second Asian Population Conference met in Tokyo in November, 1972, twenty-three Asian nations adopted a Declaration of Population Strategy for Development. It is one of the most far-reaching population statements ever endorsed at an international conference of governments. Basically, governments are urged to recognize the essential role of population and family-planning programs as a means of effectively achieving the aspiration of families and their societies and to provide information, education, and services for all citizens as early as possible. The conference recommended, in the area of policy, the following:

1. That population policy should be defined in such a way that consideration is given to: the numbers, the distribution, and the structure of human populations; marriage, family and fertility, health and mortality; mobility and migration; growth; age structures and changes; rural-urban and regional distributions and redistributions

2. That family planning be recognized as an essential means to achieve family well-being; and family planning programs, as an essential means to achieve national goals of the countries that wish to reduce their population growth rate

3. That development be viewed as an integrated process and that the complex relation of economic, social, political, and population plans and developments be assessed in the programs in every field

4. That governments provide a comprehensive and properly evaluated basis of statistical data on population and related variables to guide decisions to measure changes at all levels

5. That population and economic and social development be given a coordinated and integrated status in national planning

6. That countries establish action-oriented population development planning units appropriately placed at high levels in the administrative structure

7. That the requirements in planning be met and the increasing sophistication in methodology be provided through national institutes of population planning and development.

In examining these recommendations it is obvious that some countries are lagging behind in many areas. On top of these are the elements of international and internal migration. Governmental policies with respect to international migration seem to be based largely on concern that employment opportunities for their citizens should not be jeopardized by immigrants. Countries with strong government social service programs might not wish to face increased demand arising from migrations. On the other hand, countries might restrict departure of persons with higher education and skills. Internal migration is less easy to regulate. The settlement of nomadic people has been attempted, as has relocation of people from overcrowded, remote, and poorly endowed areas. Large-scale transfer of people for the expressed purpose of redistribution has not met with great success. Location of industries also has influenced population redistribution, but not much has been attempted in this respect.

Population policy is a policy of means and not of ends. Population measures are not a final value to which others must defer. Population measures are instruments with which to seek other ends no matter what these ends are: be they economic, political, environmental, or social, the ultimate aim must be the improvement of "quality of life." Quality of life is invoked these days as the objective to be optimized as against quantity of life in the form of population growth or population congestion.

Population policy statements can be helpful in many ways. A population statement should be viewed as an effort to legitimize ongoing work and minimize adverse political reaction. It should, however, be recognized that policy statements can be disadvantageous in some situations, as for example, where they lead to a polarization of views. But one instrument which might be considered to help the process of shaping population policy is a national commission. An example is the United States Commission on Population Growth and the American Future. With a population policy and a plan to hold population growth to a certain stipulated figure, a country should seriously consider the appointment of a population commission with the sole purpose of promoting and disseminating information pertaining to population matters. This commission could initiate and undertake population control programs, stimulate interest in demography, and advise the government on all matters related to family planning and population control. The commission could also be given far-reaching power to oversee any groups or persons who plan to promote or disseminate or distribute medicine related to family planning. As a statutory body, the commission could also help to bring about legislation which would provide disincentives to undesirable births. All in all, it is hoped that this commission would be able to transcribe guidelines provided by the population policy into a comprehensive plan and program so as to hold the population growth to a minimum.

With the availability of a plan, the appointment of a Commissioner for Population is evident. The commissioner, with adequate staff, would provide the executive arm to carry out the plans and decisions of the commission. The commissioner would have a central role in planning and coordinating all population programs. He would also be prepared to sponsor or support projects extending across the whole spectrum of population and family-planning programs, such as: training of medical and paramedical personnel; family-planning components of health facilities; use of mass communication techniques; manufacturing of contraceptive materials; establishment of special population studies as well as continuous statistical census and demographic work. He would also be the liaison among government departments such as medical and health, education, social welfare, labor, census and statistics, and others in matters relating to population.

The UN General Assembly has designated 1974 as World Population Year. The World Population Conference of governments will convene in Rumania in August, 1974, to discuss world population problems and policies and, it is hoped, to agree on a world population plan of action. It is also hoped that social workers can be active participants in this vitally important field of population as stimulators, enablers, and even as agents for social change, social legislation, and social action for the betterment of our community.

# The Use of Social Research and Social Indicators—Experiments and Innovations

## ARTHUR J. KATZ

PROFESSOR, SCHOOL OF SOCIAL WELFARE, UNIVERSITY OF
KANSAS, UNITED STATES

THE FUNDAMENTAL and well-accepted value of the social welfare and social work professions is protection and maintenance of human life. This ultimate value becomes, therefore, a criterion to direct policy decisions for social welfare purposes. Closely connected to, and often indistinguishable from, the value of preservation of human life is "quality of life." The existence of life is often synonymous with concern about its quality. Indeed, the quality of human life may at times influence the will to live and can be closely correlated to the process of existence itself. Life quality is variously perceived as self-fulfillment, the fullest development of individual potential or enrichment.

Perhaps the most general definition of quality of life relates to the "well-being of people as individuals or in groups, and to the well-being of the environment in which these people and groups live." [1]

In 1972 a symposium, "The Quality of Life Concept," indicated that at the present time there is no consensus as to what quality of life is or what it means. Consensus only exists that the quality of life concept is important, there is a need to define it, and it is significant as a potential new social decision-making factor. [2]

It is sometimes stated that policy-makers often are misled by

[1] The Environmental Protection Agency Office of Research and Monitoring, Environmental Studies Division, *The Quality of Life Concept* (Washington, D.C.: U.S. Government Printing Office, 1973).
[2] *Ibid.*

inadequate interpretation and by bad information. Social information is often based on obsolete concepts and inadequate research. A critical challenge, therefore, is the search for quality of life indicators which can help to gather new information useful to evaluate the past, guide the action of the present, and plan for the future.

The personal dissatisfaction expressed by large numbers of people form the heart of the problem known as the "quality of life question" in the United States, as in some other nations. The new emphasis currently being developed under the title of "the social indicators movement" attempts to look beyond merely economics to factors of empathic and social concerns in an effort to deal with these expressions.

Attempts to define quality of life have resulted only in criteria being advanced as follows:

Quality of life refers to an indefinite number of states of being and does not imply an evaluation of life styles.

There are as many different life states as there are individuals (i.e., there is no single universal quality of life criteria extant in any society at any given time).

Quality of life refers to a subjective state of the individual and can only be partially explained by using such terms as "happiness," "educated," "welfare," "self-fulfilled," "satisfied," "purpose," etc. The same holds true of their opposites: discontent, illiterate, frustrated, apathetic, alienated, etc.[3]

Attempts to create more specific definitions have produced the following notions about quality of life:

1. It is a function of the objective conditions appropriate to a selected population and the subject of attitude toward those conditions held by persons in that population.

2. It is concerned with a person's sense of well-being, his satisfaction or dissatisfaction with life, or his happiness or unhappiness.

3. Happiness, when related to material comforts, suggests having money left over after taking care of basic necessities and having the necessary time and opportunities for spending

[3] Anton B. Schmalz *et al.,* "Social Indicators," report to National Science Foundation (New World Systems, 1972).

it in a pleasant way. Having a maximum range of choices for a way of life is another aspect.

4. It is an objective measurement of the difference between an individual's state of being as he perceives it and his aspirations, desires, and needs.

5. It is a multidimensional entity of many components: quality of housing, education, health care, and so forth.

A search for defining the quality of life concept involves gathering, ordering, analyzing, and interpreting data related to such life goals. These efforts describe the organized activities which have come to be known as the "social indicators movement."

What are social indicators? A recent definition states:

Statistical time series that measure change in significant aspects of society. Thus, a social indicator may be a time series which at present contains very few points. The aspect of society it measures may not be deemed "significant" by all observers and the "society" involved may be no larger than the population of a census tract. But the social indicator expresses something about the composition, structure, or functioning of that society and expresses it in quantitative terms that can be compared with similar measures in the past or future.[4]

The general tendency in the United States in dealing with issues of quality of life or social development has, in the past, been primarily related to economic indicators such as the gross national product (GNP) and the Consumer Price Index. These have been available to decision-makers in order to measure the progress and the health of the nation. However, the failure of these indicators to account for noneconomic factors has led to the quest for a new set of measures known as social indicators.

Traditionally, the economists' approach to defining quality of life was to interpret quality in quantitative terms. Increasingly, they also have recognized the need to incorporate qualitative factors in their technical analyses. Economists are beginning to note that such concepts as production and distribution, goods and services, commodities and performances, are integrally related to the human actors who control them

---

[4] *Social Indicators Newsletter,* Social Science Research Council Center for Coordination of Research and Social Indicators.

and who in turn are controlled by them. Generally speaking, the top priority for most nations has been economic health. Consideration of the humanistic elements of life, social consciousness, and social indicators has generally come about after the basic problems of economic survival and growth have been dealt with.

Economic measures in the United States and other industrialized nations have always been the major indicators of prosperity and well-being. As long as the GNP rose, it was assumed that the prosperity and well-being of the individual were also rising. There is, however, no evidence that economic prosperity has a high correlation with the state of social well-being or the solution of social problems and social ills. Widespread social unrest in the United States and other countries, and the questioning of the legitimacy of certain traditional institutions, has stimulated a major reexamination of socioeconomic, environmental, and behavioral phenomena both within and outside the economic contexts.

Attempts to predict purely economic futures are highly complex. Since each GNP item behaves differently, one can question the meaning of the GNP. Even per capita GNP is not a sound index since it corresponds to national production rather than consumption. It is possible to devise a way of translating national income accounts like the GNP into a more meaningful expression of well-being, that is, an index of quality of life.

Another frequently quoted definition of social indicators in the United States comes from the volume entitled *Toward a Social Report:*

A social indicator may be defined to be a statistic of direct normative interest which facilitates concise, comprehensive and balanced judgments about the condition of major aspects of a society. It is in all cases a direct measure of welfare and is subject to the interpretation that, if it changes in the "right" direction while other things remain equal, things have gotten better, or people are "better off." Thus, statistics on the number of doctors or policemen could not be social indicators, whereas figures on health or crime rates could be.[5]

[5] U.S. Department of Health, Education, and Welfare, *Toward a Social Report* (Washington, D.C.: U.S. Government Printing Office, 1969).

Much of existing social statistics cannot, however, be considered as social indicators since they are merely records of public expenditures on social programs or quantity of inputs for socio-economic purposes. "It is not possible to say whether or not things have improved when government expenditures on social program or the quantity of some particular input used increase." [6]

Another statement defines social indicators as measurements of transeconomic social phenomenon: "It is normative (or finalized) and is integrated in a self-consistent information system." [7]

Functions of indicators have been described as information, prediction, problem description, and program evaluation, monitoring social change and systems mapping. Social indicators can be seen, therefore, as part of the concepts central to the generation of an information system descriptive of the social system.

The Organization for Economic Cooperation and Development (OECD), which recently completed the first phase of a multiphase program to develop internationally comparable measures of the quality of life, saw the problem as follows:

Better techniques are required to measure and understand the incidence of the costs and benefits of technology among the various social and economic participants involved; an important prerequisite for this will be adequate information on economic and social trends and impacts. Increasingly, sophisticated social indicators should be evolved to minitor these trends and impacts and to provide a system of "early warning" of growing imbalances, social disbenefits, dissatisfactions and emerging social needs. Major efforts should be stimulated to devise social indicators that will permit social components to be fully taken into account when evaluating cost and benefit in technological innovation. [8]

The object of phase one of the OECD effort was to agree on a set of social concerns of importance to the governments of

[6] *Ibid.*

[7] Bernard Caces, "The Development of Social Indicators: a Survey," in *Social Indicators and Social Policy,* Andrew Shonfield and Stella Shaw, eds. (London: Heineman Educational Books, 1972).

[8] "How to Measure Well-Being," *The Organization for Economic Cooperation and Development Observer,* June, 1973.

member countries. The list of concerns is the agenda for phase two, having as its objective the development of statistical indicators which will correspond to the concerns. An initial exchange of views has begun in regard to health indicators. The twenty-four concerns developed in phase one are grouped into eight major areas: (1) help in individual development through learning; (2) employment and quality of working life; (3) time and leisure; (4) command over goods and services; (5) physical environment; (6) personal safety; (7) the administration of justice; and (8) man's place in society. Acknowledging the impracticality of developing a single indicator of gross national well-being, OECD expects that each of the twenty-four social concerns can be represented by one indicator.

The Social Science Division of the National Science Foundation in the United States has awarded some $5.5 million in support of forty projects related to social indicators. The goals of this research program are to lay a scientific ground work for social indicator development and to build a community of research interests.

Current international developments in the social indicators movement is reflected in the following brief review.

*Social Indicators 1973* was published in February, 1974, by the Statistical Policy Division of the U.S. Office of Management and Budget. It is composed of statistical time series selected and organized to describe social conditions and trends in eight areas: health, public safety, education, employment, income, housing, leisure and recreation, and population. In each area several social concerns are identified. In the area of health, these concerns are good health, long life, and adequate access to medical care. In the area of public safety, they are freedom from crime and the fear of crime. Statistical indicators are selected for each concern based upon two criteria: (1) the indicators must measure individual and family (rather than governmental or institutional) well-being; and (2) they must measure end products of, rather than inputs into, social systems.

Most of the indicators in the book are time series showing

national totals aggregated by age, sex, and race. While most of the data in the charts are from federal statistical sources, other data sources were utilized as well. A second edition of the report is planned for 1976.

*Social Trends No. 4, 1973,* published by the Central Statistical Office of Great Britain, is the fourth annual volume containing tables and textual material. Many of the tables have been repeated in all four editions. New data are added as they become available; in particular, data from the new general household survey. Coverage of topics of particular current interest vary from year to year. Among the new tables are job satisfaction by sex and age group, reasons for absence from work, and work stoppage due to industrial disputes by industry in the employment section; migrant flows by sex, age, occupation, citizenship, and region in the population section; and data on attachment of earnings, average waiting time for defendants, and types of sentences for various crimes by age of offenders in the justice and law section.

*Données Sociales,* published in France, is the first of a planned series of annual reports from the Institut National de la Statistique et des Etudes Economiques. It contains data organized to show trends in French society through the functions of production, consumption, and distribution of social goods and services.

One section ("Population Active") describes the world of work including characteristics of the working population, occupational mobility, employment conditions, wages and salaries, industrial strikes, occupational industries, and so on. Another ("Modes de vie, Modéles Culturels") examines the changing consumption patterns of the French people since the Second World War. Data on family budgets, household possessions, vacations and other leisure activities, education, housing, and health are presented.

A third section ("Disparités et Équilibres") focuses on the processes which contribute to the stability of society. Data on public expenditures for social welfare distribution and redistribution of income, as well as on patterns of marriage, fertility, and family structure, social mobility, and criminality, are presented. Data in all sections are broken down by sociopro-fessional class in addition to other descriptors. The report dis-cusses probable causes and consequences of the trends which the data display and suggests systematic linkages among the various social processes they describe.

A Scandinavian survey entitled *About Dimensions of Welfare: an Exploratory Analysis of a Comparative Scandinavian Survey*, published in 1973, is a general survey of welfare values in Denmark, Finland, Sweden, and Norway. The survey was con-ducted in the spring of 1972 and financed by the Social Science Research Council of each participating country. A na-tional probability sample of the population ages fourteen through sixty-four was interviewed.

The basic welfare values used in the survey were cat-egorized as follows: (1) having; (2) loving; and (3) being.

"Having" corresponds to the general notion of level of liv-ing and is measured by two indexes: number of persons per room and income. "Loving" encompasses the individual's feel-ings of belonging, attitude toward neighborhood and friends, and evaluation of opportunities to establish new and satisfac-tory relationships. "Being" denotes self-fulfillment and in-cludes measures of the individual's feelings of uniqueness, op-portunities for self-development, and daily activities. The measures used in the analysis include an index of perceived security and support, happiness, anxiety and complaint scales, and an index of perceived societal conflicts. The study places strong emphasis on cross-national comparability of data collec-tion and analysis, and gives a broad definition to the concept of social welfare.

The Federal Republic of Germany has recently published its first official volume of social statistics, *Gesellschaftliche Daten 1973*. It contains extensive analyses of the social data, mostly from government sources, which are organized into chapters on population, health, education, science and research, em-ployment, income, consumption and standard of living, physi-cal environment, social environment, participation, adminis-tration of justice, and public finance.

In Japan the economic planning agency has recently published *White Paper on National Life 1973,* subtitled *The Life and Its Quality in Japan,* the seventeenth statistical report on Japanese society. The paper focuses on social problems with a view to social welfare policy design. It deals with changing patterns of family consumption, followed by examinations of the health problems of the aged, inequalities of educational opportunity, problems associated with retirement, urban housing conditions, environmental pollution, and vulnerability to accidents, crimes, and natural disasters. It examines the structural components of the recent rapid inflation of the Japanese economy and the resultant problems for the consumer, the wage earner, and the natural environment.

In considering the use of social indicators in policy and planning, Richard Rose points out that the social indicators movement raises the prospect that the skills of social scientists can become more relevant to the activities of government, and therefore possibly more responsive to social needs. He adds, however, the following caution: "It would be ironic if efforts to introduce social indicators, like efforts to introduce PPBS, taught social scientists more about the needs of politicians than it taught politicians about the needs of society." [9] Rose questions whether there is a real demand for indicators, or rather that social scientists are building up this notion of demand in their own minds. He also wonders whether the social indicators concept is "purpose built for political use." [10]

Social indicators should be measures of concepts, not raw facts. They can only have significance by virtue of reference to a larger body of ideas. The concepts which indicators refer to must form part of one or more social theories. Therein lies a major weakness, for the pace of social theory development is indeed a slow one. Some indicators can be multipurpose and relevant to political issues; others are single-purpose and seek to explain social phenomena. Policy-makers do not need to manipulate or react to all of these.

Rose's general proposition is that policy indicators will be

[9] Richard Rose, "The Market for Indicators," in *Social Indicators and Social Policy,* Shonfield and Shaw, *op. cit.*
[10] *Ibid.*

used when their utility to policy-makers is greater than the cost of using them. The costs of using information are not necessarily measured only in money terms, but in other such scarce resources as time and those arising from value conflicts or political contestation. Rose's formula involves such factors as the cost of obtaining information, the cost of consumption, the cost of value conflict, the cost of action, the cost of inaction, and the utility of information.

The essential problem which social indicators attempt to meet is not a new one. The question that has always faced public policy decision-makers has been how to optimize their decisions by basing them on accurate and adequate information. The problem of information is central to effective decision-making. However, as Henriot has pointed out, it is not truly the unique or the most important problem.[11]

The purpose of social indicators is to provide as clear and empirical a picture as possible of the social conditions of the nation or the community. However, merely a collection of uncoordinated pages from the statistical abstract is hardly adequate.

Social indicators must be distinguished from social statistics. The latter are purely descriptive. Social indicators have a close relationship to the goals and objectives of a society, especially those which have been clearly articulated as national policy. Social indicators must attempt to include some sort of qualitative data, such as measurement of social participation, belonging, and satisfaction. Finally, social indicators must emphasize the social costs of developments lest only the economic aspects be considered.

The root of contemporary social problems, at least in the United States, seems not to be primarily a lack of information but rather a conflict of interests. Henriot is critical of the recent literature on social indicators which argues that challenges which are arising from social problems in the United States can be met through the medium of adequate information. This seems to be an oversimplistic notion. Knowing alone

[11] Peter J. Henriot, "Political Questions about Social Indicators," *Western Political Quarterly*, June, 1970.

is not an automatic solution to social ills. At least two other factors are crucial, namely, understanding and doing.

It has become increasingly clear that administration cannot effectively be divorced from politics, neither in theory nor in practice. Means are not independent of ends, and ends (matters of values and interests) are basically political.

Leaders of the social indicators movement in the United States who have contributed to the literature seem to display a common orientation characterized by commitment to long-range planning involving an attempt to manage the environment in a rational fashion. They seem to be committed to reform (change within the existing structure) and thus seek amelioration rather than radical transformation. There is little doubt of their interest in changing social conditions, attacking the problems of poverty and racism through programs of positive government assistance.

The proponents of social indicators must also face up to the danger inherent in their management bias which suggests a tendency toward elitism. Concentrating power in social science techniques can place a strain upon the traditional democratic process. An antidemocratic elitism is not inevitable if those who have the social planning-management biases and social accounting expertise assume positions of authority. There is inevitably the danger that people who develop the "best" programs for a society may tend to impose them upon the rest of the population who neither understand nor want these programs. Information, particularly social information, is not politically neutral.

Currently, no one is suggesting the direct utilization of social indicators in the overt management of society; however, the possibility exists:

From Machiavelli and Adam Smith to modern social researchers, social scientists have been politically oriented. In their "applied" roles or moods they have addressed themselves to the ruler; intermittently [only have] they turned their attention to the troubles of less privileged groups among the ruled.[12]

An overview of the literature within the frame of the social indicators movement presents a picture of social scientists

[12] Harold W. Wilensky, *Organizational Intelligence* (New York: Basic Books, 1967).

engaged in research interested in improving the human condition, seeking rationality and order. However, such efforts may possibly produce the very same problem which they hope to address.

Is social information the key factor in policy decision-making? Having the knowledge, is one then free to make the most efficient and soundest decisions in policy and planning? Examining the possibilities of using social information in developing countries, it is important to understand that the social indicators movement comes out of the more highly developed societies, and that there is neither an adequate theory nor a model that can be quickly transplanted.

In discussing national social development the following definition seems critical:

Development means many things; it means dams and factories, roads and canals, bush clearing, electrification, soil improvement, universities, secondary schools, primary schools, sanitation, research and a multitude of other activities and achievements. But above all, development means people . . . the preparation and activation of people is the cause of economic and social development.[13]

Itzhak Galnoor [14] points out that there is very little of a conceptual framework to guide efforts of nations toward social development. Is the soft and imprecise social indicator "liberty of the people" a critical factor? Can this determine other economic and social conditions?

Latter-day scholars confine their observations to data that could be incorporated in quantitative models and compare nations according to their economic characteristics. . . . Unfortunately, the comparative and cross-cultural analysis studies made by some social scientists have not been used much in the challenging area of development planning.[15]

A broadened social definition of development must take place, and the efforts of the UN in the area of comparative social research are extremely helpful in that direction. Comparative scholars have begun to introduce social information

---

[13] Leopold Laufer, *Israel and the Developing Countries; New Approaches to Cooperation* (New York: Twentieth Century Fund, 1967).
[14] Itzhak Galnoor, "Social Information for What," *The Annals,* January, 1971.
[15] *Ibid.*

to cross-national research. Galnoor also makes a distinction between social information designed to be used for understanding society on the one hand and for policy-making on the other. For purposes of development, however, this distinction does not seem useful or meaningful since at the present stage of the art of social information it makes more sense to talk about multipurpose social data capable of meeting different needs.

These contemporary efforts known as social indicators are geared to improve our social information systems. They should be supported. Understanding and doing begin with a sound base of knowing. The more efficient and effective our knowledge base, the greater opportunity we may have for sound policy decisions, planning actions, and program operations.

Social indicators have excellent promise for aiding in this effort although, to be sure, the technology is currently in its infancy. To interpret social indicators as a panacea with magical properties is a mistake. They are only an instrument. The skill, knowledge, and values of those who will make functional use of this tool are of critical significance.

However, we have already seen some interesting positive developments in redirecting purely economic concerns for national development to include human and social factors. Any movement which develops a high order of technology and a cadre of technocrats potentially can develop into an elite power structure. Those in control of a social information system could therefore be in a critical position to manipulate social policy.

At the same time, the value to be gained from social indicators can contribute soundly to the research efforts of those who labor on behalf of making our social systems more responsive to the needs of the human condition.

*Reports of*
*Commissions and*
*Special Meetings*

# Commission I. The Role of Social Welfare in Economic and Social Development—Targets and Programming

*Chairman:* Richard B. Splane, *Canada*
*Vice-chairman:* Kim Hak Mook, *Korea*
*Rapporteur:* Joseph Ben-Or, *Israel*

THE MEMBERS of Commission I were undaunted by the magnitude of their assignment. Their task was to consider the role of social welfare in economic and social development. And while they were asked to give special attention to targets and programming, further guidelines required them to consider the extent and nature of social welfare participation in the planning and assessment of developmental policy and the extent and effectiveness of measures to increase people's participation in decision-making and in the provision of services for themselves. They were further called upon to consider how welfare personnel could most effectively act as proponents of social action and as facilitators of communication.

The term "social welfare" is used to include the wide range of policies and services designed to bring about ways of life acceptable to individuals, groups, and communities, sometimes thought of collectively as the "social aspects of development" and including policies and services designed to strengthen individuals, groups, and countries, confronted with economic, physical, mental, or social disabilities, together with those aimed at influencing the remedy of conditions leading to dependency.

In undertaking their assignment they began by examining the situation in many of the countries represented on the commission and in so doing encountered wide national differences not only in degrees of development, measured in economic terms, but in a wide range of other factors: levels of education; internal cultural and linguistic differences or, put more positively, the degree of national cohesiveness; political ideologies; forms of government; degrees of freedom of expression and political action; access to resources; access to technological skills and services; and freedom from internal or external economic domination.

There were also wide differences in the extent to which members felt that social welfare was currently succeeding in influencing economic and social development. Some members felt that far too little progress was being made in moving from the dominance of economic development at any cost—development, that is, achieved with scant attention to social, cultural, and environmental factors. Others painted a more optimistic picture, citing national plans which reflect an increasing consciousness of social factors. But none of the members of the commission was satisfied with the degree of progress being achieved in and beyond their own countries. Many remedial measures were discussed:

1. Widening their own social welfare horizons

In this connection, members looked critically at the definition of social welfare used by ICSW in this and earlier conferences, regarding it as inadequate in its lack of reference to social policies and in its failure to amplify the concept of community.

2. Improving the level and quality of general education through whatever endeavors are required to extend education to the total population and to ensure that education reinforces sound human values

3. Improving social welfare education and training in ways that will provide social welfare personnel with these various skills and abilities:

    a) Ability to help people to develop as individuals and in groups

    b) Ability to translate human values into social relationships and programs

    c) Ability to analyze social situations and problems

    d) Ability to comprehend political structures and processes and operate effectively within them, without abandoning the goal of bringing about needed political change *e*) Ability to collaborate with others in converting micro realities into humane and viable macro policies and programs.

4. Utilizing effectively a wide range of resources which have particular applicability to developing countries:

*a*) The UN and its specialized agencies and a wide range of nongovernmental agencies like ICSW itself

*b*) Multilateral and bilateral aid where this is available and is free of damaging restrictions

*c*) Professional and technical experts where these are capable of relating their expertise to the real conditions and needs of the country

5. Encouraging and utilizing research:

*a*) On problems of human need

*b*) On the consequences of various economic policies, such as those involving the movement of labor (that is, people) across national boundaries

*c*) On the success of experimental or pilot projects

*d*) On the applicability of various indices of welfare and "diswelfare."

6. Establishing social security programs and taxation exemption measures in developing countries that are appropriate to the level of national development and meet a wide spectrum of income and service needs.

This report refers to those measures discussed in the commission as "remedial." That term is not used in a disparaging sense. These, and similar measures that were touched on, are meritorious and indeed essential.

On the final day of the discussions three members expressed what probably all were feeling: that the measures which had been discussed fell short of the compelling needs of people in developed and developing countries alike. The members were reminded of the challenge presented in the address on participation in development by Sugata Dasgupta and no less forcefully in the report of the Conference Working Party.

The group's attention was drawn to those recommendations of the Conference Working Party that related to the elimination of poverty and excessive inequality of wealth and power

and the vast world-wide wastage of human and natural resources.

This led the members in the final hours of their collective
deliberations to reach the view that more radical measures
than had been discussed earlier were required and that the
focus must indeed be upon participation—participation having as its goal self-management. Particular attention was given
to one of Africa's most interesting experiments in participation, that being pursued in Tanzania and especially within the
Lushato Integrated Rural Development Project. This may well
prove to be the prototype for action in many parts of the
world.

More complex problems stand in the way of meaningful
participation in developed countries, notably those that provide the base for multinational corporations. Members of the
commission, however, were able to cite examples of citizen
and worker participation, including producer and consumer
cooperatives, employee participation in industrial policies and
management, and student participation in the operation of
colleges and universities.

There is evidence that participation of these and related
types has been increasing in many countries. Members of
Commission I, however, came to the view that the pace is un-
acceptably slow. Their message to the conference is that the
social welfare field must take wise and vigorous action through
the various measures discussed by the commission. More fundamentally, the social welfare field must take the lead in moving radically toward these objectives: a world free of poverty
and a world in which all are able to participate fully and freely
in all that touches upon their economic, cultural, and social
well-being.

# Commission II. The Role of Central and Local Government and Nongovernment Organizations in Development—How to Encourage Participation in Development

*Chairman:* Gert Nulens, *Germany*
*Vice-chairman:* James R. Burress, *United States*

THE MEMBERS of Commission II were drawn from a diversity of cultural backgrounds and operate in varied political systems. We included members from countries at very different stages of economic development and using a variety of developmental means.

Some countries have a well-developed network of nongovernmental agencies. Others have few such agencies, or agencies inherited from colonial times whose role in the new society is not fully clear.

Whereas some members emphasized the importance of presenting the people with a range of choices, others stressed that the reality may be a choice between subhuman conditions and the first steps to upgrade the condition of life to offer greater human dignity.

In such circumstances, the applicability of the conclusions we can draw is severely limited. Nevertheless, it is possible to identify some common operating principles and many common problems; and to identify means which, if appropriately adapted, offer ways of meeting these problems.

## THE PRESENT ROLE OF CENTRAL GOVERNMENT

The degree to which central government plays a planning and directive role varies from country to country. Few coun-

tries are without central government control in the following
areas:

1. Setting national goals
2. Setting national priorities
3. Establishing national development plans
4. Formulating legislation
5. Distributing resources
6. Promoting voluntary and/or self-help projects integrated
   within national plans
7. Ensuring proper use of resources of finance, skills, and
   manpower
8. Setting standards
9. Evaluating programs.

The way in which decisions are made, or should be made,
was the concern of another commission. This commission
wishes to stress that the central government, which sets the
operating terms for a wide range of activities, must be open to
the participatory process, be prepared to allow freedom to organize to meet social needs, be responsive to the needs and aspirations of the people and to the nongovernment agencies, in
so far as these represent the needs and aspirations of the people.

The commission also recognized the political nature of central government decision-making, and while not recommend-
ing political party alliances, believed that the social welfare sector as a whole (including both the government and the
nongovernment sector) must be aware of issues related to political power and must recognize and claim its place in the national planning process.

THE PRESENT ROLE OF LOCAL GOVERNMENT

The commission decided not to spend time in attempting to
clarify the various levels of government operating in the countries represented in the commission. When referring to local
government, the commission had in mind those tiers of government—districts, divisions, municipalities, and so forth—
which are (or should be) in close touch with the people they
serve.

The task of local government, briefly stated, is:

1. To influence central government policies and programs to ensure that local needs are being met
2. To adapt national policies and services to local needs
3. To plan the allocation of locally raised resources where these are available
4. To deliver or make available services on a decentralized and personalized basis
5. To relate to nongovernmental agencies and self-help groups in the local community.

As with central government, the commission stressed the importance of the participation of the people, individually, in groups, and in organized structures, in the development of local plans and in administration.

THE ROLE OF THE NONGOVERNMENT AGENCIES

The view taken of the place of the nongovernment sector within the total service provision varies. To a considerable degree, this variation is determined by availability of resources rather than on ideological grounds, though ideology is the determinant in some countries. Generally speaking, we can identify three models:

1. *Nongovernment as supplementary to government.* Here the assumption is that the main service provision is, or is ultimately planned to be, provided by government, and the role of nongovernment agencies is to fill any gaps in this provision on a long-, medium- or short-term basis.

2. *Nongovernment as complementary to government.* In this model, the two sectors are seen as operating side by side, each performing the functions best suited to its organization and mode of operation. Overlapping within and between the two sectors may occur but is not encouraged. Much stress is placed on the need for coordination of service provision.

3. *Nongovernment as a competitive service.* This model stresses the desirability of presenting opportunities for client choice and the avoidance of dangers of stagnation and low-quality service, which monolithic service structures present. Here both sectors may provide the same general types of service,

and the client is offered a choice between a government and a nongovernment service or between different nongovernment services.

Those holding this view believe that what they describe as "the cult of coordination" tends to reduce experimentation, quality of service, and public accountability.

Clearly, the competitive model is available only to societies with sufficient resources to permit its development. In the developing countries the level of resources currently available means that the principal priority must be to offer at least one type of service to meet the most outstanding needs. Duplication or competition is a luxury which cannot yet be seriously considered.

On the other hand, decisions on whether nongovernment is seen as supplementary or complementary do need further study. While governments have frequently themselves initiated service in many areas, the nongovernment sector has spearheaded development by moving in to meet needs as they become evident. In time, the government, convinced of the need, and with resources now available, takes over the responsibility for the service and offers it on a much wider basis. This is not necessarily to be regretted since it frees the nongovernment sector to move on to other areas of need.

While this broad trend is accepted, it remains true that even if government were able to provide adequately and at a good level of quality and flexibility all the services needed by the people, there would remain areas of work which are more appropriately undertaken by nongovernment agencies. There has been insufficient study of the criteria on which such judgments might be made. While inflexible and ideological criteria could be a disadvantage, some broad criteria to assist planning decisions could be developed.

The commission had insufficient time to develop this theme in detail. However, it considered issues such as:

1. The relative situations between government and nongovernment on questions of resources (money, skills, manpower), accountability, responsibility, flexibility, good

communication, willingness to reach out into the community, and ability to deal rapidly with disaster situations
2. The capacity to develop universal services offered to citizens by right (sometimes called social utilities)
3. The situations in which government and nongovernment might cooperate to provide different aspects of a particular service
4. The need at times to provide a nonauthoritarian image for services for, or on behalf of, certain kinds of deviant or oppressed groups.

These are but a few of the issues which need detailed consideration. The commission wishes to stress the undesirability of undiscriminating judgments. Not all government departments are inflexible, incapable of rapid action or of reaching out into the community. Some nongovernment agencies are rigid, conservative, and paternalistic. The issue is which kind of service and with what qualities can at any one time meet the needs of the people responsively, and in a way which offers them human dignity.

THE INFLUENCE OF GOVERNMENT AND NONGOVERNMENT
ON ONE ANOTHER

Clearly, the position of government in power and resource terms gives it considerable control over the operations of the nongovernment sector. There are many factors involved:
1. The setting of over-all national plans into which the nongovernment sector must fit
2. The legislation upon which services are based
3. The allocation of resources: which services are given subsidies and which are denied; what terms are attached to the subsidies
4. The provision of professional staff and consultant services
5. Registration requirements
6. Requirements for reports
7. Standard-setting
8. Audit arrangements.

Many of these factors can be seen in terms of assistance by government to the nongovernment sector, and as such they are highly desirable. However, they must also be recognized as potential controlling mechanisms which can be used actively or less actively, according to circumstances.

The existence of these controlling mechanisms means that if government policy is or may become paramount, then the means by which the nongovernment sector can participate in the formulation of policy and administrative practices is of key importance. The question of policy-making needs full consideration.

The matter of administration can more readily be dealt with through joint consulting arrangements, either bilateral or multilateral, and such arrangements are clearly essential. The particular mechanism of a national council of social service will be discussed later.

NONGOVERNMENTAL INFLUENCE ON SOCIAL POLICY

The commission started from the premise that while some governments (national and local) are closely attuned to the needs of the people, many are careless of individual rights and needs. The nongovernment sector must therefore at all times be vigilant.

1. An important first step is to exert continued pressure on governments to adopt social-development-oriented policies; that is, policies in which economic and social policies are seen as organically related parts of a single process of development aimed at social progress in all its dimensions. In many countries economic progress alone is the dominant policy, with social progress as a secondary benefit which all too frequently fails to reach the low-income sector of the population. Both government and nongovernment sectors of social welfare have a responsibility constantly to restate the need for total social development policies.

2. It was noted that in many countries the activities of nongovernment agencies is looked on with suspicion by government. Such agencies want to see their role clarified and full recognition given to them as partners in development. It is

recognized that where resources are limited, governments will expect to have a strong say in where such resources (including international aid) is directed. However, from the viewpoint of the functioning of nongovernment agencies, the agencies need opportunities to participate in the preparation of national plans, the setting of guidelines for financial and other resources, assistance in standard-setting and similar areas.

Further, so far as resources allow, the nongovernment agencies should be given freedom to innovate, to experiment, and to relate to all levels of government and to people's organizations. At the same time, the nongovernment agencies must examine themselves to ensure that in determining their own policies and programs they are open to participation processes by the people they serve. The dangers of middle-class domination and failure to communicate with people at the grass roots is ever present unless active steps are taken to overcome these tendencies.

3. Those working in nongovernment agencies have a special responsibility to provide means by which the people, particularly the most oppressed, can express their needs to government. In some countries such opportunities are provided by government initiative. However, in many countries where governments take action which is detrimental to the deprived and inarticulate, or fail to offer them protection against the actions of others, then workers in the nongovernment sector must consider whether they can take action such as:

*a*) Pressure for government action

*b*) Organizing mass media campaigns

*c*) Training community leaders

*d*) Organizing, through community development processes, those who are being oppressed to enable them to take action on their own behalf

*e*) Advocacy for oppressed groups.

Nongovernment agencies, social worker groups, groups from other professions (lawyers, doctors, town planners), religious groups, trade union, farmers cooperatives, and citizen groups of various kinds all have a responsibility to be active both alongside and on behalf of the least articulate, to ensure their human rights. This responsibility remains even if it endangers the personal status of the groups and individuals concerned. If we are preaching a philosophy of human rights and human dignity, we cannot stand aside when these are attacked.

4. For purposes of direct participation by those with least access to resources many and varied means must be sought and promoted by government and nongovernment alike. In rural areas this is particularly difficult to achieve. The self-employed, living a marginal existence, have few resources and little energy to spare for participatory processes; yet experience has shown that participation can be achieved.

Particular attention must be paid to developing such processes in rural areas, since in the developing countries the majority of the population is rural. In urban areas in many countries people who lack access to resources are forming associations of various kinds, and these have much potential for determining their own needs and putting forward to government their own viewpoint.

5. Commission II is suggesting that there is room for productive conflict as part of the participatory process. It is also suggesting that old forms of organization reshaped and new forms of organization of a flexible nature must move forward to aid the people in securing greater control over the quality of their lives.

NATIONAL COUNCILS OF SOCIAL SERVICE (OR WELFARE)

Commission II was asked to give special attention to national councils of social service. While not suggesting that national councils are to be regarded as the sole means of influencing government policies, it was seen as appropriate to consider the potential of this form of organization.

It was noted that it exists in many countries and in a variety of forms:

1. National councils which are government-sponsored operate as joint councils between government and nongovernment (often chaired by a government representative) and act as a channel of communication and a means of coordinating

the nongovernment sector. It was considered that in many (though not all) cases these councils are limited in their freedom of action and in the scope of their activities. In some countries, such organizations have been felt to be inadequate and new forms sought.

2. More independent national councils are councils of voluntary social agencies whose principal function is to act as an arm of government in allocating resources and coordinating services and as a consultative mechanism between government and nongovernment agencies. These, while restricted in scope, can provide a valuable forum for communication between agencies and between government and nongovernment.

3. There are national councils with a central priority to operate as in the previous section, but which in addition, through committees, by means of seminars, surveys, studies, and so on, seek to frame desirable social policies and to put these before government, using formally established networks of communication.

4. There are also national councils that seek to involve a wide range of community organizations, both social work and nonsocial work, and direct their attention to all those social arrangements which affect the lives of people (including, for example, the taxation system, the legal system, town planning) and which aim to be a public forum for the expression of a community viewpoint on social development.

It was noted also that while some councils act for the particular interests of the nongovernment agencies (an interest which is unfortunately not always coterminous with the interest of the most underprivileged), others have sought to involve within the organizations those who directly represent client groups and people's groups.

Further, some national councils operate mainly as capital city councils, whereas others have found means of establishing branches throughout the country or have sought other means of relating directly with the needs of rural people and people in smaller cities and towns.

The commission does not consider it appropriate to prescribe the form and method of operation a national council should take. Rather it considers that each national council should evaluate its role in relation to:

1. The needs of the country concerned
2. The extent that it is participatory in its decision-making
3. The scope of its membership
4. The extent to which it has independence in relation to government
5. The extent to which it is efficient in its operation.

If the national council is relevant, participatory, efficient, and independent, it forms a vital resource for the country as a whole, for government and nongovernment action and in relation to the UN and its intergovernmental organizations.

Commission II has had many communication problems in its discussion, but its underlying spirit has been based on a common commitment to human rights and human dignity, to a belief in government and community responsibility to reach out to meet the needs of the people, and to a belief in the right of the people, through participation, to share in decisions which affect the quality of their lives.

# Commission III. Ways and Means of Encouraging Participation of Local Communities and Individuals in Development

SECTION A (ORIGINAL TEXT IN FRENCH)

*Chairman and Rapporteur:* Jean Marc Irvin, *Switzerland*

FIRST AND foremost, participating means sharing, having an equal share of resources, difficulties, and worries. The essential elements of participation are: openmindedness; listening; discovery; patience; awareness—a communal birth, at a group pace, of a new reality; self-awareness—awareness of oneself in relation to others, what one has, what one does not have, what is acceptable and is not, and what it is possible to work out together in order to permit personal and collective fulfillment and a better life for oneself and others.

Participation, therefore, implies a mental attitude different from the normal, both for individuals and groups, which is capable of coping with the constant tensions between oneself and others and between different groups. Dynamics are needed which allow for continuous evolution, moving from one new situation to another new situation, according to plans worked out together.

This conception of participation emerged without difficulty from discussions of the commission, which had a rich membership of nearly twenty countries from four continents. It appeared obvious, however, that participation involves different aspects according to whether it is being established in industrialized countries or developing countries, in a liberal or an authoritarian regime, and whether or not there is an existent economic infrastructure. There is no rigid model for participation; its dynamics and application to a particular local, regional, or national situation require constantly alert thinking and precise knowledge of the realities that need to be confronted and overcome.

## THE DANGERS AND OBSTACLES OF PARTICIPATION

If participation essentially means sharing, and thus corresponds to one of man's fundamental desires, it also—paradoxically—provokes fear, both individual and collective. It is threatening to the extent that sharing means renouncing part of what one has in order to develop a new group dimension. This may lead to subtler or cruder versions of the following:

1. Paternalism, which is frequently present even when efforts are made to avoid it
2. Technical, professional jargon in which experts unconsciously enclose themselves
3. Propaganda which makes insidious use of information, and recruits participation for clearly determined economic and political ends
4. Fear of the power structure, whether formal or informal, of being criticized, being confronted.

Ignorance and indifference also represent major obstacles to participation. Indifference, implying the refusal to make any effort, loss of confidence, an awareness of being overtaken by things, and feelings of impotence, is a grave threat which can only be overcome when men understand that they are not blind objects in economic development or in the political machinery but rather actors in control of their own destinies or the destiny of the community.

## WAYS OF PARTICIPATING

We are not going to present an exhaustive list of ways of encouraging participation of local communities and individuals in development, but have selected a few examples:

1. *Setting up a pedagogy of participation.* This should be started at the family level. Although this is not easy for either developed or developing countries, it is urgent, considering the acute crisis of the family structure inherited from the past.

Such pedagogy develops a constant exchange between people who learn to give as well as to take, encourages awareness of one's own potentialities, of local culture, of human and material resources at the community level. Although frequently informal, it is precise and tries to develop techniques which encourage communal work situations and helps the emergence of a new form of leadership which no longer depends on power or knowledge but on one's way of being and of acting upon others.

In this way pilot experiments can catch on and spread, extending the necessary dynamics and impetus. Furthermore, this pedagogy can enrich indigenous models of participation within local cultures, particularly in the Third World. The commission considered that this was important.

2. *Development of supple structures.* Such structures would encourage at all levels mutual exchange and coordination of everything that contributes to community development. However, the grass-roots community cannot live through new relations alone. Participation cannot accept orders which are imposed from outside, whether work techniques or projects are to be established. Participation cannot operate within a pressure group; it cannot bear to be held back.

Of course there are nuances here and differences between developing and industrialized countries. All the same, it is clear that participation is not possible without the organization of constant exchange between the grass-roots communities and the higher echelons. At this latter level, where a system of delegation automatically appears, it is particularly necessary for two-way communication to be ensured, from the grass roots to the top of the hierarchy, and from the top of the hierarchy to the grass roots. Otherwise, delegation becomes a screen which obstructs all possibilities of evolution within determined projects.

The commission considered it important that all structures of social welfare should be developed on the lines of this form of organization, favoring maximum coordination of all elements concerned in the social sector.

3. *Encouragement of study and research.* Community develop-

ment and the economy are interdependent. Both, in fact, have to take each other into account; one precedes or follows another. It is of course unthinkable that economic conditions of the community could be ignored when community development is going to occur.

On this subject, a fundamental requirement is also the redistribution of resources. If the grass-roots groups do not have a share in, or some control over, economic development, participation becomes a trap. The commission therefore considers that this interdependence should be systematically studied and taken into consideration in planning and carrying out development programs.

4. *Development of social training at all levels.* This should be done according to the values that have to be promoted. Such training requires discipline and methods of intervention which are likely to encourage a global approach to situations. It should prepare social workers, in the widest sense, to look for causes of social deficiencies and to attack them. They must be capable of interdisciplinary actions, coming out of research into needs, which are constantly reappraised. The commission considered this point fundamental.

### SECTION B (ORIGINAL TEXT IN SPANISH)

*Chairman:* José Zambrano Jara, *Venezuela*
*Vice-chariman:* Maritza Navarro, *Panama*
*Rapporteur:* Augusto Galli, *Venezuela*

PARTICIPATION IS increasingly perceived as a value; it is a worth-while goal so far as theory, methodology, and social practice are concerned. All of the commission's delegates agreed that participation should be encouraged and promoted, both as a right and as a duty of public and private institutions as well as of communities and individuals.

In practice, however, participation is restricted by profound structural, societal, cultural, and political limitations. In this sense, we can hardly talk about implementing participation in development when:

1. The mass media are essentially aimed and directed at consumerism.

2. Local, regional, and national realities are partially or totally unknown.

3. Formal and informal education, socialization, and enabling, which ought to constitute the backbone of the participation process, do not further it and instead spread antiparticipative concepts.

4. The convenience of social classes or castes, as well as of pressure groups, does not permit participation or renders it largely impossible. This is even more true when there is no participation of workers in social affairs and no participation of the concerned population in the establishment of educational and other programs.

5. National, regional, and local planning is imposed vertically.

These indicative, but on no account exhaustive, limitations have been studied by the commission and led to discussing the question of the need to try out and create more efficient methods of participation toward development, especially in a society where the promotion of man takes second place to that of the economy. Be this as it may, given the accelerated economic and social changes which we are going through in the world today, politics and social programs—both as goals and as means of development—assume a double function. It is not only a matter of simple acceleration of the gross national product's growth rate, but rather of a real attempt to integrate all the social factors involved in the transformation of the economy—culture, social rules, political institutions, and social structures—within the national development plans directed toward changes in the social system so as to attain a participative and developed integrated society.

These aims comprise simultaneously the double goal of strengthening and expanding the economy which is at the service of the population in its entirety and of promoting man and society—both capable of deliberately and consciously integrating themselves as objects and beneficiaries of all the processes and goals of the development.

From what has been said before, it is obvious that there is no sense in talking about social development as opposed to economic development since they are interdependent variables of one and the same process. Thus it can be stated that making the objectives and means of the economy compatible with the requirements and aspirations of society, as well as promoting and directing social behavior in conformity with the efforts and limitations implied in any expansion of the productive process, is a task that is more urgent today than ever before.

Consequently, taking participation into account, a social policy demands not only that one should deal with health, housing, education, and social security but also that work should be a means to the fulfillment of the human person and permit access to all goods and services. However, we must realize that this would not be possible so long as the population does not play an active, conscious, organized role in every process of national development, both on the decision-making and the execution levels.

The still unsatisfactory conditions existing in health, nourishment, housing, education, social security, and other aspects of the standard of living are not isolated cases, but rather part of a more complex framework of social and economic marginality, stemming from: the lack of productive jobs; the inadequate system of distribution of income; the chronic institutional and operational limitations of public and private sectors with regard to taking care of social problems; organized services; and obtaining an adequate return from available resources, and so on.

At the same time, this entire situation makes for an unstable rate of growth of the economy as well as for an unequal distribution of wealth. This last factor, together with the nonincorporation of a large part of the population—both urban and rural—into political activities, public services, cultural benefits, and so on, implies a phenomenon of marginality, that is, a phenomenon of nonparticipation which characterizes current development processes. This gives rise, in terms of the increasing expectations created but not satisfied, to increasing conflicts. The practical consequences of all this in relation to the development process are quite varied. Thus we can point to the fact that because the marginal population does not participate in decision-making or in determining the development strategy to be followed, there is a danger that the marginality will go on unabated. On the other hand, nonparticipation gives birth to psychological, social, and political situations of systematic resistance to the tasks of development.

These maladjustments between the growth of social marginality and the limited capacities of national systems to incorporate the population politically and economically not only pose the problem of social justice and of an increase of social conflict but also determine a structural rigidity which affects decisively the vitality of national economies and the importance of current models of development. In this context, the participation policy and programs acquire the greatest strategic importance, particularly as instruments of global development policies, since they are meant to generate new social workings capable of rendering the objectives and means of economic growth compatible with those of social benefit. That is why participation must constitute an ensemble of integrated efforts intended to stimulate change in the socioeconomic and cultural system that will allow for the deliberate and conscious incorporation and participation of man as subject in all the processes and aims of development. Action in this field includes every activity (traditional or not) which has to do with the collaboration and the participation of the population in:

1. The production and wealth distribution process
2. The adequate use of the goods and services which tend to raise the standard of living
3. The cultural and social organization of communities with the aim of creating channels that will permit participation in the decision-making processes
4. The deliberation and mobilization of individual and collective potentialities in search of motivations and attitudes favorable to development
5. The encouragement of positive values, creative attitudes,

and cultural manifestations as well as the enjoyment of scientific and technological knowledge

6. The coordinated action of the different public and private organizations which in every country cooperate in the fields of promotion, organization, and community development.

These elements and others that have not been mentioned could serve as a basis for a participation policy with two main goals: to achieve community participation in the tasks of planning and carrying out development; and to accelerate the incorporation of the population into the processes of production and distribution of wealth and to ensure for them the benefits of development as well.

The first of these goals implies community participation in the tasks of planning, organizing, and carrying out development; it also implies a process of change and alteration of the current structures of decision through which will be attained an awareness and organization of the population, with the aim of facilitating and ensuring a genuine and adequate representation and participation of all sectors of society.

The second goal implies active participation in the productive processes by means of steady, adequately paid employment; in access to the market and the guarantee to obtain goods and services which correspond to the actual demand and are in the interest of the community, as well as in that of the national and local public services.

Consequently, it becomes more and more important to study, try out and determine:

1. Channels allowing for genuine participation and not pseudo participation
2. Juridical instruments that will guarantee participation
3. Social strategies capable of promoting the transformation of social structures obstructing development
4. Social organization models which will serve as a basis for achieving the cohesion of the community, by means of a consciousness, a responsibility, and a solidarity which will facilitate the formation of an integrated and participative society.

These objectives will require certain aims such as:

1:(*a*) analysis of participation experiences in various countries; (*b*) study of relevant institutions and their achievements; (*c*) study of the realities of each country; and (*d*) study of the techniques and methods employed.

2:(*a*) formulation and testing of a methodology of education for participation based on social reality; (*b*) formulation and testing of structures of participation which will complement the said methodology; (*c*) designing and testing programs of popularization of human values through mass media and the different ways of expressions in use in each culture; (*d*) designing and testing specific forms of enabling at the level both of institutions and of social welfare agencies; (*e*) determination of methodologies for community organization, coordination of institutions or agencies, education of the community and institutions, and the popularization of human values.

3:(*a*) integration of the process and the structure of participation into the national planning systems; (*b*) establishment of national participation policies or plans; and (*c*) determination of agencies for planning and carrying out the participation policy.

Lastly, the commission considered that participation constitutes an over-all strategy and a common effort which, through its objectives and functions, involves every sector of the administration; its aims will be reached with the help of sectorial actions operating through specific agencies and programs. Of course, the nature and characteristics of social phenomena in various countries and their communities will always be taken into account. The programs, taken as a whole, must be directed toward serving urban, semirural, and rural areas, and include economic, social, cultural, and sociopsychological aspects.

Taking all of this into account, it can be said that the best way to encourage participation is through participation itself.

# Commission IV. Participation in the Promotion and Delivery of Services

*Chairman:* Mrs. Pratiblia Patil, *India*
*Vice-chairman:* Mrs. Zenab L. Elneggar, *Egypt*
*Rapporteur:* Ralph E. Pumphrey, *United States*

IN AN international gathering of workers dealing with human needs it is easy to agree on abstract global values and objectives such as the dignity and worth of the individual, altruism, integrity, self-help, and mutual involvement. Difficulty arises when people from different countries try to find applications of similar values and objectives across the variety of cultural and social-economic stages of development they represent. In traditional Africa the community took care of the individual; and the individual took care of the community. The pattern has differed in other parts of the world. To some extent regional patterns will be discussed here, but for the most part we have been content to present examples of operational applications of principles as a basis for further exploration.

## RELATIONS AND RESPONSIBILITIES OF GOVERNMENTAL AND NONGOVERNMENTAL ORGANIZATIONS

As reported, some countries rely almost exclusively upon governmental organizations to provide services, while others rely preponderantly upon nongovernmental organizations for at least the operational aspects of service. The range of such nongovernment agencies in all countries probably is somewhat similar to that in the United States. There, it was noted, in addition to the traditional service agencies, there are consumer organizations and organizations based on ethnic lines. Much service is also being given by profit-making organizations. The majority of countries rely upon delivery of service under a variety of arrangements by which both governmental and nongovernmental organizations participate.

In the African region the closest structural interdependence was reported. In several countries strong governmental planning and financing structures operate at the national, district, and local levels. At the same time, much reliance is placed upon voluntary and private agency activities, but these are organized primarily at the local level and are cleared through the governmental structure. In Kenya, there is a National Council of Social Service which coordinates the activities of the small, local voluntary organizations as they participate in the national objective of cooperative self-help—"Harambee." National voluntary agencies may deal with problems such as family planning, child care, and so on, for which a government has not yet assumed responsibility, so that in this role the voluntary agencies serve as pressure groups on the government. Through the ruling party organization, a government may seek to promote decentralized self-help projects at the local level.

In Egypt there is an added component in that the 7,000 voluntary organizations are organized into federations at the local, district, and national levels, parallel to the governmental structure. At the national level, the Minister of Social Affairs serves as president of the national federation, thus providing the key link for participation in planning, and exchange of information, proposals, and plans between the two structures at all levels.

In all these structures there is provision both for the initiation of proposals for self-help projects based on felt needs and aspirations at the local level, with consideration for supplementary funding by appropriate governmental units, and also for the transmission of national aspirations and plans to the districts and local communities to help them in setting their own priorities.

Even in countries which rely primarily on governmental structures, note was made of the value of voluntary agencies in supplementing government programs, and in meeting needs outside the range of government programs, such as those of refugees in Taiwan. On the other hand, in countries which rely heavily on private agencies to provide service, national interests may be served through subsidy of nongovernmental organizations.

## AID TO COMMUNITIES

In general, the industrialized countries did not speak on this issue. In the developing countries much emphasis is placed upon self-help projects, based on community decisions and investment of effort and money, which are given supplementary financial and/or technical assistance by the local, district, or national government. The assignment of community development workers to help the communities recognize and articulate their needs and aspirations is an important ingredient in the process. Some, if not all, countries, encourage voluntary agencies to participate at this level of providing community development and technical assistance. An exception to the pattern of community development work was noted in Vietnam, where most of the nongovernmental and almost all of the governmental activities are directed to the relief of immediate needs without utilization of the traditional sources of mutual aid, especially for the care of orphans or the promotion of self-help activities which could mitigate in a constructive way the massive problems of unemployment. Schools of social work are now beginning to train workers at all levels for these forms of social effort, but much help is needed to avoid consolidating a general atmosphere of dependency.

## ROLE OF LEADERSHIP

Two principal characteristics of leadership were noted: vision, which sees beyond the immediate difficult situation to the possible solutions; and the ability to communicate, so that the aspirations of those with whom the leader is working can be accurately determined and passed on to others. The danger was recognized that leaders may be chosen on the basis of status and hence will not truly represent various segments of the community. They may be, consciously or unconsciously, self-serving. Hence functional leadership should be encouraged from various groups such as youth, women, the aged, rather than attempt to achieve a composite leadership. Leaders in the developing countries are chosen by their own groups, but their success is dependent on the cooperation and support of the community. They are given training courses in leadership skills. The length and complexity of these courses varies according to the previous education and experience of the leaders. Women from rural areas may only have a week of training at first. These leaders are given responsibilities within limited areas and cooperate with neighboring leaders within a larger structure. Emphasis was placed upon the importance of education in the basic virtues of integrity and honesty.

In more developed countries the emerging importance of the role of the social worker as an instrument of social change in situations where the traditional societal structures have broken down was noted. Such workers have to play a role similar to that of the village worker in transmitting to people of power and authority the needs and aspirations of those who would not otherwise be heard. This means that social work education must be much more oriented to political science and decision-making than in the past, to help the people with whom they work to develop and exercise power.

It was noted also that leaders need to study carefully and utilize incentives and motivations to effect change. Illustrations were given of the great impetus to education and hence to living standards provided by that type of benefits given to veterans in the United States after the Second World War; and of the apparently successful rehabilitation of prisoners through parole to attend a university.

PARTICIPATION OF MINORITY AND ETHNIC GROUPS

The importance of finding ways not only to select leadership but to gain participation and expression by any group which is not a controlling majority was recognized. In Japan national instrumentalities are established for this purpose with self-selected representatives from the various minority groups. This again was seen as a matter of power, and in India minority groups are assured of proportional representation in legislative bodies. It was noted that participation requires changing attitudes of the elite through education as well as stimulating involvement of all groups.

INNOVATIONS

A few particular innovations were mentioned. Community centers have introduced family life education, and also programs of teaching grass-roots leaders to be themselves teachers of their neighbors both in basic literary and in household and other skills. Canada reported innovative work programs for youth and adults. Youth groups or groups of unemployed adults can propose work projects for the benefit of the community. Some remarkable results have occurred in the form of projects for day care of children, senior citizen centers, transportation of the aged and handicapped, building a greenhouse for a home for the aged, and so forth. In addition to wages for the members of the group, an additional percentage is allowed for materials and supplies.

GENERAL THOUGHTS

Constant reference was made to the ethical and moral undergirding of social welfare services, particularly in efforts to achieve participation. Such values are built into many national programs, as illustrated by the Kenya national slogan of "Harambee." But various religious beliefs also bring such values to the services they sponsor. While others might not be willing to go so far in their personal or institutional commitments, there was universal recognition of the validity of the position of Mahatma Gandhi that only by each man bringing the basic problems to which he is subject under control can the social objectives toward which we strive be achieved.

More specifically, it can be said that people must have a part in the decisions that affect their lives. This means that:

1. People should be informed and educated to be aware of decisions affecting them, *and* encouraged to express their ideas and aspirations.

2. Leaders must learn to share the power of their positions so that their decisions represent the aspirations of the people.

3. Political and economic decisions should be made in light of, not in conflict with, social welfare goals. These goals should be formulated with as direct participation as possible by the people being served.

4. Social workers at all levels must fully understand that their mission is to help individuals and communities to stand on their own, and *not* to allow the individual or community to become dependent. Dependency works against the development and participation of individuals and communities.

5. Leaders at all levels *must* receive regular and continual training in human values, honesty, and integrity.

# Commission V. Implications for Training and Education in the Encouragement of Participation in Development

*Chairman:* Dr. Abdul M. Shawky, *Egypt*
*Vice-chairman:* Thomas C. Y. Lee, *Hong Kong*
*Rapporteur:* Marguerite Mathieu, *Canada*

AT THE first session twenty-eight delegates were present, from twenty different countries.

## RELEVANCE OF EDUCATIONAL SYSTEMS

Relevance is herein discussed as a quality which makes education responsive to the needs of individuals in a given social situation. The crisis in today's educational systems seems to be universal in that goals, teaching methods, and skills of teaching staff are outdated for participation in the development of social structures for social changes; educated people are not adequately equipped to set up and participate effectively and efficiently in the necessary processes of their country's development.

In developing countries, the lack of relevance between educational models imported from other cultures and the need for indigenous leadership was seen as a matter for great concern. It was also considered that many of the systems of Western education were autocratic in matters and in content, and did not meet the needs of these societies for participation.

The teaching profession can no longer rely on social prestige in playing a leadership role in society and must think through its appropriate place and contribution in a participatory society.

*Educational goals.* Education's first goal should be personal growth and social awareness. Education should be seen not only as teaching to read and to write, or transmitting technical skills, but as a means for imparting skill in human relationships, a basic disposition to participation. Thus, through a scientific humanism, education should enable people to enter into a relationship of basic trust with their fellow men.

Education should be functional and continue throughout life. Education should aim at widening, deepening, and focusing participation. Participation should also be seen as an end in itself and as a satisfactory, fulfilling, and enjoyable experience.

Such a definition of educational objectives calls for a revolution in educational systems, that is, in institutions, structures, curriculum, pedagogy, and so on. We need to acknowledge the conflict which exists in education throughout the world and to identify factors which create opposition to change. The technological explosion and the search for the scientific approach are in direct opposition to a long-honored form of learning in which a charismatic master transmitted his knowledge as definitive truth or dogma to his unquestioning students. Then education was not concerned with particular participation.

It was agreed that educational goals have to be defined by each country in compliance with its over-all goals for development, its set of values which will provide guidelines for the organization of its educational system. The tendency, too often prevalent in developing countries, to rely on a definition of goals imposed by some external agents was denounced as most ineffective. If a country determines its own sequential, short-term, and long-term goals, the suggestions and ideas of external experts could then be modified and adapted to the country's goals and resources.

*Educational institutions.* These are conditioned both by the nature of the knowledge to be transmitted and the nature of the country or the prevalent social conditions where educational experience has taken place. The nature of the knowledge has probably a more determining influence. Science with its methods of inquiry and appeal to demonstrable phenomena for its legitimization comes into conflict with metaphysical knowledge with its appeal to eternal wisdom vested in persons and in traditional institutions. Though the technologies of science can be transferred (regardless of the results) across cultures, the relationship of man to knowledge, and the corresponding relationship between teacher and learner, is not so simply transferred. One major reason in that there are fundamental conflicts between the two kinds of realities. This is particularly significant where participation is adopted both as a means and as an end. The social sciences and social work meet compounded problems because the subject matter and its legitimacy are value- and culturally laden and the manner of its teaching and its practice deeply involves (or should involve) a participatory relationship.

*The Family.* The first institution in which human interaction is learned, the family, has a primary role in preparing and encouraging all members to participate both in decision-making and in implementing these decisions in day-to-day living. All social institutions within the community need to carry forward the goals of motivating, preparing, and enhancing the abilities of members to participate in planning, policy-making, and implementation in the community concerns.

OBSTACLES TO PARTICIPATION

Predetermined attitudes toward our social and personal roles create mental blocks to the acceptance of participation. Some of these are belief in the superiority of the ruling classes, the glorification of competitiveness, and so forth.

The lack of capacity or know-how for participation is as important an obstacle as prejudice, if not more so.

The professions, in general, have not encouraged participation. They are too class-conscious and adopt a superior and paternalistic attitude.

In all institutions, whether the family, the school, or the community at large, there exists a dominance-submission, hierarchical cycle which tends to be self-perpetuating. Educational institutions and programs foster much more competition than participation.

Participation is also hampered by the problems associated

with underdevelopment and the uneven distribution of power. Education and planners in education need to analyze the power structure through specially devised research methods as the basis for designing appropriate educational systems to prepare for participation. Still another obstacle is that as yet we have not found tools and methods which can effectively and efficiently involve the total community.

It was suggested that the promotion of participation refers to a collectivist society and that the society we live in is a competitive and individualistic society. Therefore, the problem is to find ways of penetrating the social structures to counteract the deeply entrenched competitiveness and to promote cooperation for participation.

But participation can best be learned through participatory activities. Pilot projects are urgently needed to develop new techniques and new models. We need also to evaluate current projects.

To foster participation we need to involve all the cagegories of power structures, including influential groups in a society.

TRAINING OF SOCIAL WORKERS FOR
PARTICIPATION IN DEVELOPMENT

Several changes are required in education for social work in order to foster participatory skills. Although participation has always been a goal in social work practice and education, social workers are more skillfull in talking about participation than in giving it.

Learner-centered and problem-solving rather than subject-matter-centered programs, flexible curricula designed to meet student career interests rather than rigid standard curricula, a greater emphasis on the integration of practice, and experience in teaching were all offered as suggestions for developing capacities for participation. Achievements in schools of social work in involving student participation in curriculum planning and interdisciplinary collaboration will, it is hoped, be extended to all education. Education must reconcile teaching methods with the declared goals of participation.

RECOMMENDATIONS

1. To achieve the required changes in the educational institutions, this commission urges ICSW to encourage pertinent governmental and voluntary organizations to stimulate educational institutions to enhance student participation and to emphasize preparation of students for participation in social development.

2. The commission suggests that ICSW stimulate pilot projects in various regions focused on particular problems related to participation and, furthermore, that ICSW encourage social researchers to undertake comparative evaluation of these projects, from which new knowledge, principles, and skills might be derived.

3. The commission challenges the position noted in the Conference Working Party report and recommends that ICSW *not* dichotomize vocational training or job training and education for general enlightenment.

4. The commission urges ICSW to undertake the collection and dissemination of information on experiments in education for participation now under way at all levels of informal and formal education.

5. The commission recommends that members of ICSW be alerted to the existence of the vast and rich source material such as has been collected by UNESCO in preparation of the report on education, entitled "Learning to Be."

6. The commission recommends that more emphasis be given to the use of mass media in preparing people for participation in social development.

# Commission VI. Planning and Utilization of Research Information in Development

*Chairman:* James A. Goodman, *United States*
*Rapporteur:* James Oglethorpe, *Zambia*

A STATEMENT on the role of social research in development planning issued by an international organization, and prepared by a group of strangers meeting for the first time in brief and sporadic enclave, must of necessity exhibit an unevenness and inconsistency both in context and in presentation. In spite of these shortcomings, the commission provided the opportunity for its members to carry on a stimulating and searching conversation based on our various experiences in the fields of research and planning. Although we did not even attempt to achieve a consensus, or to distinguish strictly between the research experiences and needs of the so-called "developing" and "developed" countries, or to address ourselves specifically to any given situation, we would like to belive that the views contained in this statement are of a level of generality which will make them usable in a wide variety of situations, both nationally and internationally.

The specific national conditions that contribute to economic growth, the elimination of poverty, and the participation of individuals and groups in the processes of national development must be understood and analyzed in the context of the "real" resources available to a given nation. Planning for the enhancement of individual and group potentialities is a complex undertaking. As many people as possible should be encouraged and enabled to participate according to their capabilities in activities related to development. Rising expectations on the part of the world's people in regard to having their needs met, their voices heard, and their spirits uplifted must

be responded to honestly and forthrightly by their governments. Research can often be used as a tool to gather and
analyze appropriate information to be presented to the people
in clear and unmistakable language. In this way the people
will be in a position to make a variety of responses to their
governments. The important consideration here is to ensure
that they are informed and have an intelligent basis for alternative responses to their social situation.

Research, which is seen as a problem-solving activity, is itself
a problematic concept. The kind of research carried out will
depend on the context. For example, research carried out in a
university often differs from that done by government agencies. The former frequently tends to be too academic to be of
much use to policy-makers and planners. This need not, however, necessarily be the case. Academic research can, if it ab-
stains from isolating itself artificially from the social and political environment, be done in a manner which will be of
immediate use to policy-makers. This will require a change of
approach on the part of both researchers and planners. Researchers and planners will have to enter into a "contractual"
relationship with each other. This involves seeing research as a
continuous process of feedback, an open-ended dialogue. The
researcher must listen to the needs of the planner when designing his program of research, and he must periodically
report back to the planner on the progress being made in a
language the planner can understand. Moreover, he must not
think that his task ends with the presentation of his research
findings. He also has a responsibility for the use being made
of his research. Since policy-makers usually do not have either
the time or the inclination to wade through long and technical
documents, it would be helpful if every research report relating to development could be accompanied by a simplified
summary of its conclusions.

Policy-makers and planners, for their part, should be realistic about their expectations regarding research as an instrument for development. The function of research is not to
give definitive answers to policy questions, but rather to clarify
the issues and identify the alternatives which will enable the

policy-makers to arrive at decisions and the planners to plan for the implementation of those decisions. If this were accepted, not only would undue reliance upon research be avoided, but spending on research would be less prodigal. As it is, an indigestible surfeit of research material exists in the world.

All too often it is assumed that research requires a great deal of money and experience. What is forgotten is that the most valuable resource for social research is the people themselves for whose benefit the research is being done. This does not imply that people not educated in the techniques of research can without further ado participate in programs of social research. But an essential ingredient of any social research worth its salt is education: as the people participate in the research program, and as the researcher explains the goals and methodology of the research program, they will find themselves going through a learning process which will enrich their lives far more than the mere presentation of results arrived at without their informed cooperation.

A close and continuing relationship among the people, researchers, and policy-makers also entails a clear understanding of the social goals of the country in which research is being conducted. It is up to the policy-makers to state these goals in general terms as an expression of the national philosophy. But a general statement of goals is insufficient for the purposes of development planning. They need to be analyzed in operational terms. This is a main task of the social researcher, to assist in the process. Indeed, all social research should, as a matter of course, be preceded by a quest for an explication of the value system undergirding the research.

The exact connotation of the term "social research" is not altogether clear. It may be described as "research into the social problems of development." This implies—a fact not always readily perceived by economic planners—that development involves social problems and, what is more, that development has a social dimension which, if ignored, leads to costly mistakes. The underlying assumption of all social research should be that development in human terms is a continuing process of discovering and unfolding the potentialities of people working within the context of a more human set of values and leading to an improvement in the quality of life for all within a society's chosen life style. Seen in this context, the elimination of poverty, a primary goal of development, cannot be achieved merely in terms of economic growth. Economic growth, inestimably important as it undoubtedly is, must be subordinated to social goals. The task of social research in ensuring that these goals are in the forefront of the minds of those responsible for development plans lies in monitoring these plans in the light of indicators that may be designed for this purpose.

This should not be interpreted in a legalistic sense. Movement toward the achievement of social goals cannot be measured in the same way as economic growth. For one thing, the factors involved in social development often elude quantification. They are "soft" as opposed to the "hard" facts of economic growth. Consequently, they need to be approached differentially, unobtrusively, in a questioning as well as a measuring frame of mind.

The foregoing description of what is meant by social research should not be taken to entail a necessary conflict between the spheres of interest of social and economic planning. The social researcher has as little right to divorce himself from the economic facts of development as vice versa. Indeed, it is important that the social researcher should be versed in the exigencies of economic planning if he is to succeed in making his point. The ideal is an interdisciplinary approach to development planning.

Something should also be said about the low priority and lack of coordination from which social research suffers in many countries. There is, on the one hand, a dearth of reliable information for planning purposes in newly independent countries, and on the other hand, a surfeit of information at international levels which awaits interpretation and application. We agree with the statement in the report of the International Social Services:

New research patterns have to be developed, participation in studies has to be improved and findings of research need to be taken into account in planning social welfare measures. Coordination of research, particularly between international bodies, is urgently needed.

If participation in research by the peoples of the world could, for example, be extended to international social research, the vexing question of world poverty might be seen in an entirely new light. For one of the major obstacles in tackling poverty on a world scale is the monumental ignorance among most of the affluent about the real conditions of poverty in which the majority of the word's people are condemned to live. Social research in a participatory sense could contribute toward changing the attitudes rooted in such ignorance.

RECOMMENDATIONS

With the foregoing considerations in mind, the commission wishes to recommend to the ICSW Executive Committee adoption of the following resolutions:

The XVIIth International Conference on Social Welfare held in Nairobi, July 14–20, 1974 RESOLVES THAT:
  a) In view of the low priority enjoyed by research into the social problems of development, and the lack of coordination of such research as is being done, governments be requested to establish councils for social research in their various countries; or, alternatively, to permit and support the establishment of such councils under the auspices of national councils for social welfare,
and
  b) In view of the fact that a great deal of information is prepared by the United Nations and its agencies, but much of it is not known or readily available to those engaged in social research in their various countries, the ICSW use its good offices at the UN to expand and make more readily available the social research findings of the UN organizations, especially those of the UN Research Institute for Social Development, to the social research organizations in various countries.

# Commission VII. The Essential Problems of Urban and Industrial Pressures on Rural Societies

*Chairman:* Mrs. Anta Toure, *Senegal*
*Rapporteur:* Simone Hoffeurt, *France*

REPRESENTATIVES FROM the following countries, both industrialized and developing, attended this commission: Australia, Belgium, Canada, Egypt, France, Federal Republic of Germany, Haiti, Senegal, South Vietnam, Upper Volta, and Zambia.

The commission noted that as in the past, industrialization continues to be synonymous with centralization of both secondary and tertiary activities, as well as with large-scale urbanization. A large imbalance has thus been engendered between the development of urban and rural areas, with extremely grave repercussions on the populations of countries as a whole.

However, this seemingly inexorable curve appears to have reached its peak and to be falling, either because of pressure by governments (in Vietnam, for example, the creation of agrotowns) or because of pressure by people (in developed countries, for example). The commission mentioned, though, that this latter phenomenon only applied to populations which have attained optimum satisfaction so far as consumer goods are concerned. Those which have not attained it are still highly susceptible to the attraction of urban centers.

In order to stem a haphazard form of development, the commission considered that the time is ripe for governments of all countries to make a politico-economic choice, involving not just encouraging industrialization and the resultant urbanization, but rather determining a policy of global development for the country, integrating human and social costs with data on productivity and increase in the gross national product. Certain developing countries pointed out, however, that their governments, which are subject to the pressures of underdevelopment, have relatively little freedom in deciding on the setting up of decentralized forms of industrialization; they are subject to pressure from large economic—often multinational—groups.

PRESSURES AND CONSTRAINTS OF INDUSTRIALIZATION
AND URBANIZATION

The modernization and mechanization of agriculture liberate work forces. In countries practicing policies of industrial concentration, this causes migration and excessive urbanization.

The commission is aware that in implanting industry, and particularly so-called "heavy" industry, certain factors have to be taken into consideration: proximity of raw materials, geographic and climatic conditions, existence of a large labor force. On the one hand, it is possible to develop lighter industries in a more decentralized way, providing there are good basic services and infrastructure within a country. On the other hand, industry is becoming more and more complex; technological and scientific advancement requires an increasingly qualified work force.

The rural work force does not have the necessary qualifications and is underprivileged, compared to those in urban areas; hence the need for investments to be made in technical training. The big city has great prestige for rural populations and is a real pole of attraction for them.

Technical, economic, political, social, and cultural information is elaborated and programmed in the urban centers and diffused to rural populations via modern methods. This tends to lead to the uniformalization of aspirations in rural and urban environments for better living conditions, improved health services, access to education and culture. Although life may in some ways be more pleasant in the country, the people

in nonconcentrated areas, wishing to have access to the same
goods as urban populations and unable to achieve this locally,
feel constrained to emigrate to the urban areas to avoid being
citizens of second-grade areas. The overestimation of the values of the urban milieu implicitly encourages massive migrations in all countries, with a consequent increase of social and
psychological problems.

CONSEQUENCES OF INDUSTRIAL AND URBAN CONCENTRATION

A policy of unplanned, large-scale, industrial and urban
concentration leads to a large imbalance between rural and
urban populations, the latter being privileged in all fields.

*In the economic field.* Rural migrants in competition with
urban dwellers are often relegated to the least considered and
worst paid jobs. The inadaptation of supply and demand gives
birth to latent unemployment.

*In the field of health.* Rural zones are badly equipped with
regard to services for safeguarding health, preventive medicine, and treatment of illnesses. Doctors are fewer in the country, since they are attracted to the urban areas by higher
salaries and the better health equipment required by more
specialized medicine. There are fewer general practitioners as
doctors become more specialized. However, in some smaller,
less spread-out developed countries like Switzerland, some
doctors are beginning to return to the rural areas. In some developing countries—for example, Vietnam and the Republic
of China—a progressive system of services is being set up: in
the large rural centers and average-sized towns less sophisticated services are available for treatment of less grave illnesses, for diagnosis, and for preventive medicine; more sophisticated equipment is available in the large centers for
treatment of serious illnesses, after an initial diagnosis has
been made locally.

*In the educational field.* Again, rural areas are under-
equipped, the large schools being concentrated in the large
towns. Education which is insufficiently pragmatic and is ill-
adapted to the real needs of the country has two consequences: the brain drain toward those countries where the

demand is higher and the devaluation of degrees and qualifications.

*In the social field.* Many migrants do not fulfill their ambitions of attaining a better life, hence the birth of multiple frustrations. In developing countries there are two kinds of social repercussions:

1. Young migrants, particularly young men, cannot find well-paid work and are driven back upon expedients. Subject to psychological difficulties, they frequently turn to delinquency. Young girls naturally aspire to the same advantages as their urban sisters, but more often than not only find badly paid domestic work. Forced to increase their limited resources, they often turn to prostitution. Although young people accumulate difficulties in the towns, they are reluctant to return to their villages and lose face.

2. In developing countries, particularly in Africa, the virtues of hospitality are still very strong. It is usually families already installed in the urban milieu, themselves of reduced means, which look after the new arrivals. When such families have insufficient resources, their increased responsibilities can cause serious financial and social stress.

Rural residents who migrate to the urban areas are insufficiently aware of, or prepared for, the problems they will encounter. In the towns themselves the welcome structures are insufficient to permit migrants to develop the possibilities of adapting to, and integrating into, the environment.

The commission believes that in the light of demographic growth, particularly in certain countries where its level is higher than that of economic growth, we have perhaps reached a stage where it is necessary to reconsider the level of ambition of world populations for the possession of consumer goods. Improved living conditions will be attained by the populations of countries as a whole if there is coherent planning of industrialization and services, even if economic progress has to be slower.

Furthermore, in order for people to be able to participate and exercise necessary and discerning pressure on their political representatives and public services, they must be sufficiently well-informed on the technical, economic, human, and social levels. Only when they are fully informed and aware of all the different elements involved will they be able to become credible partners in participation.

The social workers present at the commission's meetings feel that they have an important role to play in the development of individual awareness. The most useful contribution that social workers can make is to place themselves above the particular problems within which they are often confined, and to arrive at a more global conception of the needs of people and the necessary ways of meeting them. Social workers should help people analyze their needs, that is, use their leaders to make their aspirations felt; this important and demanding task will enable communities to make themselves heard and understood.

RECOMMENDATIONS

Unfortunately, all the ideas and illuminating examples brought up by participants cannot be included in a synthesis report. The commission thinks, however, that the recommendations which it has formulated should provide the quintessence. These recommendations are of two kinds: some are of a more general nature for the attention of governments; others are more specific in the form of suggestions.

Participants were agreed in their reaffirmation that governments must be aware that in the field of industrial development it is vital to take into account social and human costs and not be confined to the strict notion of economic profitability.

In order to preserve economic equilibrium between urban and rural areas the commission recommends that the mechanization of agriculture, particularly in developing countries, should progress only in judicious harmony with industrial development according to each country's individual capacities. This should avoid the phenomenon of large unemployment, both in rural and urban zones where a migratory movement which is not planned according to needs provokes grave social effects.

It would be preferable to envisage using the labor force liberated by mechanization for the development of light local industries, beginning with those which can manage with less qualified labor. In order to facilitate industry in rural areas, the commission considers it necessary to recommend to governments that they dedicate a more important part of their national budgets to infrastructures, while involving the population in their construction.

With regard to education and training, the commission recommends that greater importance be given to the training of middle-management professionals who are in short supply in certain countries.

In order to stem the brain drain evident in certain developing countries it would perhaps be more sensible to import teachers than to send young people abroad, some of whom, attracted by the higher salaries, never return. The risk of the brain drain decreases if already trained and experienced individuals are sent abroad to perfect their knowledge since they are more likely to return.

In the health field it is necessary to rediscover family medicine and to consider that schools are excellent places for spreading elementary notions of hygiene and preventive medicine. Often medical and sanitary equipment in isolated rural zones is insufficiently used—or used too late—because the people living there do not have much confidence in it.

The commission suggests that doctors take into account psychological data and popular beliefs and that they do not neglect a certain form of collaboration with healers, sorcerers, and midwives. Examples cited showed encouraging results.

Conscious of the heavy burden of social services on local and government budgets, the commission suggests that in order to reduce certain categories (nurseries, day care centers, and so forth), one might reconsider the notion of segregating housing according to age as is practiced in developed countries, and reconsider the idea of an extended family in which each member could be used according to possibilities and capacities.

The commission hopes that research will be undertaken in this area.

# Interministry Cooperation on Promotion of Social Welfare and Development

*Chairman:* Dr. G. Hendriks, *the Netherlands*
*Rapporteur:* Mrs. Nana A. Apt, *Ghana*

THE ORIGINAL meeting of ministers responsible for social welfare scheduled for the afternoon of Wednesday, July 14, had to be canceled due to nonavailability of simultaneous translation facilities. The meeting was therefore rescheduled for the afternoon of July 18.

This meeting, attended by eight ministers and six deputy ministers responsible for social welfare, began with a personal apology from Reuben C. Baetz, President of the International Council on Social Welfare, for the confusion over arrangements at the previous meeting. He explained that ICSW was totally unprepared for such a large ministerial participation at the conference since previous attempts to have the participation of ministers at their conferences were not very successful. He apologized on behalf of himself and the Council and promised better planning at future conferences for such an important meeting.

The Honorable Minister of Cooperatives and Social Services of Kenya, Mr. Masinde Muliro, also apologized on behalf of his government, explaining that his government was not officially aware of the presence of so many ministers at the ICSW conference.

Introducing the subject of the meeting, Dr. G. Hendriks referred to the Conference Working Party report and quoted the following:

The nature of social work requires a problem-oriented and multidisciplinary approach. Although it is helpful for social work research dealing with social development to use tools of various disciplines, it is necessary to organize research in institutes and university departments devoted primarily to the problems of social development and methods of solving such problems.

He drew attention to the gradual but steady growth of social work methodology from the traditional individualistic approach to a community-oriented and multidisciplinary approach. Policy-makers and administrators, he explained, are now more and more looking at the community as a human entity, and there is a move from bilateral approaches in social welfare to multilateral approaches. Similarly, he said, more and more nations are seeking to implement social welfare measures in the very environment where people live, thus moving away from traditional institutional care to community care in order to keep people as much as possible in their own community. Consequently, there is now a move from the specialized welfare worker to a multipurpose worker. In view of the community-oriented approaches of our time, there is a need for a multipurpose approach in social welfare services in areas such as health, education, employment, housing, welfare, and so on. These, he concluded, were some of the fundamental issues underlying the main subject of the afternoon discussion; for the field worker and the administrator are equally looking to the policy-makers for the means and guidance to these interdisciplinary approaches in social welfare.

The afternoon meeting was planned with two features: country statements and discussions.

Country statements were made by representatives from the following countries: Yugoslavia, Kenya, Vietnam, Ireland, the Netherlands, Ethiopia, Gabon, Mauritius, Venezuela, Israel, and the United Kingdom. There was also a special statement outlining the role and function of the Commission of European Communities by the meeting's resource person, Dr. Patrick Hillery.

Basic issues drawn from the statements of the country representatives themselves within the context of the actual situations faced by each country confirmed the issues highlighted earlier by the chairman on the need for interministry approach to social welfare.

In spite of the variety of backgrounds of speakers, it was clearly acknowledged that integration of social welfare services should be seen as an integral part of social welfare policy in all countries. In the context of social policy, interministry cooperation was seen by an African member as the total commitment of the whole gamut of ministries of government to promote maximum welfare of the maximum number of people through the development and promotion of agriculture, health, labor, welfare, housing, and so on. Ministries responsible for these various sectors promoting the well-being of citizens and community at large definitely need to work closely together. To another African member, one means of ensuring effective interministry cooperation was to examine ways and means of cooperation right at the planning level of any development project. Such projects, he explained, as those relating to population control, going back to the land, urbanization and employment problems, and rural development need the concerted efforts of various government agencies in both the planning and the implementation in order to eliminate additional problems. To be able to bring about a rise in the quality of life, he concluded, all government ministries have to be involved in social welfare services.

Supporting the need for concerted planning, another African member added that planning and implementation constitute two phases of interministry cooperation, both of which need equal attention to ensure realistic and effective national social welfare programming. He cited duplication and overlapping of services as creating conflict in African ministries and local communities.

An Eastern European member advocated the following measures as being necessary for effective cooperation in social welfare: decentralization of administration and systematic reduction of the role and function of the state and creation of awareness for self-management.

Another member from Europe added that while it was acknowledged that interministry cooperation was an essential element in national development, functional approaches are needed both at government and nongovernment levels, including the universities, in a concerted plan to improve the well-being of citizens.

Regional cooperation between nations was also give prominence in the country statements. As concluded by one member from Europe, it is now more and more realized among nations of the world that economic expansion is not an end in itself. Nations, he stressed, should also seek cooperation at regional levels. The need for regional policies for cooperation throughout the world was clearly emphasized.

At the end of the country statements, it became immediately clear that problems of social welfare in the various countries represented at the meeting were as diversified as the geography of these nations. Actual situations, tensions, and problems in these countries naturally called for their priorities in social welfare programs. Thus the problems of migrant workers, poverty, social deprivation, and the handicapped are in the developed countries as much a priority as the problems of rural development and rural migration plus a host of other urbanization problems facing developing countries. In the war-ridden areas of some developing countries in the Far East, priority is given to social welfare resettlement programs for refugees, orphans, and migrant workers from the rural areas. Similarly, a boom in oil production in a South American country which is causing grave problems in housing, health, and social disorganization is determining the country's priorities in social welfare.

In the discussions that followed the country statements, we were made aware that some interministry cooperation already exists in some countries. In Venezuela for example, the government's plan of action for social welfare and rural development generates close cooperation among the various ministries of health, agriculture, education, development, and public works and construction. All these ministries have the financial backing of both the central state and the municipal government. Plans for development are coordinated by a ministerial office at presidential level named the Central Office of Planning and Coordination:

All efforts are directed to the development of rural villages with all public services including education, health services, social development and community organization in order to obtain public participation on social welfare programs together with full employment targets, especially in agricultural development.

Venezuela is further establishing a multidisciplinary postgraduate course on social services and health for social scientists, social workers as well as medical doctors, dentists, and other paramedical professionals to prepare them for an interdisciplinary approach in the implementation of health programs. Similarly, in Vietnam there is an interministry council involving ministries of education, public health, and agriculture in their plan for rehabilitating their war-ravaged country.

Other countries, aware of defects in cooperation in national development, are making efforts to correct the situation. For example, Gabon has recently organized a seminar to examine defects in the country's cooperation for social action.

CONSENSUS

The consensus of the country statements and discussions may be stated as follows:

1. Interministry cooperation is an essential element in national development throughout the world.

2. Within the framework of the over-all stated policy of national governments for development, functional approaches are needed in the solution of problems and for an efficient development of services.

3. Social welfare depends on cooperation between local communities and local government. Therefore, both government and nongovernment bodies, including the universities, should be included in a concerted plan to improve the well-being of citizens.

4. There is a need for regional policies for cooperation between nations throughout the world.

RECOMMENDATIONS

In view of the shortcomings of this meeting, as explained above, and as a guide for planning for the next conference, to be held in Mexico in 1976, the following recommendations were made:

1. For Mexico, a small working group should be set up to plan a detailed program for meeting in order to get maximum participation from all nations. It would be necessary, for example, for this kind of meeting to send out questionnaires to countries to explore what possibilities of cooperation existed prior to the meeting.

2. It was further recommended that for Mexico, a detailed program for this sort of meeting should be sent to invited participants well in advance so that they could prepare properly for the meeting. As it turned out in Nairobi, most of the participants were not really sure what was expected of them at the meeting.

3. It was felt that the subject matter, "interministry cooperation," was relevant to all ministries of government and not only to social welfare so that in future, invitations to such a meeting should be extended to other government ministries as well.

4. The problem of drug addiction is becoming a world-wide concern. It was therefore recommended that drug addiction should be included in the agenda for the next ICSW Conference.

# Report on the International Congress of Schools of Social Work

## E. MAXINE ANKRAH

IASSW REGIONAL REPRESENTATIVE FOR AFRICA

THIS CONGRESS was unique not only because of venue but also because participants from developing countries were in the majority. Most important for social work education was the consensus that social work education stands at a crossroads although the direction is clear. The goal set in Latin America, Africa, and Asia, as well as by educators in North America, Europe, and Australia, has been adopted. That goal is an education that commits the profession to social change and human and societal development. A universal consensus on the objective greatly facilitates a determination of means.

Discussions on social change and development are in vogue. What, therefore, is the developmental focus with which the social work educator must be concerned and what are the implications for professional roles and institutional change? Social work practice has traditionally been tied to agencies and institutions. These are the starting points and have served to demonstrate the efficacy of the profession. If there is a new thrust, do the social welfare services and present fields of practice reflect the change in terms of an emerging "developmental" frame in which to work? A final aim, but one of paramount importance, is the consideration of some concomitant imperatives in educating for change and development.

### THE CURRENT STATUS OF SOCIAL WORK EDUCATION

Does the social work educational system encompass the capabilities for the required rigorous examination, reorientation, and the projection of a new thrust? This hitherto rhetorical question was answered informatively and optimistically by

Dr. Katherine Kendall, Secretary-General of IASSW, who reported on a comparative analysis of material obtained from seventy-nine schools of social work in sixty-five countries.[1] Not since 1950, when the UN published the first international survey of training for social work,[2] have social work educators had an opportunity to take a holistic view of the field. Dr. Kendall, therefore, not only presented social work education as it appeared in 1972, the period of data collection, but also placed it in a broad historical perspective spanning twenty years.

From Dr. Kendall's paper we learned that social work education increasingly is education within the university structure. Financing of education varies, but more and more the government is a chief and indispensable source of funds. With considerable variation, the trend around the world is toward requiring higher qualifications and longer training. Admission requirements show no dominant pattern. Educational objectives indicate future directions. While the broad curriculum framework has altered little, the content change has been substantial. School faculties are used creatively, and some experimentation is occurring despite support and supply problems.

In its quest to attain a developmental approach, the profession of social work strives for relevance as well as excellence. Toward achievement of this goal, preparation for social work practice is, on the whole, taking longer periods of time in all regions of the world. There appears to be much greater stress placed on academic credentials than, as formerly, on the personal attributes of the new recruits. Where there is still an interest in these, the emphasis is not so much on personal psychosocial facts as on societal expectations and the potential of the individual to act responsibly and independently.

*Educational objectives of social work.* Given the diversity noted, can we discern any significant new directions? Schools are highlighting such values as social responsibility for the profession as a whole as well as for the individual practitioner. Em-

---

[1] *World Guide to Social Work Education*, comp. Patricia J. Stickney and Rosa Perla Resnick (New York: International Association of Schools of Social Work, 1974).

[2] Katherine Kendall, *Training for Social Work: an International Survey* (Lake Success, N.Y.: United Nations, 1950).

phasis is also placed on the centrality of human togetherness and ways of creating structures and systems that foster human potential and true community. Authenticity is gaining importance as Asians seek to "indigenize" education and practice, as Africans search for a professional *modus operandi* that responds to local needs, and as Latin Americans in their educational programs reject imported ideas, structures, and practices that do not conform to their notion of the authentic or the indigenous.

Curriculum patterns and content show a number of changes, each of which has a bearing on social work education, and also show a number of changes, each of which has a bearing on the social developmental approach toward which education is being geared. The central figure upon whom so much depends is the educator. First and foremost, social work education *is* the social work educator. The discussion of faculty, therefore, was highly significant in the review published in the *Guide*. It is a scarce resource, due in part to the increased number of schools of social work. Many different organizational patterns were discovered in the various schools, with both part-time teachers and part-time students and a growing use of team-teaching. A positive trend is emerging, however: most of the full-time staff in the seventy-nine schools have social work qualifications.

SOCIAL CHANGE AND SOCIAL DEVELOPMENT

The second plenary session reiterated the fact that social change is a universal phenomenon, long-term and often detrimental in its effects. Social change is often a consequence of unplanned economic change, and one of the concerns of social work educators is that the impact of both economic and social change may be felt most strongly by the most defenseless. A recent illustration is the oil crisis, an unplanned economic change forced on everyone. In developed countries peoples and governments were able to cushion the shock somewhat and cope with the rising prices by channeling additional funds into the system. Most of the developing world, where there is a concentration of people at the subsistence level, has had to accept the inflated prices. This, in turn, has had profound repercussions, not only on their economic well-being but on their social and, in some instances, their political life as well.

The focus of the Congress, however, was not just on the impact of changes in the developing world. We were concerned with the effects of social change on human development, the development of persons as a whole, a subject covered brilliantly in the keynote address by Dr. T. Adeoye Lambo, Deputy-Director General of the World Health Organization. Our concern reaches beyond the "victims" to the "normal" persons whose potentialities may never be realized because of social and structural maldistributions and political and economic disenfranchisement. Our basic premise was that change favorable to persons implied their acting on and mastering change, making it work in their interest.

But what has been our action? There seemed a consensus that as a profession we have been primarily on the defensive, responding to consequences rather than effecting change itself. Since we have not organized training to deal with this phenomenon, our contributions to planned change have been marginal. This, it was agreed, is not an adequate response. There is now a call for the profession to attack the causes rather than the symptoms. It is also recognized that as long as our educational curricula are to a large extent outmoded and not relevant to the needs of society, we will be unable to produce social workers whose orientations differ greatly from an essentially remedial approach. It was further pointed out that the functions of social welfare that these programs necessitated were based on a narrow perspective of the goals and the very nature of social welfare itself. We were urged, therefore, to examine our welfare concepts since these would indicate the direction in which training should be moving.

Developmental social welfare is a concept of this decade. It is significant that in the XVIth International Congress the term "social development" was hardly used, but since 1972 the concept of social development has pushed its way more and more into the central thinking of social work education no less than in social welfare itself. It is no longer a *laissez-faire* trend but an orientation systematically pursued.

What, then, is developmental social welfare and how does its function differ from the remedial and rehabilitative programs? Most important, how is it translated into social work education?

During one plenary session, several characteristics were noted:

1. Developmental social welfare encourages institutional change as opposed to social work maintenance of existing social structures. That is, instead of the social welfare system waiting quietly in the background, it contributes positively to changing the system, both qualitatively and quantitatively.

2. Developmental social welfare has a change outlook, from a purely therapeutic or micro level to the community and societal or macro level of concern and action. The tendency toward dichotomizing man and his society was challenged, for it was felt that such dichotomizing does not serve to relate the client systems to the societal systems; it does not foster an understanding of the linkages between the individual and his community.

3. In developmental social welfare, more permanent systems of social welfare services and programs replace the *"ad hoc-ism"* of the present time. It extends itself to the community as a whole in a regular and systematic way. In order to do so, developmental social welfare streamlines its methods and techniques. It seeks to become efficient. It is prepared for change and responds to it by providing adequate and continuing services.

Social workers must be ready in order to be involved in, and to contribute to, such a process of deliberately planned social transformation toward predetermined goals. What, then, has been social work education's response thus far? Although social development has become more and more of a central concern of education for social work, up to the present time acceptance of the need to relate social work education to social development goals, tasks, and strategies has remained a rather weak trend in the curricula, except, perhaps, for some new developments in Asia and Latin America. This is because the process of a comprehensive review of curricula and systematized training has not occurred fully everywhere, and therefore our practice has not yet begun to reflect this trend toward a developmental welfare approach universally.

One problem is that we have not translated the knowledge gained from the experience of the last few years into our curricula. Second, there is the problem of identifying social development roles for social workers, for these must evolve from the context of national developmental goals, programs, and employment opportunities.

INSTRUMENTALITIES FOR HUMAN DEVELOPMENT,
SOCIAL CHANGE, AND SERVICES

Dr. Lambo reminded us that any valid starting point in educating for new roles must be man himself. He noted that it is all too easy to pay lip service to commitment to human development; it is much more difficult to translate that commitment into national policy and professional activity. Yet, if we are considering instruments through which the social work profession can demonstrate the developmental thrust through social welfare, we have to recognize that the best and most crucial instrument for change and the provision of service is man himself. Our task is really to establish meaningful contact with man. In most countries of the developing world, 70 percent to 90 percent of the people live in the rural areas, yet the profession can hardly claim to have developed an effective rural practice. We have questioned whether an urban-based training suits rural-oriented agencies and services, and such considerations have led to a two-pronged exploration. One was of the concept of the people's participation in strategies for change and human betterment; a second was for services as vehicles that would include a practice that had the potential of viewing man and his transforming capacities in a new light.

A social development specialist suggested at a plenary session that if rural development programs are to be successful, they must meet criteria of social feasibility; that is, they must be desired by, and acceptable to, the majority of the people who will be affected by them. Such criteria can, we were told, be "assessed partially by the tangible benefits" and also in terms of the successful application of technical prescriptions at the grass roots. An additional criterion, comprehensiveness, requires that developmental programs take into account the entire social, economic, and political context of the immediate environment. The speaker concluded that these criteria can be met by assuring that opportunities for participation by the people are created at every stage of the development process.

It is, however, a mistaken notion that only rural people in developing countries need opportunities for "popular participation." An educator described the traditional paternalism that prevails in one highly developed country. Paternalism generally leaves little room for spontaneous action. Indeed, spontaneous action is suspect; involvement for social action, initiative groups, community organizations, and many other modern forms of self-help are viewed there with suspicion and alarm by the authorities, politicians, and even by segments of the social work profession.

*"Indigenization."* Innovations that maximize people's potentials and contribution, as a developmental approach requires, are therefore not the concerns of developing countries alone. Developing countries are taking the lead, however, particularly in efforts to arrive at local solutions. This confers special significance on the movement toward "indigenization," not only of practice, but of social work education as well.

What clearly emerged was agreement on the concept of an indigenous approach as a process of relating social work functions and education to the social realities of a country in such a way that a unique and local approach results.

Although it was agreed that indigenization is a desirable goal, it was recognized that obstacles have hampered satisfactory achievement. Among the most critical obstacles is the lack of indigenous training materials. This deficiency is most keenly felt in education for social development. Within the last two years, considerable strides to rectify this have been made in the Asian region. Using family planning as a point of entry, schools have undertaken curriculum reviews with the aim of

relating curricula effectively to efforts toward national progress. Much new material has resulted from an international
IASSW family-planning project. It is also true that a number
of innovations have led to new methodologies in social work
(communication skills, for example) and an increasing use of
the media, audiovisual aids, and so on, but caution is urged in
transferring methods and materials. It was thought that, in
general, borrowing from other cultures should be kept to a
minimum. Some educators concluded that psychosocial expla-
nations, ideas, and behavior derived from Western cultures
particularly should not be sought in response to the problems
and needs of developing countries. Rather, we should seek to
discover those phenomena acceptable to, and derived from,
the daily life of the people. Such locally derived concepts and
responses should then be introduced into the curriculum.

*Developmental services and fields.* Many educators expressed
concern that the traditional agencies for which most social
workers have been trained do not lend themselves readily to a
new developmental thrust. Perhaps of greater consequence is
the absence of any social welfare infrastructure in many developing countries. This suggests that unless the social work profession in general and schools of social work specifically lead
the way toward creating opportunities and instrumentalities
for development programs, there will be little possibility for a
future infrastructure at all.

Is the creation of new channels of service a possibility for
schools of social work? Is this a feasible undertaking? If so,
how does it work? Are there precedents? This last question
can be answered, "yes," in the form of community multipurpose centers.

In one plenary session we heard a description of a center
program in Iran that had been initiated by the school of social
work in Teheran. This move was in response to a perceived
need for permanent institutions for change. Thus, the school
went into communities barren of services and filled with people having little hope, and began to set up comprehensive
community service centers which now act as catalysts. The
people are encouraged to determine their own priorities and

goals. An aroused, interested populace needs tools. Education of the people is thus the key purpose of the program; those who participate are equipped to be self-reliant by acquiring, through the educational process, skills and abilities needed in a modernizing society. The aim is more than individual betterment, however; another objective is to generate a sense of community that guides community forces for change and progress. Such centers also provide services in youth welfare, health, family planning, day care, adult education, and so forth. A most important result of involvement in these centers is greater acceptance of the social worker as a professional and of the profession as a major discipline to bring about change. The role and status of schools and the profession can be enhanced through a structure that brings them closer to the people.

In the transnational review we also heard of a number of settings that allow for learning and development of skills concomitant to the developmental approach. Social workers in developing and developed countries are now finding job opportunities in planning agencies and in housing estates. They work in youth welfare, trade unions, family planning, social security, urban and rural community development, literacy and adult education, migration and settlement movements, cooperatives, public health—all new fields of practice for which schools of social work must prepare the profession.

*Values.* Any program of social change and development is designed not just for the education of the mind, but also for inculcating corresponding values, ethics, and ideologies. It was therefore to be expected that a pervasive theme throughout the Congress concerned social work values. One group session delineated those values which it felt must underline actions of the social work profession and its training for social development, since we have neither a value-free nor an ideology-free profession, and our basic social values are shared with humanity as a whole. One value upheld by social work around the world, if the Congress is any gauge of this, is that the individual and the group should control their own destinies. It was agreed that there are other values to which the profession subscribes nearly universally, such as removal of injustice. We must also be aware of elements that could frustrate expression of these values in practice. It is true that there is suppression of dissent and self-expression in some societies. One group called attention to the fact that there seems to be no forum for discussing the professional plight and problems of colleagues whose human rights and dignity are withheld, eroded, or abused. This led to a number of questions, such as: under what circumstances might social workers renounce values believed to be inherent in the profession when these confront the power structure?

Another related area of concern was whether schools of social work should teach community approaches that would emphasize confrontation and conflict, or whether they should seek consensus approaches. Congress participants recognized that there can be no single answer. A strategy of involvements within the community should be chosen that would be most effective in a given situation, and the student should be taught alternative strategies. Representatives from the various regions concurred that a technique for one nation or group might not be relevant elsewhere.

Finally, some educators questioned whether the move to ensure people's participation and the emerging developmental services did not necessitate basic redistribution of power and a corresponding involvement of social workers in bringing this about. If achieved, such redistribution would in itself imply effective rendering of services. Should not the student be made aware of this prospect and the risks attached? How do we build these as yet controversial values and consciousness into an educational program? The starting point, it was argued, must be with the educators, who must believe in the values themselves. This would facilitate an educational program enabling students to discuss their own and society's values intellectually, to recognize the possible conflict between these and professional values, and to acquire the ability to deal with such conflict.

EDUCATING FOR CHANGE AND DEVELOPMENT

We have accepted the need for critical analysis and new approaches to change and development. We have recognized a responsibility to prepare the profession with a wider range of skills for creating and functioning in new fields. We must look, then, to the implications for future roles and educational emphases and strategies with an immediate bearing on new task orientations.

*Roles.* Role determinations will engage the social work profession for years to come as we experiment and gain experience in change and developmental activity. The Congress provided a number of pointers as to where we might focus our attention in training. These were projected rather than confirmed roles, however. In the participants' view, social work can no longer be limited to the direct-service role but must become a profession sensitized and equipped for a participatory role in social planning and social policy. Social workers must become "agents of change," be revelators of social needs as a result of social analysis of the realities of the people; be action-oriented or have an action perspective; be able to exercise professional functions, particularly in rural areas; and be able to work with other disciplines. For most practitioners such activity necessitates what amounts to retraining, since at present few are ready for the complex demands of current opportunities.

*Curricula.* Although the conclusion was reached that social development is a "weak" trend in our education thus far, a remedy was advocated. It was suggested that every student should be sensitized to the developmental approach, and something of a continuum was proposed: students at the pre-university level should receive an orientation to social development concepts, strategies, and fields so that they are aware of being a part of a new whole, a new outlook. For the bachelor's degree university-level students, slightly more emphasis should be put on the above, with skills programs added. At the master's and doctoral levels, students might specialize in defined areas such as policy or planning.

The curriculum review implicit in this suggestion is already in process in several countries, as described in the transnational review. A central issue revolves around teaching the methods and skills that a social worker will need to use in an integrated way. The "growing disenchantment" with the methods trinity (casework, group work, community organization) as a basis for curriculum planning was noted again and again. In response, many of the schools represented at the Congress are committed to, and have begun experimenting with, various interpretations of the integrated approach, but some are having problems in putting this approach into operation. A key point of agreement was that beginning courses should help students to think rationally about what is required in any given problem, so that they will be able to adopt whatever method of intervention is most suitable.

A number of curriculum components that have a bearing on the developmental frame of reference were isolated. Social science content is crucial, for its generalizations and theories form an indispensable element of social work education.

A social work educator *cum* social scientist suggested that social work training should acquaint students with the perspectives that the social scientists bring to their understanding of human behavior, society, change, and stability. This would allow a shift away from the sometimes overwhelming exposure to the traditional disciplines. Thus, in approaching a problem, the insights gained would equip the student to ask how the sociologist, the psychologist, or the political scientist would begin to think about the situation. Such perspectives should lead the social workers to a better understanding of the possibilities and limitations of their practice and provide some essential background for the application of their disciplines to human and societal problems and with change. Such practical problems as economic and social development, changing family patterns, and so on, are areas of immediate concern to social workers, and their study would suggest leads to useful content. Perhaps, the most promising development both for social scientists and for social workers is the converging identification of problems of interest to both disciplines and for which systematic exploration and thinking are necessary. In jointly asking questions and discovering answers, knowledge useful for the social sciences and for social work practice is being generated.

*Social policy and social planning.* Skills preparation for policy analysis and formulation and planning is no less urgent. Several noteworthy observations emerged, among them the following. Social policy has two parts: a statement of social goals and people's aspirations; and a determination of strategies to achieve these goals. Social workers in all countries believe in popular participation in goal-setting; but at the point of determining strategies, more specific knowledge and expert skills are called for, especially in reaching the power elite. Although it is desirable to know these strategies, we have yet to acquire prime power roles. We are now in positions of teaching people to "convert micro power into macro power," and the profession itself must learn to convert its own micros into macros. One point of entry to the centers of power, where plans are adopted and policies implemented, may be more effective participation in policy-planning and administrative spheres.

The fact that professionals in any discipline seldom begin at the top poses an obvious problem in locating the appropriate nexus for training. Although we considered that the preparation for policy and planning and administrative tasks should be training at the higher levels (B.A., postgraduate), there was accord on the need for *all* social work training to provide some exposure. For in the development field, social policy and planning activity reach from the grass roots to the loftiest chambers of power. Continuing education was advocated for dealing with practitioners who need updating.

*Research.* Before we pass on our supposed "knowledge," we need to be sure that it is based on experience and evaluated in practice. How much is clearly established about how best to deliver our services? How much and what type of effort do we need to secure what results? Are we really going in the right direction to discover how best to educate for change and development? Such questions challenged schools to examine their research offerings.

The increasingly popular emphasis on understanding and utilization rather than production of research was considered to be an inadequate response by educators from Africa and Asia. Participants explained that upon returning home after training in Western countries, they are obliged to collect data, plan and initiate services, and contribute policy guidelines for social development based on sound data. It is, therefore, imperative that they produce and participate in relevant research, and that they have the preparation to do so. A format that will require further elaboration was put forward by a discussion group focused on research. Classroom teaching which "tacked research on" or perpetuated a division between research and practice was challenged, as was the tendency to see research as a field only for social scientists. Thus, there was a strong idea that research should be promoted within the social work profession itself, by social workers, and with emphasis on relevance and change.

*Field learning.* Given the increased stress on the social development theme and the ensuing expectations that students will be able to function in various contexts, integrative field training as well as classroom learning was deemed essential. Toward this aim, several new patterns and models are emerging. Through background papers and discussions we learned that field instruction is changing from "more specialized, narrowly focused placements to multipurpose, unstructured, and community-based placements." Educators are now seeking to develop "generalists with an innovative approach" rather than specialists. To do this, the community service center model has provided an invaluable vehicle and is thus being created, or rediscovered, in developed as well as developing countries. Participants were made aware that the lack of supervisors with skills and orientation commensurate to that of the faculty and school hamper training, especially in developing countries. Many social welfare administrators, and many agencies in which students are placed, lack the necessary flexibility to permit innovation and experimentation. Where schools rely mainly on nonagency placements and faculty supervision of field learning, the staff is often greatly overburdened. Nevertheless, rather than lessening in importance, the field work component has assumed a more central place as social work education's laboratory for change in theory, in method, in skills, in students, and, ultimately, in the profession itself.

*Interdisciplinary contexts.* Social development is a task which no profession can accomplish in isolation from other disciplines. This perception emerged many, many times in considering services, curriculum, teaching, and so forth. Despite our recognition of the interdisciplinary character of social work in social development, we had to face the unpleasant truth that we know little about this significant sphere. If a developmental curriculum and an educational program are dependent upon educators identifying pertinent skills and techniques as well as the essential knowledge base, it is not enough just to bring members of several disciplines together. We have to know more about how to promote interprofessional work, which requires deepening our understanding of other professions; we have to know that theories and concepts from the social sciences relative to team practice need to be explored further to be incorporated in our teaching; that in addition to foundation courses, field learning experiences must feature joint training; and that special attention must be given in centers of learning (in international councils and seminars) to the difficulties that partnerships between professions create and to ways of promoting teamwork. We realize that we have not said or heard the last word on this most crucial area in the developmental strategy of training and practice.

Our conceptual formulations suggest that we are seeking to systematize our thinking. Field innovations reveal a search for reliable venues for testing ideas and theories. The new fields of services into which we now enter attest to a growing readiness to stretch ourselves. It is my optimistic view that the social work profession will find in this moment of change its most glorious opportunities.

# Report on the Symposium of the International Federation of Social Workers

## MAURICE PHILLIPS

### ENGLAND

WITHIN THE over-all theme of the symposium were three topics:

1. The philosophical concept of social workers
2. The goals, objectives, and function of social workers
3. The means to achieve the goals.

The idea was to have an integrated approach to a main theme, and speakers were well-briefed as to the part they played. The structure for dealing with the topics was very imaginative in that there were three "open" and three "working" groups for each topic. Membership of the working groups was prearranged, and each group comprised fifteen members from the "old" countries and fifteen from "new" countries. In each working group two case studies were presented, one from an old country and one from a new country. The group was split into "old" and "new" subgroups, and each subgroup discussed the case study appropriate to it while the other subgroup observed. In this way similarities and dissimilarities between old and new countries were more easily distinguished. The same procedure was adopted for each of the three topics under discussion, with the membership of each group remaining constant. Opinion varied as to the usefulness of this approach, but it was generally favored. Membership in the open groups was not predetermined, and so those people not assigned to a working group could "float" between open groups and listen to the speaker of their choice. Three papers were given under each topic heading, so nine major papers and eighteen case studies were presented.

The keynote speech was given by J. Riby-Williams of the

Economic Commission for Africa, a member of the Program Committee of ICSW. While he dealt mainly with current difficulties in Africa, many of the issues he raised proved prophetic in the light of the symposium itself.

The theme of the symposium was "The Changing Role of Social Workers in a Changing Society." Mr. Riby-Williams made it clear how rapidly societies, particularly in Africa, are changing and questioned whether social workers, who, he suggested, have low status as a profession, were doing enough in speaking out about the contribution they have to offer. He urged them to examine their role within the hierarchy of other systems which will be brought to bear on the problems of coping with technological, political, and economic changes and, with the associated difficulties of unemployment, poverty, and large-scale population growth.

Other key questions he raised were:

1. Can we afford the luxury of picking up social casualties when the job of comprehensive social planning and development confronts us?

2. To what extent do developing countries need to differ in their approaches from those adopted by more developed ones?

3. What roles should a social worker play in addition to the remedial one?

4. Does the imprint of a European approach to training inhibit the emergence of more appropriate indigenous responses to local problems?

5. Is social action going to be a major response as part of the trend away from specialization?

The first major question can be summarized as: Casework— is it enough? There seemed to be general consensus that it certainly is not. It was described variously as irrelevant, inadequate, a luxury. One participant said that "casework is not a substitute for food—or for an education." There was also a feeling that we must not "go overboard" and that a multimethod generic approach is necessary. All countries seemed to echo this, with different emphasis in one area or another, according to local variations. Group work and community methods are seen to play a major part by all countries, and more especially in the developing ones.

The question of the differences and similarities between countries occupied a good deal of the time. Some of the similarities were identified as:

1. Casework is not enough, and may be too expensive for any country.

2. The goal of social work programs is social services for all, not just for the poor or disadvantaged; this includes rural areas and rural development.

3. Politics is "the name of the game."

4. Mutual accommodation is needed in developing for technical assistance, use of experts, and exchange programs, which will be satisfactory both to grantor and grantee countries.

5. There are common human problems found in widely differing societies at different stages of development.

Some of the differences identified were:

1. Self-help is stressed by developing countries, even when it is clearly inadequate to fill gaps. Developed countries lean more on initiating private demonstration projects, for which public funding is sought.

2. Most of the "experts" from abroad are nonexperts and themselves need education in the ways of a developing country.

3. Use of so-called "volunteers" varies widely in different societies and is not at all comparable.

4. The "colonial" pattern of private social services, described as white, middle-class, and racist, and the related council of social agencies pattern, is inappropriate for developing countries and must be discarded.

5. Developing countries feel that they start from a different base, and that two parallel lines will never meet.

In identifying these similarities and differences I have drawn heavily on Dr. Virginia Little's excellent summary of the first two topics of the conference.

A third major question has to do with how social workers can influence others, and what roles they need to adopt in order to do so. Among others identified were those of: enabler, advocate, educator, consultant, social problem finder and researcher, change agent, social action leader, and political influencer.

Obviously, not all these roles can be developed fully in one person or necessarily by one country, and circumstances will dictate how far in which direction such roles are played. Two interesting examples came from Sweden and the Philippines. In Sweden, training courses for social workers now include a major physical and social planning element so that social workers can more effectively understand and interpret planning propositions to their clients, and can also contribute to the discussion from the social work point of view in terms and language easily understood by the planners. In the Philippines, social workers are being trained in small-scale business management and accounting techniques so they can better advise leaders of cottage-industry community enterprises. Such self-help schemes, which are essential to the economic well-being of large numbers of people, have often foundered because of a lack of knowledge or understanding of certain basic principles which social workers will soon be able to offer, along with their own more specific contribution.

The role of national associations of social workers also received close attention. It became clear that if social workers are prepared to come together and identify and agree on key issues which they present jointly through a national association they can be a powerful influence on the political decisions which have to be made. The need for IFSW to take the lead to fulfill this role was emphasized; also, hope was expressed that in time IFSW might itself exercise an influence in advising countries of the priorities they ought to consider and in supporting national associations in the task of promoting social work values and knowledge.

The style, content, cultural bias, and impact of social work training received close attention. There seemed to be general dissatisfaction in this area, and two more quotes from Dr. Little seem appropriate. First, "If there are deficits in social work practice and in role behavior, they are mainly attributable to deficits in training. Modern training programs should include more and better training in social policy and planning."

Secondly, "Social work training abroad is considered largely irrelevant for developing countries, or at any rate requires considerable adaptation to be of practical use." It was interesting to note that the International Association of Schools of Social Work Congress came to similar conclusions.

Finally, there were two cautionary warnings. The first came from a United States delegate and emphasized the dangers of overplaying the extent of differences between developed and underdeveloped countries. The dangers of polarizing attitudes and thinking are very great and should be avoided at all costs. He said that America is a "so-called developed" country, but in the push for development at all costs important social values have been lost and America today is "maldeveloped" and is still developing in ways which cause serious concern. He suggested that younger countries have the opportunity to try fresh approaches which might preserve essentially old-fashioned values like morality and a sense of personal obligation to others. If possible, efforts should be made to avoid the pitfalls of militarism and materialism, and development should be a slow creative process rather than being rapid and destructive.

The second caution came from Latin America where involvement of social workers with social planning and social action has proceeded faster than changes in attitudes on the part of various government regimes. This has had the result of lowering still further the credibility of social workers, who have been seen as dangerous and subversive. In one country, this has resulted in one school of social working training being closed down. Involvement with social planning must therefore be linked to what the market can bear, and serious pitfalls await if this is pushed too far too soon.

It was much regretted that the Latin American presence at the symposium was not more in evidence. It was suggested by one speaker that Latin America feels far away from the rest of the world, and lonely. In coming to Kenya I think all of us have realized the extent to which the support of our respective conferences has boosted the confidence and feelings of support of our African hosts. We will be taking so much away from Africa that it is good to feel that we may have offered something however small in return. My fervent wish is that something of the same process will occur again in Mexico in two years' time, and that I will return from there with the same degree of hope for the future of social work as I do now from Kenya.

*Appendix*

# International Council on Social Welfare

## EXECUTIVE COMMITTEE

## PROGRAM COMMITTEE

Chairman: R. B. Lukutati, *Zambia*

J. A. Ahouzi, *Ivory Coast*
Andrée Audibert, *France*
Mr. Beejmohunsing, *Mauritius*
Maria de la Luz Perales de Borro,
  *Mexico*
Sybil Francis, *Jamaica*
V. Ganeshan, *Malaysia*
Douglas Glasgow, *United States*
Zena Harman, *Israel*
Mary Clubwala Jadhav, *India*
Falilou Kane, *Cameroon*
Yoon Gu Lee, *Korea*
Virginia C. Little, *United States*
Daisaku Maeda, *Japan*
Patricia Nye, *Hong Kong*
J. K. Owens, *United Kingdom*
Rudolf Pense, *Federal Republic of*
  *Germany*
Manuel Perez-Olea, *Spain*
Susan Pettiss, *United States*
Norbert Prefontaine, *Canada*

Sayom Ratanawinchit, *Thailand*
J. Riby-Williams, *United Nations*
  *Economic Commission for Africa*
Luz E. Rodriguez, *Panama*
Charles I. Schottland, *United States*
A. H. Shawky, *Egypt*
Teresita Silva, *International Federation*
  *of Social Workers*
Herman Stein, *International Associ-*
  *ation of Schools of Social Work*
André Trintignac, *France*
Jimmy Verjee, *Kenya*
Gustav Vlahov, *Yugoslavia*
Mebrahtu Yohannes, *Ethiopia*

Reuben C. Baetz, President, ICSW
  (*ex officio*)
Kate Katzki, Secretary-General,
  ICSW (*ex officio*)
Dorcas Luseno, Assistant Secretary-
  General for Africa (*ex officio*)

## INTERNATIONAL STAFF

Kate Katzki, *Secretary-General*
Maria Augusta Albano, *Assistant Secretary-General, Latin America and*
  *Caribbean Area*
Sharad D. Gokhale, *Assistant Secretary-General, Asia and Western Pacific*
Dorcas Luseno, *Assistant Secretary-General, Africa*
Marie Antoinette Rupp, *Assistant Secretary-General, Europe, Middle East,*
  *and Mediterranean Area*
Alden E. Bevier, *United Nations Representative*
John Macdonald, *International Headquarters Consultant*
Marie-Cecile Larcher, *Administrator, Europe*
Helene Ogurek, *Administrative Secretary, International Headquarters*